D1569039

INTERNET LAW
IN A NUTSHELL

By

MICHAEL L. RUSTAD

Thomas F. Lambert Jr. Professor of Law &
Co-Director of Intellectual Property Law Concentration
Suffolk University Law School

WEST®

A Thomson Reuters business

© 2009 Thomson Reuters
        610 Opperman Drive
        St. Paul, MN 55123
        1–800–313–9378
Printed in the United States of America

ISBN: 978–0–314–19522–7

TEXT IS PRINTED ON 10% POST
CONSUMER RECYCLED PAPER

PREFACE

Just about every law school offers one or more courses in Internet Law, Cyberlaw, E-Commerce Law, or the allied field of Computer and Information Technology Law. Numerous graduate programs and business school also offer courses with a heavy emphasis on Internet law and governance. This nutshell summarizes key cases and statutes and up-and-coming developments taught in most Internet law classes as well as some undergraduate and graduate classes. When I began teaching Internet Law in 1994, I found it difficult to find enough Internet cases and statutory developments to fill out a two-credit law school class. Today courts hand down consequential Internet-related cases on a weekly basis and keeping up with the field is akin to taking a drink out of a fire hose.

While this nutshell has a primary audience of law students and lawyers interested in a summary of Internet law, it is a book suitable for undergraduate and graduate studies in cyberspace, law and policy as well as e-commerce business courses. This book is for anyone who needs a succinct, but comprehensive coverage, of the featured cases and statutory developments taught in Internet Law, Cyberspace Law, or E-Commerce courses.

A decade ago, Internet law was an esoteric specialty but today it is a mainstream field of study. Business lawyers draft and negotiate Internet licensing agreements and counsel clients on drafting and negotiating digital content agreements. Intellectual property lawyers advise clients on how to protect online trademark and copyright rights and avoid infringing the rights of others. The successful resolution of cyberdisputes requires lawyers with an understanding of Internet law. We are all Internet lawyers now. Large law firms and boutique firms alike have lawyers specializing in Internet Law and law of e-commerce. Lawyers of the new millennium serve as counsel to eBusinesses, conduct website audits for online businesses, negotiate licensing agreements, and advise companies on a host of Internet law issues. This book is for general practitioners, business lawyers, and government lawyers alike who need to understand the basics of Internet Law.

ACKNOWLEDGEMENTS

Many people contributed their time and talents to *Internet Law in a Nutshell*, and I appreciate their help. Diane D'Angelo, a Suffolk University Law School reference librarian, found useful research materials on Internet governance. Marcus Hall, LL.M., a University of Lund (Sweden) law graduate, and current U.S. law student, drafted a useful research memorandum and located key UDRP domain name cases. I would like to thank Stephen Hicks and Bridgett Halay of Suffolk University Law School's LL.M. program in U.S. and Global Business Law taught in Budapest, Hungary. The Suffolk University Law School LL.M. students in this international program practice law in thirty-one countries and in all continents. I taught U.S. Contract and Commercial Law and Internet Law in Budapest during the summers of 2007 and 2008. My exposure to international LL.M. students helped me develop a more global perspective on Internet governance issues.

Special thanks to Dr. Adam Liber, who is an intellectual property lawyer with the Budapest law firm of Bogsch and Partners. Vicken B. Bayramian, a lawyer for Leman Commodities Spa in Geneva provided me useful insights on the importance of Internet Law for international business lawyers. Karolin Nelles of the Munich law firm of Schwarz, Kelwing, Wicke & Westpfahl contributed helpful suggestions about Internet-related trademark issues as well as European Union developments. I would also like to thank Edward Canuel, a doctoral student at the University of Oslo Law School, who took the time to review my manuscript.

I gained invaluable insights about Europe Union e-commerce law from Professors Patrik Lindskough and Ulf Maunschbach, who taught Internet Law with me every other year between 2000 and 2006 at Suffolk University Law School's University of Lund (Sweden) summer school. Mary Kate Donovan, Amber Holloway, Lisa Keefer, Josh Matloff, Rob Penchuk, Dan Rose, Catherine Schulte, and Rachel Tropp contributed invaluable research and editorial assistance. In addition to her position as research assistant, Lisa Keefer provided invaluable suggestions during the final stages of the manuscript. Rob Penchuk kept me informed with the most up-to-date developments with Web 3.0, wireless technologies, and emergent Internet protocol and engineering feats. Dan Rose, a patent agent in a major Boston law firm provided many useful examples for the chapters on Internet technology and Internet-related patents. My secretary, Danielle LaVita, formatted, corrected, and printed out my manuscript scores of times. I would like to thank my Internet law coauthors Cyrus Daftary, a partner at Staples and Mane, LLC, Sandra Paulsson, a Brussels, Belgium trademark lawyer with Gevers & Partners SA, and Thomas Koenig of Northeastern University who contributed to my earlier scholarship in this field.

Jerry Cohen, Christopher Gibson, Iris Geik, and Andrew Beckerman-Rodau, colleagues and friends, helped make this a better book. I would like to

ACKNOWLEDGEMENTS

thank my Harvard University LL.M. thesis advisor
Charles Nesson; William F. Weld, Professor of Law,
Harvard Law School Founder and Faculty Co-Director, and Berkman Center for Internet & Society who
inspired my interest in Internet Law. I greatly appreciate the enthusiasm of Trina Tinglum, who
edits the WESTLAW Nutshell series. I benefited
from the experience of my daughter, Erica Knowles
Rustad (Fordham University Law School, Class of
2009) who was taking cyberlaw at the same time I
was finishing this Nutshell. My family has been
supportive and encouraging, as usual. My wife,
Chryss J. Knowles, deserves special thanks for her
editorial assistance.

*

OUTLINE

XII

OUTLINE

Page

Page

*

TABLE OF CASES

References are to Pages

A

B

C

D

G

H

I

Q

R

S

T

U

V

W

Y

Z

TABLE OF STATUTES & REGULATIONS

References are to Pages

A

B

C

D

H

I

M

N

P

R

V

TABLE OF COLLATERAL AUTHORITIES

A

B

TABLE OF COLLATERAL AUTHORITIES

L

M

N

TABLE OF COLLATERAL AUTHORITIES

TABLE OF COLLATERAL AUTHORITIES

Z

*

INTERNET LAW
IN A NUTSHELL

*

CHAPTER ONE

OVERVIEW OF THE INTERNET

You must imagine at the eventual heart of things to come, linked or integrated systems or networks of computers capable of storing faithful simulacra of the entire treasure of the accumulated knowledge and artistic production of past ages and of taking into the store new intelligence of all sorts as produced. Lasers [and] satellites [among others] will operate as ganglions to extend the reach of the systems to the ultimate users.

BENJAMIN KAPLAN, AN UNHURRIED VIEW OF COPYRIGHT LAW (1967).

§ 1.1 Overview of the Internet

Benjamin Kaplan's vision in 1967 of a vast computer network storing all of accumulated knowledge is close to fruition some four decades later. The surface web is the portion of the World Wide Web that is indexed by search engines and it comprises between 25 and 64 billion Web pages. The rise of the Internet is reshaping every substantive branch of the law. Copyright law is beginning to evolve to address the treasure of accumulated knowledge posted on the Internet. The British Broadcasting Corporation ("BBC"), for example, is planning a web page that will give site visitors access to every

1

program aired over the preceding eighty years. Google Book is functionally equivalent to Kaplan's treasure trove with its colossal collection of digitalized books from library collections all over the world. Google's storage, taken as a whole is, five petabytes, 5,000 terabytes, or a quadrillion bytes of data; and it is still counting. IAN AYRES, SUPER CRUNCHER 39 (2007). Google settled a lawsuit for $125 million with publishers and authors in 2008.

Lawyers and law students can best tackle World Wide Web legal issues by learning about the Internet's history and key technical infrastructure. The Internet was solely a research and educational tool until 1991 when the National Science Foundation (NSF) lifted all commercial use restrictions, and jump-started the dot com economy. In 1990, the NSF conducted a workshop on "The Commercialization of the Internet" at the John F. Kennedy School of Government at Harvard University. In 1985, the NSF created NSFNET, an assemblage of computers for connecting research and educational institutions. The World Wide Web and dot coms were not yet in currency, and few outside the government used email, bulletin boards, or networked computers.

The NSF displaced the DoD's ARPANET beginning in 1987 when it took over its nodes to build a T1 backbone. Companies such as SPRINT and MCI later constructed their own interrelated computer networks connected to NSFNET. NSF awarded Network Solutions an exclusive contract to register domain names and allocate dot com names. NSFNET set aside the Internet for education, military, and other governmental purposes prohibiting commercial developments.

The World Wide Web is less than two decades old. In the new millennium, it is difficult to envision mass culture before the commercialization of the Internet and without applications such as YouTube, MySpace, eBay, or Amazon.com. Netscape launched Mozilla, the earliest browser, in 1994; the first online pornographers materialized that same year. Amazon.com launched its online book service in 1995. Federal and state courts have referred to the Internet in tens of thousands of court opinions. Courts are deciding novel questions raised by the Internet on a weekly basis. The Internet gold rush commercialized the web in a short period of time. In 1991, the NSF began the shift from a government operation, to a for-profit operation by lifting restrictions on commercial applications. In 1993, online shopping constituted an inconsequential allocation of shopping revenues, a mere $200 million, out of a total $1.5 trillion in retail sales. *Commercialization of the Internet*, 37 COMMUNICATION OF THE ACM 1 (1994). Many nationwide corporations, law firms, and professional associations had not yet launched homepages by 1994.

In the early 1990s, cybersquatters registered thousands of domain names of famous companies in order to convey them back for a handsome price. Domain names such as sex.com were traded, hijacked, or even converted in a Wild West style virtual land boom. Website addresses in advertisements are as memorable to television viewers as 1–800 numbers were in the early–1990s. Amazon.com, eBay, Dell Computers, and Cisco Systems grossed millions of dollar in sales per day within weeks of launching their 24/7 websites. America Online's emblematic "You've Got Mail!" became part of the lexicon made popular by the 1998 romantic comedy starring Meg Ryan and Tom Hanks.

MySpace, Facebook, and eHarmony continue to evolve as multi-million person venues, enabling cyberrating, dating and mating. Only ten years later, MySpace has as many daily visitors participating as viewers of Fox's Television's *American Idol*. In 1990, there were no browsers, hyperlinks, nor could you surf on the World Wide Web. Today, it is difficult to visualize pop culture before the Internet. Millions of Internet users purchase goods from virtual stores or online auction sites such as eBay. Forester Research's estimation of online retail sales today was $204 billion. Forrester Research, *Online Sales to Climb* (April 8, 2008) up from $200 million in 1993.

§ 1.2 The Pre–Commercialized Internet

Back in 1969, the Internet started as a research experiment to develop a computer network that could survive a nuclear attack. When it was launched in 1969, the Internet consisted of only four interconnected computers. The Internet was a project of the U.S. Department of Defense ("DoD")'s Advanced Research Projects Agency ("ARPA"). ARPANET's exceptional computer scientists developed the testing ground for packet switching technology, which permitted host-to-host computer communications. Within a decade, the computer scientists of the DoD's Advanced Research Projects Agency Network ("ARPANET") used TCP/IP to network computers across the United States.

ARPANET enabled "computers operated by the military, defense contractors, and universities conducting defense-related research to communicate with one another through redundant channels even if some portions of the network were damaged in a war." *Reno v. ACLU,* 521 U.S. 844, 851 (1997). The ARPANET matured from only four computers in the late 1960s to more than 200 computers by 1981. While the precise number of Internet users is unknown and unknowable, an estimated billion Internet users representing roughly speaking twenty percent of the world population are online.

(A) TCP/IP

The definition of the "Internet" is an interconnected worldwide web network of networks employing the Transmission Control Protocol/Internet Protocol ("TCP/IP"). Internet Protocol Numbers ("IP") encompass four groups of digits separated by periods, such as '192.215.247.50' pinpointing a specific computer connected to the Internet. This protocol is the most widely used communication system within the Internet. The current Internet Protocol version 4 has the capacity for 4.2 billion addresses.

ARPANET prefigured the Internet with its implementation of the Transmission Control Protocol/Internet Protocol ("TCP/IP"). The TCP is the data packeting protocol whereas IP is the protocol for routine packets. Each packet has a header containing its source and destination, a block of data content, and an error-checking code.

TCP/IP evolved as necessary infrastructure for file transfers, email, remote terminal access, and other vital essential tools of the World Wide Web. ARPANET combined the Internet Protocol or IP–RFC 791 with the TCP in 1978. In 1983, the ARPANET tailored TCP/IP as its common language. FCC, *The Internet Looking Back* (2008). Three years later, the Internet Engineering Task Force ("IETF"), a voluntary organization, took "responsibility for short-to-medium term Internet engineering issues, which had previously been handled by the Internet Activities Board." FCC, *Common Standards* (2008). While ARPANET prefigured the Internet with its implementation of the Transmission Control Protocol/Internet Protocol ("TCP/IP"), the IETF developed the protocol that enabled interoperability for Internet users, irrespective of the type of computer.

The TCP is the data packeting protocol whereas IP is the protocol for routine packets. A packet is a basic unit of data formatted for transmission on a packet switching computer network. Each TCP/IP packet is comprised of three parts: (1) a header containing its source and destination-enabling Internet routers to transport the packet; (2) a body, which contains the payload, or application data; and (3) the tail, with its error-checking code.

The Internet Society ("ISOC") supports the two standards-setting organizations, the IETF and the Internet Architecture Board ("IAB"). The TCP's error checking feature ensures the trustworthiness of email, web pages, and other data transfers. "The TCP must recover from data damaged, lost, duplicated, or delivered out of order by the Internet communication system." Information Sciences Institute, *Transmission Control Protocol,* DARPA Internet Program Protocol Specification RFC 793 (1981).

The TCP's positive acknowledgment system ensures that the Internet functions properly. If the packet does not arrive within a timeout interval, the data is simply retransmitted or rerouted. The receiver uses a sequence of numbers to organize segments in the correct order. This process not only sequences the packets, but it prevents duplicates. The TCP identifies broken packets by adding extra data, called a checksum, to each segment transmitted, checking it at the receiver, and disposing of damaged segments. *Id.* The TCP's asset is its reliability in delivering data without data loss or redundancy. The positive acknowledgment method, with the retransmission guarantee, is the key to the reliability of packet transfers. Information Sciences Institute, *Transmission Control Protocol.*

(B) UDP

The User Datagram Protocol ("UDP") is the alternative datagram mode of packet-switched com-

munications developed in 1980, six years after the
development of the TCP protocol. In contrast to the
TCP, the UDP is more capricious. The UDP has no
means to safeguard against transmission errors or
to confirm data receipt. However, because it does
not provide those mechanisms, it has lower over-
head and is thus faster than TCP. UDP is best
suited for time-sensitive applications where the certainty of delivery is less crucial. The protocol is of
use for streaming audio, video (including Voice over
IP), or online games.

§ 1.3 Key Internet Infrastructure

(A) Open Systems Initiative

The International Standards Organization's Open
Systems Initiative Model ("OSI") conceptualized
networking as an assembly line composed of seven
different layers or stages. OSI enables computer
systems made by different vendors to communicate
with each other. OSI's aim is to create a worldwide
open systems networking environment in which all
systems can interconnect and are interoperable.
The seven-layer model processes the data after the
web browsers or other applications make requests.
Each of the seven generalized layers performs precise functions. OSI's method is to order data for
layer-to-layer transfers, in which each layer ensures
data travels seamlessly across the network. The OSI
converts data into packets that consist of zeroes and
ones, and are transferable over the network. Like-
wise, when a computer receives one of these packets, it runs through the assembly line backwards.

After this 'disassembly,' the OSI method reassembles the data into the order sent.

(B) TLDs & SLDs

Each domain name is a chain of character strings (called "labels") separated by dots. A domain name consists of two parts: a top-level domain ("TLD") and a secondary level domain ("SLD"). TLDs are the right-hand part of a web address. For example, in the domain "IBM.com," the ".com" part is the TLD. The SLD is the rest of the address, in this example, the "IBM" part of the address. In general, the SLD may consist of combinations of letters, numbers, and some typographic symbols. Each number sequence of SLDs and TLDs constitutes a unique Internet address.

The Internet Corporation for Assigned Names and Numbers ("ICANN") approves the top-level generic domains representing the domain name's suffix. At the start, ICANN approved only six TLDs: (1) ".edu" for educational institutions, (2) ".org" for non-governmental and non-commercial organizations, (3) ".gov" for governmental entities, (4) ".net" for networks, (5) ".com" for commercial users, and (6) nation-specific domains, such as ".us" in the United States." *Sporty's Farm L.L.C. v. Sportsman's Market, Inc.* 202 F.3d 489, 492 (2d Cir. 2000).

Country-code TLDs ("ccTLD") are composed of two letters such as .se for Sweden or .ca for Canada. The ccTLDs registration procedures vary significantly depending on the country's policy preferences. Sweden, for example, had a "prior assessment" domain name system that required companies to have a corporate presence in their country before they could register a domain name. Although in 2000, Sweden updated to a more liberal policy based on a race to the registry. Most country-level registries register domain names on a "first come-first served" basis, rather than prior assessment. However, countries have enormous freedom in managing country-level domains.

In July of 2008, ICANN approved new TLDs, greatly expanding the number and possibilities of suffixes; the exact number will depend on how many applications it receives. ICANN is undecided on how to allocate these TLDs in order to monetize them for their full market value. Domain registrants will soon be able to register in non-English languages such as Chinese and Arabic. Coca Cola, for example, will be able to register .coke and IBM. com can register .IBM as a TLD. In 2009, registrants will be able to use TLDs such as .travel or .computer, as well as suffixes for cities, i.e. .Miami or .NYC. This planned TLD expansion will likely result in another gold rush of domain name registrations.

(C) Links

Links are the virtual brick and mortar essential to creating a "single body of knowledge, and what makes the Web unique." *ACLU v. Reno*, 929 F. Supp. 824, 836–37 (E.D. Pa. 1996). Website visitors make use of links to surf from one website to another simply by clicking on hypertext as opposed to typing in Internet addresses. "Typically the linked text is blue or underlined when displayed, and when selected by the user, the referenced document is automatically displayed, wherever in the world it actually is stored." *Id.* at 836.

(D) Telephone & Cable Modems

Internet users access the Internet using two chief methods: (1) by a dial-up connection, and (2) by a broadband connection. A computer user's dial-up access begins with the computer modem attached to the customer's computer. A modem is an uncomplicated communications device for transmitting data over an analog telephone line. A modem modulates the digital data of computers into analog signals, transmittable over telephone lines. The modem then demodulates or transforms the data back into digital signals ("modulator/demodulator"). Cable modems and digital subscriber lines transmit data at "broadband" speeds of 5 million bits per second (five Mbps). Wireless microwave links, or WiFi, operate at up to 540 million bits per second. In 1999, the Internet was able to transmit at a speed of 2.5 Gbps, less than a decade later, software engineers beta tested transmission speeds of more than 10 billion bits per second (10 Gbps).

(E) Bandwidth

Broadband is a much-expanded pipeline for the transmission of digital data. High bandwidth enables quick transmission and high volume transmission. The measurement unit for bandwidth is bits per second (bps). The first modems developed in

1958 had a capacity of only 300 bps. Modern modems using standard phone lines have the capacity to transmit data at up to 56 thousand bits per second, or 56 Kbps. In contrast, the Federal Communication Commission ("FCC") classifies broadband speeds as ranging from 200 Kbps, or 200,000 bits per second, to six Mbps, or 6,000,000 bits per second.

(F) DSL

Digital Subscriber Line ("DSL") includes high-speed data transmission of digital data over regular copper telephone wire. Businesses use faster broadband, including Higher–Data–Rate Digital Subscriber lines ("HDSL") and Very–High–Data–Rate Digital Subscriber Lines ("VDSL"). DSL features an uninterrupted, high-speed connection directly to an Internet Service Provider ("ISP"). Asymmetrical Digital Subscriber Line ("ADSL") is broadband for principally residential users. ADSL allows faster downstream data transmission over the same line used to provide voice service without disrupting regular telephone calls using that line. *Id.* "Downstream" refers to data sent from the ISP "down" to the PC; conversely, "upstream" is data transmission from the PC to the ISP. Symmetrical Digital Subscriber Line ("SDSL") is a broadband application with equal downstream and upstream traffic speed used by many businesses.

§ 1.4 Applications of Networks

(A) FTP & HTTP

The File Transfer Protocol ("FTP") is the principal Internet protocol for copying and transmitting data and images from one machine to another over TCP/IP. FTP transmits files from computer to computer on the Internet. A Hypertext Transfer Protocol ("HTTP") is a high-level protocol, like FTP, enabling users to transfer files from one machine to another over TCP/IP networks. HTTP interprets and classifies metadata in files, which in turn, enables browsers to exhibit hypertext files as web pages in HTML.

(B) GIFs & JPEGs

The Graphics Interchange Format ("GIF") displays bitmap images on World Wide Web pages. The .gif is a filename extension, which pinpoints the type of file. GIF format uses 256 different colors and is useful in HTML applications. The Joint Photograph Experts Group ("JPEG") developed this format as an image coding system often used for transporting color photographs and paintings, as opposed to line drawings incorporating "wavelet" technology. JPEG compresses images to 5% of their regular size.

(C) PNG

Computer scientists developed the Portable Network Graphics ("PNG") format in January 1995, shortly after Unisys, Inc. began charging licensing fees for its patented LZW compression scheme. The World Wide Web Consortium ("W3C") holds the rights to this alternative compression scheme, but freely grants non-exclusive licenses to use the format for any purpose-free from royalties. The W3C develops interoperable technologies including specifications, guidelines, software, and tools.

(D) PDF

Adobe Systems developed The Portable Document Format ("PDF") in 1993 to accommodate a range of fonts, images, and 2–D vector graphics. Adobe Systems holds several patents on the PDF format but grants a royalty-free license for developing software complying with the specifications.

(E) Computer Audio

A user can transfer audio files over the Internet in many different formats. Users may choose WAV files, based on the Waveform audio format as well as compressed-but-recoverable formats such as the Free Lossless Audio Codec ("FLAC") and Apple Lossless Audio Codec ("ALAC").

(F) MPEG & MP3

The Motion Picture Expert Group ("MPEG") sets standards for compressing and storing video, audio, and animation in digital form. MPEG developed the MP3 and MP4 highly compressed formats. MPEG–1 is a standard for CD–ROM video whereas MPEG–2 is a standard for full-screen, broadcast quality video whereas MPEG–4 is the standard for video telephony. MPEG–1 Audio Layer 3 ("MP3") is a digital audio encoding format. MP3 does not signify the borderland between MPEG–2 and MPEG–4, but is short for MPEG–1, Layer 3 Audio. MP3 is able to compress WAV audio making audio files easily downloadable. CD burners make it possible to convert MP3s into customized CD tracks.

§ 1.5   A Brief History

(A) Inventors of the Internet

Tim Berners–Lee, while employed at the Europe-an Particle Physics Laboratory in Geneva, created the World Wide Web ("WWW"). He authored the first software code used for real-time communica-tions graphics and text processing. W3C, *Who's Who at the World Wide Consortium* (2008). He conceptu-alized the World Wide Web developing its inimitable URL structure, hyperlinks, and the first web brow-ser in 1992.

Berners–Lee is the George Washington of the World Wide Web, as well as its Thomas Jefferson and James Madison all rolled into one. Jon Postel, another Internet architect, developed the User Data Protocol ("UDP") providing a "procedure for appli-cation programs to send messages to other pro-grams with a minimum of protocol mechanism." Jon Postel, *User Datagram Protocol* (1980). Dr. Vinton Cerf and Dr. Robert E. Kahn, architects of the Internet, developed the TCP/IP communications protocol used to transport data. The TCP/IP com-bined with Berners–Lee's invention created the most world-shattering information technology.

Al Gore was infamous for his *CNN Late Edition* interview in which he claimed to be the inventor of the Internet. Gore exaggerated his role when he said he "took the initiative in creating the Inter-net." While Vice President Gore did not invent the Internet, he does deserve credit for his leadership in promoting the new technology before and during his service in the Clinton Administration. As a Congressman, Gore advocated high-speed networks, which prefigured the information highway. Scott Rosenberg *Did Gore Invent the Internet?*, SALON, Oct. 5, 2000. Robert Kahn and Vinton Cerf, Internet framers, described Gore as one of the forward-looking members of Congress "who deserved credit for early recognition of the importance of the Internet." *Id.* Vice President Gore marshaled the resources of the federal government toward the adoption of the new technology at a critical period.

(B) W3C

The originators of the Internet worked collaboratively as the World Wide Web Consortium ("W3C") developing specifications for writing eXtensible Markup Language ("XML") code, as well as the template for Web 3.0 languages. Nigel Shadbold, Wendy Hall, and Tim Berners–Lee, *The Semantic Web Revisited.* IEEE COMPUTER SOCIETY (2006). XML is a programming language enabling users to create custom-made tags organizing and delivering content more efficiently. XML is a metalanguage prefiguring ever more sophisticated markup languages. Today, the researchers of the W3C continue to upgrade XML as well as other WWW standards. Web 3.0 consists of three elements:

IDs. Machines need a unique, consistent way to identify a thing or concept. For example, if I mention "Bill Clinton," how does a machine know that this is the same person as President William Jefferson Clinton? People can usually tell by context, but a machine needs that unique identifier.

New web standards. Web 1.0 and 2.0 were built on standards like HTML, XML, and CSS. Some new standards have been developed specifically for expressing metadata and metadata relationships. Standards such as RDF, OWL, SKOS and Dublin Core are used to define metadata in a machine-readable way.

Ontology. These shared classifications, relationships and logic will allow machines to integrate distinct data sets and extrapolate new, unexpected information from stated information. Think of it as a hyper-glossary.

Rachel Lovinger, *Web 3.0 is on its Way: Why Should You Care?* MASS HIGH TECH (Sept. 26, 2008) at 1.

The HTTP, created in 1990, is the prevailing protocol for transferring application-level protocol for distributed, collaborative, and hypermedia information systems. In 2008, the W3C released HTTP/1.1, that resolved problems in the original protocol. The W3C continues to create projects involving cross-community data integration of information related to video, audio, images, and other media objects.

(C) Web 1.0 & 2.0

Web 1.0 corresponds to the earliest stage content-based Internet with little interactivity other than file sharing and writing in guest books and on comment forms. Under Web 1.0 the owner of the website was one and only publisher. Web 2.0 describes the contemporary WWW in which the Internet is interactive, individuated, and user-generated. Web 2.0 launched a "social revolution" transforming the Internet from a content-based forum to one based upon social interactivity. Web 2.0 users connect through blogs, social networks, Wikis, and email, and work collaboratively. Comedian Stephen Colbert lampooned the mis/dis-information potential of Web 2.0. Colbert made up the term "wikiality" as the reality existing if you make something up and enough people agree with you—it will attain "truthiness." He instructed all viewers of the Colbert Report to edit the Wikipedia entry on African elephants to triple their number in a six month period.

(D) Web 3.0

Web 3.0 expresses the potential of the World Wide Web as more sophisticated than the current web. Web 3.0 uses groundbreaking languages such as the Resource Description Framework ("RDF") and the Web Ontology Language ("OWL"). RDF is a standardized language of the web, which enables computer systems to infer or extrapolate relationships between databases and computer users. The Web 3.0 language fashions the multi-tiered representation behind a web page using Universal Resource Identifiers. The semantic web is beginning to advance out of Web 2.0 formats of XML tagging, folksonomies, and microformats to the computer readable format of RDF and OWL. The RDF is

layered on top of the HTML and other WWW protocols:

> RDF gives meaning to data through sets of 'tri-
> ples.' Each triple resembles the subject, verb, and
> object of a sentence. For example, a triple can
> assert that 'person X' [subject] 'is a sister of''
> [verb] 'person Y' [object]. A series of triples can
> determine that [car X] [is brand] [[Toyota]; that
> [car X] [condition is] [used]; that [car X] [costs]
> [$7,500]; that [car X] [is located in] [Lenox]; and
> that [Lenox] [is located in] [Western Massachu-
> setts].

Shadbolt & Berners–Lee, *Web Science Emerge, Id.*
at 79.

This triple structure is foremost in helping Internet users yield far more focused searches. *Id.* The
W3C describes the semantic web as the use of
common formats for integration and combinations
of data. Web 1.0 was about the exchange of documents whereas Web 3.0 or the semantic web enables a person to "move through an unending set of
databases which are connected not by wires but by
being about the same thing." W3C, *Semantic Web
Activity* (2008). The semantic web will only be possible to the extent that content providers follow the
RDF and other Web 3.0 protocols.

(E) Folksonomy

A "folksonomy" refers to a community of users
allowing shared tagging of individuated keywords to
documents. Tagging photographs and tailoring content are the central qualities of Web 2.0's folksono-

mies. Flickr, for example, is a photo sharing folksonomy where members tag and share photographs. Similarly, *43 Things* is a folksonomy developed specifically for collaborative goal sharing. These folksonomies permit users to be Janus-faced content creators by personalizing content by informally tagging or book marking information with keywords.

(F) Microformats & XML

Extensible Markup Language ("XML") is a microformat to transport and store data. The HTML is the visual web format enabling authors to create web pages using a very simple and intuitive programming language. The creator will place hypertext links between objects and documents. The W3C continue to fine-tune Dynamic HTML, Cascading Style Sheets ("CSS"), and the Extensible Markup Language ("XML"). XML, unlike HTML, allows users to create their own formatting tags and converts data into indexed data.

(G) Second Life

Second Life is a virtual world with millions of users creating avatars, or virtual personalities, interacting in depictions of cities. Second Life enables avatars, representatives of the website visitor, to engage in virtual business transactions, interact in communities, and buy virtual property using Linden Dollars. Users create their own businesses, communities, and exchange virtual goods and services. Second Life even has a Linden Exchange to convert Linden dollars to U.S. dollars. Basic membership is free but Second Lifers who wish to buy virtual land or earn weekly stipends must pay for that privilege ($6 dollar a month). Members receive a bonus of $1,000 in Linden Dollars for upgrading to the premium service. Linden Research reports over 12 million members as of September 18, 2008.

Judge Richard A. Posner's avatar in Second Life is a "balding, bespectacled cartoon" who teaches copyright law, the law of terrorism, and other topics in a virtual world populated by humanoid animals, supermodels, and intermittent fireballs. *Bragg v. Linden Research, Inc.*, 487 F. Supp. 2d 593, 593 n. 4 (E. D. Pa. 2007). Second Life suspends or terminates the accounts of members automatically if their actions violate its terms of services. The service sends e-mail notifications when Second Life suspends or terminates users because of Abuse Reports. Second Life also illustrates Lessig's concept of law as norms, because current members determine what conduct, such as combative behavior, constitutes deviant behavior. This virtual life also illustrates code as law because administrators have digital locks on the services and use code to lockdown accounts of recidivist spammers and other wrongdoers.

Second Life publishes the twenty-five most recent disciplinary actions taken against members on its website, and infractions are primarily violations of community standards, though some issues could be resolved by employing tort remedies or the criminal law in egregious cases. Administrators suspended a Second Life Member's account for three day for repetitive spamming which they classified as "a breach of the peace." Second Life also terminated users for breaches of norms such as gambling, profanity, harassment, misrepresentation, devising "ad farms," or engaging in combat. An 'Ad Farm' is Second Life advertising, or content created solely to inflate prices for Second Life virtual parcels. Ad Farms interfere with the use and enjoyment of virtual parcels by spoiling the view of others. No court has extended the tort of nuisance to ad farms or other obnoxious virtual activities interfering with user's use and enjoyment of Second Life communities.

Virtual worlds are steadily gaining popularity and have developed into a billion dollar economic and social force. "It will be much harder for a business to distinguish itself when it does decide to move into a virtual world if it is competing against hundreds of established knock-off vendors." Benjamin Duranske, *Rampant Trademark Infringement in Second Life Costs Millions, Undermines Future Enforcement* (2008). Second Life's official policy is to allow Second Lifers to own intellectual property rights in any content they create on the service, including avatar clothing design, objects, and designs.

Courts have yet to consider cases involving the monetization of virtual property rights in the real world economy. Users on a Japanese online auction may buy or sell virtual goods. No company has filed a trademark infringement lawsuit for misuse or abuse of their trademarks in virtual worlds. It is also unclear whether companies will need to monitor Second Life to avoid dilution or even abandonment of trademark rights. No court or commentator has explained how copyright law might address works of authorship "where millions of people are contributing tiny additions to existing content" on Second Life. Shadbolt & Berners–Lee, *Web Sciences Emerges, Id.* at 79.

§ 1.6   World Wide Web Applications

(A) Search Engines

A search engine is a program searching web pages for precise keywords and the results assign links to web pages matching search terms. When I want to listen to my son's music, I can find it by typing the keywords, "James Rustad," and "music." The web browser uses a search engine to locate all web pages on the Internet containing these keywords. Users can download and listen to James' original songs and learn about his latest gigs at www.jamesrustad. com. Search engines such as Google create lists of websites corresponding to the searched phrase, "James Rustad." These lists allow the search engine to provide faster searches, because the sites are all cataloged in the search engine's memory which negates the need to access the web to compile search results." *Healthcare Advocates, Inc. v. Harding, Earley, Follmer & Frailey,* 497 F. Supp. 2d 627, 631 (E.D. Pa. 2007).

Some search engines index each discernible word on every web page, while others index by invisible metatags. Metatags are HTML tags that provide information describing the content of the web pages a user will be viewing. Search engines allow website owners and administrators to control their positioning and description in search engine results. Litigants have not been successful in pursuing tort-based interference with contract or First Amendment-based causes of action, against search engines for manipulating results or search engine bias. Oren Bracha & Frank Pasquale, *Federal Search Commission? Access, Fairness and Accountability in the Law of Search*, 93 CORNELL L. REV. 1149, 1207 (2008).

(1) Google

Google is the foremost Internet company and two out of three Internet users worldwide use this search engine. "Google earns most of its revenue from fees it charges advertisers to display advertisements on Google.com or on third party websites." *Viacom Intern. Inc. v. YouTube Inc.*, 253 F.R.D. 256 (S.D. N.Y. 2008). In September of 2008, Google released Chrome, its own browser, that performs functions "only on the desktop—email, spreadsheets, database management." Chrome is emblematic of "the coming era of cloud computing or Internet-based computing." Steve Levy, *The Google Browser*, WIRED 144 (Oct. 2008). Google's market share is bigger than the respective market shares of Boeing and Coca Cola combined. In May of 2008, Google unveiled Google Health, which has sophisticated software enabling users to upload and store medical records. Consumers have password protection and can access medical records from anywhere. Hardly a week goes by when Google does not announce some new Internet application or service.

(2) Mozilla Firefox3

FireFox3's browser features clever add-ons such as One Click–Bookmarking, and Instant Website. Firefox3's Full Zoom capacity gives users the ability to view web pages up close. Mozilla Corporation administers FireFox3, which is a multi-user collaborative community of software coders and users. The popularity of Foxfire3 is evidenced by the average of 14,000 downloads per minute during the first month of its launch in 2008.

(B) VoIP

Voice Over Internet Protocol ("VoIP") uses the Internet and its TCP/IP network to transmit telephone signals rather than using the long-established public switched telephone network. VoIP transmits voice and data streams simultaneously whereas traditional networks send out a single signal at a time. VoIP has advantages in cost and flexibility for long distance services. *Clark v. Time Warner Cable*, 523 F.3d 1110, 1112 (9th Cir. 2008). One shortcoming VOIP has in relation to customary telephone lines is the inability of emergency service providers to find out the location of an Internet caller. In early 2008, the system operators mistakenly routed an emergency call sent on Internet telephony to a call center in Ontario rather than Alberta, Canada. This misrouted 911 call resulted in the death of an 18–month old. Zulekha Nathoo, *Internet Phone Company Investigates Failed 911 Dispatch*, CBC NEWS, May 1, 2008.

(C) Portals

The term "web portal" signifies the entry point for web browsers. A portal is the initial page that loads when a user starts up their web browser. The term "web portal" was first used to describe the homepage of ISPs such as Yahoo!, Excite, MSN, Netscape Netcenter, and AOL where users begin their web surfing. Portals typically provide email, news, shopping, finance, sports, music, television, weather, and countless other sources of information. Google is a portal on steroids with its powerful individuated sites tailored to particular audiences such as enterprises or non-profit organizations.

(D) Email

Email is one-to-one messaging from computer to computer. Email relies on an address scheme specific to computer networks. The "at" symbol or @, first proposed in 1971 as a protocol, continues to be used in email addresses. Email relies on packet switching and just-in-time reassembling at delivery. Sending an email to Michael Rustad at Suffolk University Law School requires the sender to type mrustad@suffolk.edu in the address line. "Mrustad" isolates the specific user, Michael Rustad. The @ symbol is the connector of the specific email recipient with the latter part of the address.

This part of the email address represents the computer network on which Michael Rustad is a member. "Suffolk" in mrustad@suffolk.edu signifies Michael Rustad is affiliated with Suffolk University; the .edu suffix identifies Suffolk as an educational institution. Similarly, the most popular endings of email addresses in the United States are .com, .edu, .mil, .net, .org, and .gov, but domain name registrants may also register names ending with .aero, .biz, .com, .coop, .info, .museum, .name, .net, or .pro.

(E) Wikis

Wikipedia's collaborative format has morphed into diverse multi-user recursive encyclopedias tailored for different substantive topics or areas of interest. "Wiki users create general categories and then classify their contributions. Singular category names refer to specific objects of discussion, while plural ones refer to broader discussions or topics." A. Michael Froomkin, *Habermas@Discourse.Net: Toward a Critical Theory of Cyberspace*, 116 HARV. L. REV. 749, 761 (2003).

(F) Listservs

Listservs are electronic bulletin boards enabling users to download and exchange information. Many law schools require their students to enroll in class listservs used to post announcements and to encourage discussion on a 24/7 basis. Law professors post supplemental readings, student questions, and their responses on class listservs whether on Twen, Blackboard, or other administered sites. Suffolk University Law School, for example, hosts a listserv for the American Association of Law Schools Tort Law & Compensation Systems Section. This law professor's listserv is a simple automatic mailing list for AALS section members so they will simultaneously receive information such as a roundup of recent tort scholarships, tort law bibliographies, calls for papers, or announcements of tort law conferences.

(G) Usenets

Usenets or newsgroups are "electronic discussion group[s], serving as a bulletin board[s] for users to post universally accessible messages, and to read and reply to those from others." *Religious Tech. Ctr. v. F.A.C.T.Net, Inc.,* 901 F.Supp. 1519, 1524 n.4 (D. Colo. 1995). A bulletin board system ("BBS") is an electronic forum where users exchange mail, messages, and files. Bulletin boards are videotext systems providing quick access to information held in databanks.

(H) BitTorrent

BitTorrent represents the next generation of Peer-to-peer file-sharing applications displacing one-to-one FTP communications protocol. BitTorrent speeds downloading time by separating files into many segments and then transmitting them over a network. Beginning in 2004, the Motion Picture Association of America ("MPAA") filed many actions against websites linking to illegal content. In addition, the MPAA and RIAA are pursuing thousands of lawsuits against college students and other recidivist downloaders around the country using BitTorrent.

§ 1.7   Social Network Websites

Social network websites ("SNS") represent an entirely new paradigm in the history of the World

Wide Web. "Email led to instant messaging, which has led to social networks such as Facebook . . . and the emergence of user-generated portals such as YouTube." Nigel Shadbolt and Tim Berners–Lee, *Web Science Emerge*s, SCIENTIFIC AMERICAN 76 (Oct. 2008). Digital natives coming to age in the new millennium are conversant in the digital language of computers, video games, and the Internet. Marc Perensky, *Listen to the Natives,* EDUCATIONAL LEADERSHIP 8 (Dec. 2005–Jan. 2006). Perensk writes:

They're already busy adopting new systems for communicating (instant messaging), sharing (blogs), buying and selling (eBay), exchanging (peer-to-peer technology), creating (Flash), meeting (3D worlds), collecting (downloads), coordinating (wikis), evaluating (reputation systems), searching (Google), analyzing (SETI), reporting (camera phones), programming (modding), socializing (chat rooms), and even learning (Web surfing). *Id.* at 10.

Digital natives embrace MySpace, Facebook, Cyworld, and Bebo. Linkedin.com, for example, builds employment or prospective employment networks among law students, faculty, graduates, and other contacts. A recent sociological study of digital natives confirms the centrality of SNS in enabling new connections mediated by digital technologies. Digital natives meld digital and real-space identities in a 24/7 social environment. JOHN PALFREY & URS GASSER, BORN DIGITAL: UNDERSTANDING THE FIRST GENERATION OF DIGITAL NATIVES (2008).

(A) Facebook.com

Facebook is a Social Network Website ("SNS"), enabling users to create their own user-generated page to connect with other people with similar interests. Facebook allows a user to have friends, post photos, blog, create groups, chat instantly, post comments on friends, and add various applications. The homepage of Facebook contains a news feed depicting the recent activity of friends, including what photos they have updated, what events they are participating in, and what groups they have joined.

Sixty million Internet users visited Facebook.com by early 2008, the fifth most visited American website. *Connectu LLC v. Zuckerberg*, 522 F.3d 82, 86 (1st Cir. 2008). Incriminating SNS postings are often "smoking guns" in online defamation, business tort, or criminal causes of action. Criminal prosecutors examine MySpace pages to find incriminating evidence such as defendants making gang hand signs. Employers routinely check Facebook to learn more about job applicants or to uncover trade libel. A Gannett employee was fired after posting obscene comments on his MySpace page. Just as email has played a crucial role in litigation, incriminating Facebook postings can also result in criminal prosecutions. A defendant's arrogant Facebook posting of an invitation to an underage keg party was the smoking gun leading to the criminal conviction in *State v. Tonelli*, 749 N.W.2d 689 (Iowa 2008). Facebook enables 24/7 interaction and networks never before possible. Social scientists at MIT, for example, were able to use network analysis to determine the sexual orientation of Facebook users even though these users had not disclosed their preference publicly. Shadbolt & Berners–Lee, Web *Science Emerges, Id.* at 78. Social networks like Facebook also raise difficult privacy issues not yet addressed by statutes or the common law. Users who voluntarily post private information about themselves on these social network websites arguably wave goodbye to their common law privacy rights.

(B) MySpace.com

MySpace is a SNS enabling users to create profiles, blog, and rank music. Members create profiles, link to friends and invite others to join their social network. MySpace visitors upload pictures, music, and videos and create connections between new and old friends. MySpace also contains blogs with add-on images appearing alongside the user's name on comments or messages:

Once signed up, each MySpace user is given his or her own personal webpage to create. MySpace users are then prompted to post photographs and personal information on their webpage. Typically, a MySpace user's webpage is viewable by any other MySpace user. Further, any MySpace user can contact any other MySpace user through internal email and/or instant messaging.

Doe v. MySpace, Inc., 528 F.3d 413, 417 (5th Cir. 2008).

MySpace.com's browser connects persons from a given state (e.g. Vermont), or those subscribers with a shared sports preference (e.g. Boston Celtics or New York Yankees) or fan club (Paul Pierce or Kobe Bryant) to meet and share thoughts. By September of 2008, eighty-one U.S. courts considered issues involving MySpace. A city suspended a Kentucky police officer for his unofficial MySpace posting of information about his role in arresting a country music star and celebrity. Prosecutors frequently introduce MySpace pages into evidence in criminal cases. In *In re K.W.*, 666 S.E.2d 490 (N.C. App., Sept. 16, 2008), the North Carolina appellate court held that the trial court improperly excluded evidence from a minor's MySpace page. The MySpace page contained suggestive photos of the young girl to which she captioned: " '[I] may not be a virgin but I still gotta innocent face.' " *Id.* In *J.S. v. Blue Mountain School Dist.*, 2008 WL 4279517 (M.D. Pa. 2008), a fourteen year old impostor created a false MySpace profile of her school principal portraying him as a pedophile and a sex addict. When the student was suspended, she filed a claim stating she had a First Amendment right to post this content. The court ruled the student could be punished at school for the web page created off-campus. MySpace won a default judgment for $505,000 against a spammer misusing its social network website. As of September 2008, eighty-one U.S. courts had considered at least one issue involving MySpace. Many judges, law professors, and jurists are *"digital immigrants"* who have adapted to the Internet.

(C) Twitter

Twitter is a free micro-blogging service allowing users to send "tweets," or text-based posts under 140 characters, from the website, or via instant messaging or cell phone text messages. Hillary Clinton and Barack Obama sent "tweets" to backers and potential voters in the Democratic Party's 2008 Presidential primaries. To date, no court has considered legal issues such as copyright issues of content tweeted. Courts may rule the very short length of tweets is an occasion to apply the Copyright Act's fair use doctrine.

(D) YouTube.com

YouTube allows users to add video clips, to share the millions that have been added, and to search and view video posts. My son, James Rustad, posted some of his live musical performances on YouTube. Content providers such as major record labels and movie studios license content on YouTube's service. The Center for Social Media created a Code of Best Practices for video sharing compliant with current court interpretation of the doctrine of fair use. YouTube video uploads are transmittable by email, blogs, and mobile devices. Users tag their uploaded videos creating a sizeable, user-friendly video database.

YouTube's website allows anyone with Internet access to sign up for an account. A family, for instance, might post a video of a child's soccer game in California so grandparents may view it Illinois. Similarly, "young writers might write, film and produce their own television show and broadcast the episodes in serial form online, as in the case of the show 'lonelygirll5,' which drew millions of viewers on YouTube." *Doe v. Geller*, 533 F. Supp. 2d 996, 1001 (N.D. Cal. 2008). YouTube is referred to in thirty-two state and federal cases as of September 22, 2008. As you study cases arising out of websites, consider whether it makes a difference that the cause of action occurred in a virtual world rather than in the bricks and mortar world. The issue of whether the Internet requires new governance theories, or is old wine in new bottles, is the subject of Chapter Two.

CHAPTER TWO

PERSPECTIVES ON INTERNET LAW

§ 2.1   Overview of Internet Law

In 1897, Nikola Tesla invented telegraphing without wires, which made it possible to send out electrical signals for the unbelievable distance of twenty miles. That same year Oliver Wendell Holmes Jr. wrote an essay on the common law sketching more than six hundred years of Anglo–American cases. Oliver Wendell Holmes Jr., *The Path of the Law,* 10 HARV. L. REV. 457 (1897). "The law embodies the story of a nation's development through many centuries. In order to know what it is, we must know what it has been, and what it tends to become." *Id.* The Internet law of the twenty-first century landscape consists of less than two decades of cases, statutes, international agreements, and cross-border jurisdictional rules. However, Internet law also consists of software code, sociological norms, and the rapidly evolving market. Internet law or cyberlaw is the study of how online activity affects long-established doctrines in jurisdiction, choice of law, contracts, torts, criminal law, intellectual property, privacy, and regulation.

"The emergence of a global network of interconnected computers able to access, store, process, and transmit vast amounts of information in digital form has already altered our cultural landscape and in the decades to come, may help to transform many of our assumptions about communication, knowledge, invention, information, sovereignty, identity, and community. PATRICIA L. BELLIA, ET. AL., CYBERLAW: PROBLEMS OF POLICY AND JURISPRUDENCE IN THE INFORMATION AGE (3rd ed. 2007). The Internet is the fastest growing information technology in world history. The number of Internet users worldwide surpassed 530 million in 2001, up from fewer than 200 million users at the end of 1998. Justice Benjamin Cardozo's 1921 description of judicial process applies equally well to the Internet: "Nothing is stable. Nothing absolute. All is fluid and changeable. There is an endless 'becoming'." Benjamin N. Cardozo, The Nature of Judicial Process 28 (1921). The Internet is a moving stream not a stagnant pond and is in the process of becoming international. An estimated 130 million Chinese people use the Internet, second in number only to the U.S. where estimates of the current Internet population range from 165 million to 210 million. Pew Institute, *China's Online Population Explosion* (July 12, 2007).

In 1996, Judge Frank Easterbrook, a Seventh Circuit U.S. Court of Appeals Judge, spoke at a University of Chicago academic conference on cyberspace law. He took the provocative position that cyberspace law had no more standing in a law school than an elective on the law of horses. He noted it was far better for law students interested in horse law to take overarching subjects such as property, torts, contract law, and intellectual property. Judge Easterbrook's broader point is cyber-space property developments dictate no reworking of basic property law. Frank H. Easterbrook, *Cyber-space and the Law of the Horse*, 1996 U. Chi. Legal F. 207.

Lawrence Lessig contends Internet law illumi-nates the entire law. In a celebrated article, Lessig took issue with Easterbrook. Lessig contends the Internet is an ideal prism to view the interconnec-tions between law, markets, code, and cyberspace. He contends there is much value in closely examin-ing the ways law and cyberspace are interwoven. Lawmakers need to reconfigure cyberspace law to interrelate with norms, markets, and software ar-chitecture. Lawrence Lessig, *The Law of the Horse: What Cyberlaw Might Teach*, 113 Harv. L. Rev. 501 (1999).

Lessig argues that cyberlaw must enlighten the entire law versus being limited to specific topics like torts in cyberspace, contracts in cyberspace, or property in cyberspace. His telescopic view of Inter-net Law is to illuminate the role norms, architec-ture, and the market interrelates with law in con-straining conduct on the Internet. Tricia Bellia and her colleagues, too, begin their casebook by empha-sizing how cyberlaw uses the "rise of the Internet to encourage [students] to reconsider various as-sumptions in traditional legal doctrine. The value of this subject is to provide "broad-based and sophisti-cated training in Internet-related legal issues while also helping to shape cyberlaw as a coherent and useful field of study." Patricia L. Bellia, et. al.,

CYBERLAW: PROBLEMS OF POLICY AND JURISPRUDENCE IN THE INFORMATION AGE 2 (3rd ed. 2007).

Topics in Internet Law often reflect competing public policies such as when intellectual property rights or content regulations clash with the First Amendment of the U.S. Constitution. "Difficult and controversial questions of copyright liability in the online world prompted Congress to enact Title II of the DMCA, the Online Copyright Infringement Liability Limitation Act (OCILLA)." *Ellison v. Robertson,* 357 F.3d 1072, 1076 (9th Cir. 2004). The issue of whether social network websites or other websites should be liable for the torts or infringing acts of their members is the equivalent of a full employment act for Internet law specialists.

§ 2.2   Models of Internet Governance

"Internet governance" is a telescopic concept used in many different contexts, applying to activities as sundry as the coordination of technical standards, operation of critical infrastructure, development, regulation, and legislation, "to name a few functions. Internet governance is not restricted to the activities of governments but also encompasses civil society." ISOC, *Internet Governance* (2008). The European Union uses the term "civil society" to refer to private organizations outside of government:

Internet governance is the development and application by Governments, the private sector and civil society, in their respective roles, of shared principles, norms, rules, decision-making procedures, and programmes that shape the evolution and use of the Internet.

Europe's Information Society, Internet Governance (2008).

The International Monetary Fund defines "civil society" to include diverse voluntary organizations such as business forums, labor organizations, local community groups, as well as nongovernmental organizations ("NGOs"). Georg Hegel's *Philosophy of Right* conceptualized "civil society" in society includes civic organization, churches, social organizations, and other voluntary institutions in the borderland between the family and the state. Hegel's thesis was that civil society was the emblem of modern society. The World Summit on the Information Society formed a large number of civil society caucuses including those representing youth, gender, scientific information, media, and cities. ICANN, the quasi-governmental authority, responsible for domain names, receives policy suggestions from civil society groups.

Most Internet theories of governance fall into five camps. The first camp is self-governing or libertarian theorists who view cyberspace as a separate sphere beyond the reach of government. A second model requires the creation of new transnational institutions premised on the idea cyberspace "transcends national borders." Lawrence Solum, Models *of Internet Governance*, Chapter 2 in MODELS OF INTERNET GOVERNANCE INFRASTRUCTURE AND INSTITUTIONS (Lee A. Bygrave et. al. forthcoming 2009) at 3.

Solum's third model is governance determined in large part by software code or Internet-related architecture. The fourth model assumes cyberspace regulation is not different from brick and mortar regulation. The final model views forward market regulation and economics as central levers. *Id.* at 7. The foremost theories of Internet governance fall broadly into one of these rival camps. Judges deciding Internet law cases often incorporate one or more Internet governance theories into their decision-making. Lawyers representing their clients need to recognize these contending Internet governance paradigms.

§ 2.3   Self–Governing Libertarian Views

The self-governing or libertarian model is best represented by the Manifesto of John Perry Barlow, a former lyricist for the Grateful Dead who thundered: "Governments of the Industrial World, you weary giants of flesh and steel, I come from Cyberspace, the new home of Mind. On behalf of the future, I ask you of the past to leave us alone." John Perry Barlow, *A Declaration of Independence of Cyberspace* (1996). He argued:

We have no elected government, nor are we likely to have one, so I address you with no greater authority than that with which liberty itself always speaks. I declare the global social space we are building to be naturally independent of the tyrannies you seek to impose on us. You have no moral right to rule us nor do you possess any methods of enforcement we have true reason to fear. *Id.*

Barlow's manifesto was that governments had no place in the flattened world of cyberspace: "In our world, all the sentiments and expressions of humanity, from the debasing to the angelic, are parts of a seamless whole, the global conversation of bits." *Id.* His thesis is cyberspace is naturally independent of state sovereignty. Barlow's utopian vision was an Internet free from government censorship.

Barlow castigated the U.S. Congress shortly after it enacted the Communications Decency Act of 1996 ("CDA"), which encouraged Internet Service Providers to block objectionable content on the Internet. Section 230 of the CDA gives service providers complete immunity for screening obscene, lewd, or otherwise objectionable conduct. He also made passing references to the German prosecution of a Bavarian service provider for objectionable content posted by third parties as well as the governments of China, France, Russia, Singapore, and Italy for erecting guard posts on the electronic frontier.

He was particularly critical of content regulations, which stretched brick and mortar precedents to censor cross-border cyberspace expression. Utopian theorists contend the Internet will be generative of the democratization of the world system, though privacy advocates worry about the potential for widespread surveillance and the emergence of a new form of the Panopticon. ISPs and broadband providers historically only examined the header section of packets for routing purposes. ISPs are beginning to use deep packet inspection to examine the underlying data enabling total surveillance of Internet users including websites visited and surfing preferences.

The English philosopher Jeremy Bentham proposed the all-seeing prison or Panopticon as an efficient method of social control because from the prisoner's point of view they were always under scrutiny. JAMAIS CASCIO, THE RISE OF THE PARTICIPATORY PANOPTICON (2005). David Post and David Johnson's classic article on the sovereign Internet illustrates the "romantic conception of cyberspace as a separate realm." Solum, *Id.* at 7. Johnson and Post focus on the border-crossing aspect of the Internet that frustrates government regulators and marginalizes territorial based law. They argue that territorially based sovereigns are unable to govern an Internet that a federal court described as "wholly insensitive to geographic distinctions, and Internet protocols were designed to ignore rather than document geographic location." *Am. Libraries Ass'n v. Pataki* 969 F.Supp. 160, 170 (S.D.N.Y. 1997). E-mail, for example, does not indicate the geographical location of the server processing the e-mail. David Post describes the intractable conflicts of law arising in Internet disputes crossing international borders:

A, in Austria, posts a file to the World Wide Web using a service provider in the Netherlands. The file is transported from the host machine in the Netherlands to C's service provider, located in Virginia, by way of intermediate machines located in Great Britain and Mexico. C retrieves the file and displays it on her screen in California. The file contains something that may be unlawful (either criminally or civilly) in California, Austria, the Netherlands, Great Britain, and Mexico, or in some of them but not others—a threat, perhaps, or an offer to sell securities, or a hard-core pornographic image, or the complete text of a poem that has fallen out of copyright in some countries but not others. Whose law applies here? Which country can rightfully assert "jurisdiction" over this communication and these parties? Can California prosecute or punish A, under California law? Can Mexico, under its law? Austria? If C has suffered harm as a result of this communication, where can C bring suit against A?

David Post, *Governing Cyberspace: Law*, 24 Santa Clara Computer & High Tech L.J. 883, 885–886 (2008).

The Internet creates what Jurgen Habermas, a leading figure in the Frankfurt School, would term a legitimation crisis eroding its authority. Jurgen Habermas, Legitimation Crisis (1975). The Internet is systematically eroding governmental authority because there is no international treaty for enforcement of judgments or any Convention providing for extraterritorial Internet enforcement. The Internet presents central validity problems for the state attempting to protect consumers and punish cybercriminals who exploit the open architecture of the Net. "To paraphrase Gertrude Stein, as far as the Internet is concerned, not only is there perhaps "no there there," the "there" is *everywhere* where there is Internet access." *Digital Equip. Corp. v. AltaVista Tech., Inc.*, 960 F.Supp. 456, 462 (D. Mass. 1997).

The Internet creates challenges for the Federal Communications Commission to regulate telephone calls because of Internet telephony. Vonage, for example, uses the Internet to carry voice over telephone calls. All Vonage customers' calls originate on the Internet, which makes it unclear whether local or federal regulators have jurisdiction over its activities. Vonage's TCP/IP architecture makes it difficult to distinguish whether the Federal Communications Commission ("FCC") or some state agency should be the regulatory authority. The Communications Act granted the FCC jurisdiction over "all interstate and foreign communication" and over "all persons engaged in such communication." 47 U.S.C. § 152(a). The FCC's position is it has exclusive jurisdiction since Vonage's service is Janus-faced with interstate *and* intrastate segments. Another unsettled issue is the power of states to govern Internet-related activities. The concept of place or the "where" does not play the same role on the Internet as in the brick and mortar world. David R. Johnson & David R. Post, *Law and Borders: The Rise of Law in Cyberspace*, 48 STAN. L. REV. 1367 (1996). In their view, the Internet's disregard for territorial borders undermines the legitimacy of law and makes national regulation a futile enterprise.

Johnson and Post assert traditional principles of law do not mesh well with the virtual world. They predict a new stateless sovereign will emerge without a clear parallel to law, based upon geographic boundaries. Geography is traditionally the decisive test for determining personal jurisdiction. Geography, however, is a "virtually meaningless construct on the Internet." *American Libraries Ass'n v. Pataki,* 969 F.Supp. 160, 169 (S.D. N.Y. 1997). Romanticists too portray the Internet as a place beyond the reach of national regulators. "The theory was not so much that nation states would not want to regulate the Internet, it was the they would be unable to do so, forestalled by the technology of the medium, the geographical distribution of its users, and the nature of its content." James Boyle, *Foucault in Cyberspace: Surveillance, Sovereignty and Hardwired Censors*, 66 U. CIN. L. REV. 177, 178 (1997).

§ 2.4 Transnational Internet Governance
(A) WGIG

Global transnational institutions, Solum's second model, are just beginning to evolve. The United Nations Secretariat established The Working Group on Internet Governance ("WGIG") to study and make proposals for Global Internet Governance. The WGIG convened the World Summit on the Information Society ("WSIS") held in Geneva in 2003 and in Tunis in 2005. CHATEAU DE BOSSEY, REPORT OF THE WORKING GROUP ON INTERNET GOVERNANCE (2005). The IGF Secretariat administers the Internet Governance Forum ("IGF"). The role of the IGF is to support the United Nations Secretary–General in carrying out the mandate from the

WSIS. The UN set up a Working Group defining Internet governance as including governments, the private sector, and civil society. Shared principles, rules, and decision-making procedures comprise civil society.

The WGIG Report examined current Internet infrastructure and institutions for the Global Internet. *Id.* at 3. The WGIG conferees agreed the "stable and secure functioning of the Internet was ... of paramount importance." *Id.* WGIG defined Internet governance as "the development and application by Governments, the private sector and civil society." *Id.* at 4. The WGIG's ideal type of Internet governance includes Government, the private society, as well as civil society. *Id.*

Shared governance is the ideal without a single government playing a "pre-eminent role in international Internet governance. *Id.* at 12. The preferred organization form is "multilateral transparent and democratic with the full involvement of Governments, the private sector, civil society, and international organizations. *Id.* The WGIG identified governance issues of the "highest priority," including:

(1) The United States Government's unilateral control of root servers without a formal relationship with any authority is a concern. Root servers are pointers for all TLDs currently managed by the Internet Assigned Numbers Authority's root zone file.

(2) The problem of ISPs at long distance or remote from Internet backbones paying the full cost of international circuits.

(3) No multilateral mechanism implements network security to all Internet-related services, and applications. This failure to develop multinational tools to prevent cybercrimes poses problems for e-commerce transactions.

(4) The need to develop a global definition of spam and to address or enforce anti-spam laws and practices is critical.

(5) The development of a "multi-stakeholder" civil society approach to global policy development requires transparency, openness, and wide participation from all stakeholders including those civil society organizations in developing countries.

(6) More resources are necessary to enable Internet management at the national level, especially in developing countries.

(7) The need for developing policies and procedures for gTLDs is a priority. Internet governance needs to address issues such as domain name space, multilingualism, and access issues.

(8) The allocation policies for IP addresses need to address the unequal distribution of IPv4 addresses.

(9) The problem of protecting intellectual property rights in cyberspace requires balancing the rights of IP owners against the rights of users. The governance issue is to cope with digital piracy without solidifying market oligopolies and "the impediments to access and use of digital content."

(10) Measures to fight cybercrime or enhance Internet security must not chill expression.

(11) The Internet must secure user's privacy giving users control over the use of the personal data.

(12) Internet governance requires global standards for consumer rights in cyberspace. Global Internet consumer rights are necessary for the trustworthy cross-border purchases of goods and services.

(13) Unresolved issues of multilingualization of the Internet continue because of inadequate standards for TLDs, email addresses, and keywords. *Id.*

(B) WGIG Models

WGIG posited four paradigms for international Internet governance, which illustrate Solum's second model of evolving transnational institutions. Each model performs functions such as audit, arbitration, policy setting, regulation, and day-to-day operational management and have a different organizational structure.

(1) Global Internet Council

The UN-anchored Global Internet Council ("GIC") would likely consist of national governments with appropriate representation that would eventually displace ICANN's Government Advisory Committee. The GIC would first identify public policy issues relevant to Internet governance and work with existing organizations much like the process overseen by the WGIG. The GIC synchronizes Internet public policies and oversees Internet resource management for intellectual property, domain names, Internet security, and cybercrime as well as development issues.

The GIC, for example, would supervise IP addresses, introduce new gTLDS, and delegate ccTLDs. The ccTLD is a country code top-level domain such as .us (United States) or .de (Germany). The GIC would also set public polices as to "spam, privacy, cybersecurity, and cybercrime" currently not addressed by other intergovernmental organizations. This entity would oversee all Internet public policy issues including trade and intellectual property protection.

(2) No Specific Oversight

The "no specific oversight" alternative would augment ICANN's current Government Advisory Committee as the predominant organization to set policy. The augmented multinational forum would create transparent space to resolve current issues. The forum would seek "full and equal participation of stakeholders." *Id.* at 14.

(3) International Internet Council

The WGIG third alternative is a multilateral International Internet Counsel to replace ICANN's Government Advisory Committee still dominated by the United States. The IIC would aspire to advance public policy issues as to Internet resource management and access issues. The IIC will resolve Internet resource management issues and institute transparent, and democratic decision-making in a coordinated way.

(4) Mixed Model

The mixed model conceptualizes government as leading and developing public policy development with oversight by the Global Internet Policy Council ("GIPC"). The GIPC is government-led with participation by civil society and the private sector only in the role of observers. *Id.* at 15. The World Internet Corporation for Assigned Names and Numbers ("WICANN") will also displace ICANN and the preeminent role performed by the U.S. Government's Commerce Department. It is unclear which of these Internet model theories will emerge as the dominant paradigm.

§ 2.5 Internet Law & Code, Markets, & Norms

Internet law scholars tend to fall into two categories: plumbers or architects. Plumbers tend to map Internet law topics to traditional doctrinal fields such as jurisdiction, contract law, torts, antitrust, or intellectual property, whereas Internet law architects map out telescopic theories about the place of Internet law in governance, culture, technological change, or historical development. Internet architects construct theories of governance whereas plumbers adapt traditional doctrinal principles to cyberspace. Lawrence Lessig's work is emblematic of Solum's third model of Internet governance based upon code and Internet architecture. Internet law consists in four interrelated modalities: (1) legal sanctions, (2) social norms, (3) the market, and (4) code or architecture. Law interrelates with the other three modalities in ordering conduct in cyberspace: software code, social norms, and architecture.

(A) Legal Rules

Professor Lessig was the Internet law visionary who drew attention to the impact of laws such as copyrights, trademarks, patents, defamation, and obscenity in their interrelationship with norms, markets and codes in shaping cyberspace rights and wrongs. Protocols are software making cross-border Internet jurisdiction ubiquitous. Just by way of example, courts have had little difficulty in stretching minimum contacts to cyberspace. To satisfy federal due process, an Internet defendant must have computer-to-computer minimum contacts in the U.S. forum where the plaintiff files the lawsuit. A retailer with a virtual store targeting a particular jurisdiction's consumers will likely satisfy the brick and mortar due process standard for imposing personal jurisdiction on an out of state defendant. The architecture of the Internet changes the meaning of jurisdiction in making cross-border transactions ubiquitous.

(B) Code or Architecture

Architecture in cyberspace is the software and hardware protocols that constrain cyberspace behavior. Lessig argues nature does not determine the shape of cyberspace. "Code does. Code is not constant. It Changes." Lessig, *Code and Other Laws of Cyberspace, Id.* at 109. The ever-changing architecture of the Internet interrelates with law, norms, and markets to comprise the social and legal controls of online behavior. Lessig conceptualizes architecture as the physical world "as we find it." He describes how the architecture of Paris and its large boulevards limited the ability of revolutionaries to protest. Another architectural example he uses is the separation of the German Constitutional Court in Karlsruhe and its capital city of Berlin. He describes how this geographic separation limits the influence of each branch on each other. The Internet is "layered architecture" which enables "specialized efficiency, organizational coherency, and future flexibility." Timothy Wu, *Application–Centered Internet Analysis*, 85 VA. L. REV. 1163, 1189 (1999).

Lessig's argument is codes and standards constrain behavior and are a part of Internet law. The basic Internet protocols are standards permitting the identification of a user, as does the user's IP address. Lessig, *What Cyberlaw Might Teach*, *Id.* at 516. The Platform for Privacy Preference ("P3P"), for example, is a protocol proposed by the WC3 enabling "persons to select their preferences about the exchange of private information." This in turn enables computer agents "to negotiate the trade of such data when an individual connects to a given site." *Id.* at 521. The P3P's architecture implemented on a website gives visitors more control over their personal information than they would have visiting a brick and mortar store. The technical specifications of the P3P strictly control the data flow of personally identifiable information of consumers. Consumers can control their private information by their choice of browser preferences.

Encryption or digital locks also illustrate the role of software code constraining and channeling Internet behavior. Digital locks prevent unauthorized users from viewing materials. It is arguable, for example, an online company's failure to encrypt data constitutes a breach of the duty to protect trade secrets of third parties. Once a misappropriator posts a trade secret on the Internet, it becomes part of the public domain. Posting information on a website destroys trade secrets. In a risk-filled Internet environment, a company's failure to encrypt software in email transmissions dictates a legal conclusion that proprietary information is not classifiable as a trade secret. In contrast, a company that encrypts trade secrets acquires legal rights. The architecture of the Internet lets government officials filter out content created by political dissidents. The term "screening software" means software programmed to limit access to material on the Internet. By way of example, I tried to download a draft for this book in a community library and was blocked by a software filter taking offense to the word, "nutshell." Community libraries' use of filtering programs illustrates code as law. Similarly, content providers use anti-circumvention software to protect copyrighted content. See LAWRENCE LESSIG, CODE VERSION 2.0 (2006). When hackers circumvent digital locks, a content creator has rights under the Digital Millennium Copyright Act's anticircumvention provisions. Lessig's point is that access codes and other software interrelate with law in countless ways. Defendants disabling access codes, for example, are subject to civil and criminal penalties. Lessig describes the Internet as one of the most regulable spaces ever devised because of its architecture and code. *Id.* at 38.

(C) Norms

Sociologists define norms as culturally appropriate ways of doing things. In 1997, two Arizona attorneys placed an advertisement captioned, "Green Card Lottery—Final One?" on thousands of usenets contrary to informal norms against commercial postings. Infuriated usenet users responded with cancel bots shutting down the spammer's mail server. The vigilantes' actions to drive a spammer off-line exemplify the power of informal norms as Internet law. Lessig gives abundant examples of how informal sociological norms serve as a means of social control in cyberspace just as in the real world. He notes how fellow Internet users flame those who violate social norms such as advertising products or services. He also notes how users employ bozo filters to block messages from too garrulous members of discussion groups. Finally, he notes how those who "spoof" another's identity in virtual reality are "toaded" or have their characters removed.

Acceptable use policies are norms-based and supplement legal obligations comprising the social control of cyberspace activities. Moderators sanction purposeful harassment or distasteful Internet postings even though such expression does not violate any law other than social norms. Social network website administrators suspend subscribers for spamming, profanity, harassment, or other breaches of Internet-related etiquette. These examples illustrate how norms serve as a form of informal social control in cyberspace. Norms bridge the gap for obnoxious behavior not classifiable as crimes or even torts. Second Life, for example enforces the terms of service agreement to remove deviant players violating community norms. The sociology of Internet governance continues to be an important source of evolving e-commerce law, as well as in virtual worlds.

(D) Markets

Professor Lessig also views the market as a significant method of control of cyberspace conduct. He favors a regime of net neutrality guaranteeing a free market for Internet content. Lessig maintains telecoms such as AT&T, Verizon, and Comcast should not be able to create different tiers of online service. Internet architecture is the software and hardware determining interoperability, services, and access. He notes how software control determines access. LAWRENCE LESSIG, CODE VERSION 2.0 (2006).

Lessig contends the furthermost challenge for cyberspace is to reconcile liberty with control; he asks how do we "protect liberty when the architectures of control are managed as much by the government as by the private sector?" *Id.* at Preface. "How do we assure privacy when the ether perpetually spies? How do we guarantee free thought when the push is to propertize every idea? How do we guarantee self-determination when the architectures of control are perpetually determined elsewhere?" *Id*.

(E) Generative Internet's Architecture

Jonathan Zittrain's work, like the work of Lessig, reflects Solum's third model because of his emphasis on how software code and architecture constrains creativity on the Internet. JONATHAN ZITTRAIN, THE FUTURE OF THE INTERNET—AND HOW TO STOP IT (2008) at 2. He conceptualizes generativity as "a system's capacity to produce unanticipated change through unfiltered contributions from broad and varied audiences." *Id*. Zittrain romanticizes the generative Internet of tens of millions of Internet users collaborating to produce code and content.

Zittrain contends the greatest threat to the generative Internet is the problem of Internet security creating "walled gardens" with Internet Service Providers such as America Online. He sees the explosion of malware as impelling the increased "appliancing in networks of control." *Id*. at 8. The lockdown of the Internet is a backlash to the security problem developing rapidly in cybercafés and schools. He contrasts the generative Apple II with it collaborative community of users with the applianced iPhone—closed and tethered to a closed network of control. He compares the PC revolution with innovation by users of Microsoft's Windows operating system to the closed Microsoft's Xbox 360 video game console. The network of control has displaced innovation by users, in part, as a backlash against cybercriminals exploiting the openness of the generative Internet. Cybersecurity creates generative dilemmas as Internet users cede autonomy and creativity to greater network control in order to feel safe in cyberspace. *Id.* at 37. Cybercriminals exploit the openness of the generative Internet causing developers to lock down cyberspace. The collaborative *zeitgeist* of the Internet accounts for much of its creative breakthroughs. Zittrain contends the PC and Internet, as engines of innovation, are threatened by "information appliances controlled by their makers." *Id.* at 5.

§ 2.6 Why Territory Matters

Lawrence Solum's fourth model of governance is local regulation. This model explains how China's national regulations of the Internet collide with the model of code and Internet architecture. "The Internet is not designed to facilitate national regulation. China's efforts to regulate content "are costly and ineffective." Lawrence Solum, *Models of Internet Governance*, Chapter 2 in MODELS OF INTERNET GOVERNANCE INFRASTRUCTURE AND INSTITUTIONS (Lee A. Bygrave et. al. forthcoming 2009) at 17. The United States Constitution and implementing legislation require courts to give full faith and credit to judgments of sister states, territories, and possessions of the United States. International comity is a doctrine dictating the broad enforceability of foreign judgments and decrees unless enforcement is prejudicial or contrary to U.S. public policy. Goldsmith and Wu describe how the French authorities were able to impose their national will on Yahoo! for enabling sales of Nazi memorabilia on its auction website because these sales had detrimental effects in France. Jack Goldsmith & Tim Wu, Who Controls the Internet? Illusions of a Borderless World (2006). The French authorities charged Yahoo! with enabling French citizens' access to "page after page of swastika arm bands, SS daggers, concentration camp photos, and even replicas of Zyklon gas canisters." *Id.*

Judge Gomez ruled Yahoo's auction website violated French law and ordered the company "to take all necessary measures to dissuade and make impossible" visits by French web surfers to the illegal Yahoo.com auction site. A Paris court ruled the U.S. portal website violated French criminal law. *Id.* at 5. Yahoo! eventually agreed to remove the material complying with the French court order. *Id.* at 6. This result confirms cyberspace is neither the Wild West nor a liability-free zone as portrayed by the utopians or separate sovereign theorists.

Professors Wu and Goldsmith describe how the French government had a special justification for extraterritorial enforcement of their local regulation because of the Nazi occupation of Western Europe during World War II. The French government enacted laws against the expression of pro-Nazi and anti-Semitic views. In 2000, two French cultural organizations, *La Ligue Contre Le Racisme Et L'Antisemitisme ("LICRA") and L'Union Des Etudiants Juifs De France* ("UEJF"), filed a complaint against Yahoo! after learning they could access Nazi materials on Yahoo!'s French service.

France made it a crime for content providers to give access to or possess Nazi memorabilia. The

Tribunal de Grande Instance ("TGI") in Paris convicted Yahoo! of making Nazi materials available to French citizens through the yahoo.com website as well as yahoo.fr. Yahoo! filed a declaratory judgment action in the Northern District of California ruling the French court order was not enforceable in the United States.

American courts generally enforce foreign judgments and honor the doctrine of international comity. However, U.S. courts will not enforce judgments contrary to important public policies. In the United States, the First Amendment prohibits the government from restraining political expression, no matter how distasteful. In *Yahoo!, Inc. v. La Lique Contre Le Racisme et L'Antisemitisme*, et. al., 169 F. Supp. 2d 1181 (N.D. Cal. 2001) the court granted Yahoo's motion for summary judgment, holding enforcement of the French court order would violate the First Amendment. The federal district court reasoned the First Amendment trumped international comity also rejecting abstention. The court refused to abstain deferring to the proceedings in France. The U.S. district court ruled that enforcement of the Paris court order was inconsistent with the First Amendment of the U.S. Constitution and therefore a violation of significant U.S. public policies.

The Ninth Circuit, however, refused to enjoin the Paris order on grounds of ripeness. The court also questioned whether minimum contacts were present to support the exercise of personal jurisdiction even if ripeness was not an issue. *Yahoo!, Inc. v. La*

Ligue Contre le Racisme et l'Antisémitisme, 379 F.3d 1120 (9th Cir. 2004). The Yahoo! court noted the French defendant's efforts to enforce anti-Semitism laws did not constitute purposeful availment in California.

After this ruling, Yahoo! agreed to comply with the French court's order to block access of the objectionable materials to French citizens. Goldsmith and Wu's thesis is Yahoo!'s decision to comply with French law is emblematic of how cyberspace is constrained by local governmental regulations everywhere. More recently, the Chinese government required Yahoo! to filter materials critical of the Communist Party regime as a condition of access to Chinese markets. Goldsmith and Wu note how, today, Yahoo! provides Chinese citizens with a censored portal to the Internet. The government blocks Chinese Internet users from accessing Taiwanese websites and other websites critical of the government. The government makes it a crime for Chinese citizens to load any foreign-made software into their computer systems. This blocking software prevents users from political organizing on the Internet. During the 2008 Olympics, the government blocked Apple's i-Tunes because athletes were listening to protest songs produced by a Tibetan activist group.

Goldsmith and Wu cite many examples of how national governmental authorities impose their extraterritorial will on cyberspace activities such as the extraterritorial impact of the European Community's Data Protection Directive. After the Europe-

an Commission, Council, and Parliament approved
a Data Protection Directive, the Member States
approved national legislation implementing the directive. Under the EU Data Protection Directive, a
company is required to get explicit consent from
data subjects as to the collection of data on race,
ethnicity, political opinions, union membership,
physical and mental health, sexual preferences, and
criminal records and must implement adequate security to protect personal information. Member
States prohibit the transfer of personal information
across national borders unless the receiving country
has implemented an "adequate level of protection."
Art. 25. The U.S. did not satisfy the European
Commission's standard for adequate privacy precautions. The Commission threatened to enjoin the
transfer of European personally identifiable data to
the United States in 1998. If the Europeans enjoined data flow between the continents, the result
would trigger a worldwide Depression. To avert this
financial disaster, the United States' Department of
Commerce and the European Commission successfully negotiated a privacy safe harbor enforced by
the Federal Trade Commission. U.S. companies receiving consumer data from Europe certify that
they comply with Data Protection Directive principles. See generally, 95/46/EC.

Even though the United States is not a member
of the European Union, U.S. companies must nevertheless comply with EU Data Protection Directive
core principles. The American adoption of European
style privacy reflects Wu and Goldsmith's thesis
that cyberspace is highly regulatable. The United

States historically prefers that the business community develop its own voluntary industry standards to protect online privacy. These extraterritorial private governance rules enforced on the Internet create a legitimation crisis for traditional sovereignty.

Hardly a day goes by without further evidence of some local authority imposing regulations on Internet users outside their territory. Further evidence for Goldsmith and Wu's thesis can be seen in the Minnesota Attorney General filing suit against an online gambling site for violating the state's gambling laws, even though a Nevada corporation operated the website. The *Granite Gate Resorts* court found an adequate basis for jurisdiction over a Nevada corporation because the site actively solicited Minnesota subscribers. *State of Minnesota v. Granite Gate Resorts, Inc.*, 568 N.W.2d 715 (Minn. App. Ct. 1997).

The *Granite Gate* court also found the web was accessible in Minnesota and the toll-free market evidenced its intent to reach Minnesota. Minnesota had an interest in providing a forum to protect its consumers. More recently, Pennsylvania's Banking Department requires all Internet payday companies to get a license and comply with state's caps on interest and fees. See also, Jack L. Goldsmith, *Against Cyberanarchy*, 65 U. CHI. L. REV. 1199, 1217–213 (1998) (noting "a nation can regulate people and equipment in its territory to control the local effects of the extraterritorial activity," by constraining, "the local means through which foreign content is transmitted)."

§ 2.7   The Wealth of Networks

Solum's fifth model is Internet governance determined by markets and economic change. The Intellectual Property Alliance's 2006 report concluded the U.S. "core" copyright industries (production and/or distribution of copyright materials) accounted for $819.06 billion or 6.56% of the U.S. gross domestic product ("GDP"). The core copyright industries accounted for nearly 13% of the total growth of the U.S. economy in 2006 leading all major industry sectors. STEPHEN SIWEK, COPYRIGHT INDUSTRIES IN THE U.S. ECONOMY: 2006 Report (2007). The shift to an information-based economy is built upon "information (financial services, accounting, software, science) and cultural (films, music) production and the manipulation of symbols (from making sneakers to branding them and manufacturing the cultural significance of the Swoosh)." YOCHAI BENKLER, THE WEALTH OF NETWORKS: HOW SOCIAL PRODUCTION TRANSFORMS MARKETS AND FREEDOM 3 (2006).

Benkler's thesis draws upon the work of Karl Marx in explaining the transformation of the world economy from one based on durable goods to a knowledge-based networked economy. The term Marxist refers to those who believe the economic structure of society constructs social reality. Professor Benkler adapts Karl Marx's *Das Kapital* in his theory of how the new computation technologies have democratized the means of production. Marx's conflict theory employed the concept of the *means of production,* to include the tools, plants, and equipment to produce durable goods. The relationship to the means of production determines social class. Marx predicted class conflict between the bourgeoisie who controlled the means of production and the proletariat who were wage slaves. He brings Marxist theory up to date for the information-age economy. The Internet is "built on cheap processes with high computation capabilities interconnected in a pervasive network." *Id.*

A larger segment of the world's population now lays claim to the means of production than under industrial capitalism. In the durable goods economy, the economy requires "ever-larger investments of physical capital." *Id.* at 5. In contrast, the information age economy allows larger proportions of the population to control the means of intellectual production. Yochai Benkler describes how "individuals can reach and inform or edify millions around the world" a result not possible in an earlier stage of capitalism. *Id.* at 4. His conception of an information-based economy runs against the grain of Marxism because it is based upon the bedrock of cooperation. He described the centrality of "large-scale cooperative efforts—peer production of information knowledge and culture." *Id.* at 5.

Benkler cites the triumph of user-driven innovation, such as GNU/Linux, as an alternative human centric economy. *Id.* He declares the networked information economy enhances autonomy and a reflective culture outside the market sphere. *Id.* at 8. The battle over the Internet pits a proprietary paradigm against an informal collaborative-net-

worked economy. *Id.* at 23. Individual and cooperative private action is displacing market-based and
proprietary action. *Id.* at 21. Benkler views most
Internet-related intervention reflecting outmoded
assumptions of a durable goods economy anti-
thetical to the collaborative social economy. The
larger battle is over the opportunity to build an
"open, diverse liberal equilibrium." *Id.* at 22.

   Professor Benkler contends a spacious commons
is a core component of a free society. However, he
describes how Hollywood and the recording industry are systematically undermining the innovation
of the collaborative-networked economy. He concludes that we should not let "yesterday's winners
dictate the terms of tomorrow's economic competition." *Id.* at 28. Consider how the competing models
of Internet governance discussed in this chapter
shape judicial and legislative decision-making in the
cases and statutory developments covered in the
next chapters.

CHAPTER THREE

CYBERJURISDICTION AND CHOICE OF LAW

§ 3.1 Overview of Cyberjurisdiction

The Internet is a cross-border medium for interstate and transnational transactions and activities. An eBusiness operating a website creates new challenges for courts in determining jurisdiction, conflict of law and choice of law. This chapter explores emerging procedural issues created by Internet activities including: (1) personal jurisdiction, (2) parties' choice of law and forum, (3) conflict of law, and (4) enforcement of cross-border judgments. Personal jurisdiction refers to the power of the court to preside over a defendant. The parties' choices of law and forum clauses are contracts where the parties agree to jurisdiction and the applicable law in advance. Conflict of law refers to the principles courts use in determining what law applies in a cross-border transaction. At present, there is no multilateral convention to resolve conflicts of law or choice of law for Internet nor is there a convention for the reciprocal enforcement of Internet-related judgments. Internet lawyers representing companies doing business in Europe must consider the impact of European Union regimes such as the Brussels Regulation, the Rome I Convention, and other e-commerce related directives if they represent businesses targeting European customers. This chapter highlights domestic and international procedural Internet-related issues.

§ 3.2 Internet–Related Jurisdiction

(A) Long–Arm Statutes

Every U.S. jurisdiction has a long-arm statute determining whether a court has personal jurisdiction over a nonresident defendant. The states have enacted one of two broad types of long-arm statutes: (1) one asserting jurisdiction over the person fully allowable by the Fourteenth Amendment in the U.S. Constitution and (2) statutes limited to specified activities such as transacting business or causing *tortious* injuries. Pennsylvania's long-arm statute, for example, claims jurisdiction to the ''fullest extent allowed under the Constitution of the United States.'' In contrast, Massachusetts' long arm statute claims jurisdiction over defendants doing business in the state or deriving substantial revenues from goods or services. Personal jurisdiction involves a two-step analysis. First, does the state's long-arm statute authorize jurisdiction over a nonresident? Second, if the long-arm statute covers the defendant's wrongdoing, does exercise of jurisdiction violate the Due Process Clause of the Fourteenth Amendment?

(B) Due Process Framework

Courts typically examine whether a defendant's online activities constitute purposeful availment by determining whether it has intentionally targeted the forum state. Mere advertising on the Internet does not constitute purposefully directing activities to the forum. Courts have had little difficulty adapting the well-worn groves of the due process framework to cyberspace. Once a court determines a defendant's conduct is subject to a forum's long-arm statute, it must next consider whether asserting personal jurisdiction over a nonresident defendant comports with the Due Process Clause of the Fourteenth Amendment. This involves a two-step process, which requires the court to decide whether each defendant has established "minimum contacts" with the forum state and whether the exercise of personal jurisdiction would "offend traditional notions of fair play and substantial justice." The U.S. Supreme Court's minimum contacts framework was first articulated in *International Shoe v. Washington*, 326 U.S. 310, 319–20 (1945). The *International Shoe* Court's landmark holding was that an out of state defendant could not be subject to personal jurisdiction absent sufficient "minimum contacts" with the forum satisfying due process.

(C) General Jurisdiction in Cyberspace

The underlying jurisprudence of general jurisdiction is a defendant's contacts with the forum are so extensive as to be the functional equivalent of a physical presence. "Systematic and continuous" activities in the forum state are required for a finding of general jurisdiction. *Helicópteros Nacionales de Colombia. S.A. v. Hall,* 466 U.S. 408 (1984). "For a website to support a finding of general jurisdiction on its own, the defendant must systematically contact the forum state through the Internet over a significant period of time." 4A CHARLES ALAN WRIGHT & ARTHUR R. MILLER, FEDERAL PRACTICE AND PROCEDURE 1073.1 (3rd ed. 2007).

General jurisdiction applies if a business entity's activities in the state are "substantial" or "continuous and systematic," even if the cause of action is unrelated to those activities. If the contacts with the forum are extensive enough, courts overlook the fact the cause of action arose elsewhere. Courts determine the presence of general jurisdiction considering factors such as the presence of physical facilities, bank accounts, agents, registration, or incorporation. Courts examine whether the defendant actively solicited business in the state's marketplace. The difference between general and specific jurisdiction is a matter of degree and courts consider "economic realities" rather than a mechanical test in determining general jurisdiction. The Ninth Circuit held L.L. Bean was subject to general jurisdiction predicated upon millions of dollars of sales with California consumers. Gator sued the Maine outdoor outfitter in a federal California court seeking a declaratory judgment its pop-up ads did not infringe L.L. Bean's trademarks or constitute an unfair business practice. L.L. Bean is a Maine corporation with its principal place of business in Maine. The famous Maine outfitter advertises in California, both by mail and over the Internet, and it sells significant quantities of retail merchandise to consumers in California. It did not have either property or employees in California. The district court granted L.L. Bean's motion to dismiss for lack of personal jurisdiction.

The Ninth Circuit reversed the district court's decision holding there was a basis for general jurisdiction over the Maine outfitter. The court predicated a finding of general jurisdiction in part upon L.L. Bean's extensive marketing and sales targeting California consumers and contacts with California vendors. In addition, the L.L. Bean website created a virtual California store satisfying general jurisdiction. *Gator.Com Corp. v. L.L. Bean, Inc.*, 341 F.3d 1072, 1074, 1076–79 (9th Cir. 2003). The U.S. Supreme Court has yet to address the circumstances in which general jurisdiction may be asserted over an online business. Like the Internet, the definition of what level of activity constitutes general jurisdiction online is still evolving.

(D) Specific Jurisdiction in Cyberspace

Courts typically use the three-pronged *Burger King* test to determine whether specific personal jurisdiction over a non-resident defendant is appropriate: (1) the defendant must have sufficient minimum contacts with the forum state, (2) the claim asserted against the defendant must arise out of those contacts, and (3) the exercise of jurisdiction must be reasonable. *Burger King Corp. v. Rudzewicz,* 471 U.S. 462 (1985). The "constitutional touchstone" of the minimum contacts analysis is embodied in the first prong—"whether the defendant purposefully established" contacts with the forum state. The defendant's contacts do not satisfy due process where they are merely fortuitous. The minimum requirements inherent in the concept of 'fair play and substantial justice' may defeat the reasonableness of jurisdiction even if the defendant has the requisite minimum contacts with the forum.

§ 3.3 Zippo.com's Sliding Scale

The interactivity test of *Zippo Mfg. Co. v. Zippo Dot Com, Inc.*, 952 F.Supp. 1119 (W.D. Pa. 1997) adapts traditional jurisdictional principles to the Internet. Zippo, the maker of Zippo lighters, filed a trademark infringement lawsuit against Zippo Dot Com, a California company whose domain name incorporated its trademark. The *Zippo* court examined whether Zippo.com's conducting of business through its website satisfied purposeful availment of doing business in Pennsylvania. The *Zippo* court posited a sliding-scale test classifying the nature and quality of the online commercial activity as the test for personal jurisdiction. At one end of the continuum are passive websites, ones that simply post information not different from print advertisements. At the other end are interactive websites, ones permitting the website owner to conduct business and interact with website visitors with a "gray zone" in the borderland.

In *Zippo.com*, the defendant used its commercial Internet website to generate about 3,000 subscribers in Pennsylvania. Zippo.com also entered into seven contracts with Internet access providers to make its services available to its customers in Pennsylvania. The term "Internet access provider" means a person engaged in the business of providing a computer and communications facility through which a customer may get access to the Internet. The federal district court in *Zippo.com* found this conduct constituted "the purposeful availment of doing business in Pennsylvania." *Id.* A website that is both interactive and transaction-oriented satisfies minimum contacts.

(A) Passive Websites

Courts will not find minimum contacts if the defendant merely posts information on a website without interactivity. *Bensusan Restaurant Corp., v. King*, 937 F.Supp. 295 (S.D. N.Y. 1996). In *Bensusan*, the operator of the famous Blue Note jazz club in New York City filed a trademark infringement suit against a Missouri jazz club with a passive website advertising its Blue Note nightclub. The owners of a small jazz club in Columbia, Missouri created a web page for their club where they posted a calendar of events and ticket information, but did not permit the online purchasing of tickets. The court reasoned the Missouri jazz club owners did not purposefully avail themselves of jurisdiction in New York by posting information on a website without interactivity or otherwise directing commercial activity in the forum.

In *Cybersell Inc. v. Cybersell, Inc.* 130 F.3d 414 (9th Cir. 1997), Cybersell AZ registered its service mark with the USPTO in 1994. In 1995, a Florida father and son formed a family business to conduct website consulting services named Cybersell. The Cybersell AZ plaintiffs were Laurence Canter and Martha Siegel, infamous spam emailers, who filed suit for trademark infringement against the Florida Cybersell. The court reasoned if the defendant's website had been interactive and they had conducted commercial activity over the Internet in the forum, they might have found personal jurisdiction. The court found Cybersell FL did not purposefully avail itself of the privilege of doing business in Arizona ruling the defendant must do "something more," specifically targeting the forum rather than merely posting a website accessible in the forum state.

The court in *Inset Systems, Inc. v. Instruction Set, Inc.,* 937 F.Supp. 161 (D. Conn. 1996) departed from Cybersell's "something more" test and based jurisdiction on a website's mere accessibility. The plaintiff filed suit against a Massachusetts company for trademark infringement based on use of a domain name. The *Inset* court found purposeful availment because the defendant directed advertising into the state and its toll-free number made contact with citizens in every state on a 24/7 basis. The *Inset Systems* court held the posting of Internet advertisements was the equivalent of doing business in Connecticut. The court compared the Internet's continuous presence to television and radio advertising. The problem with this expansive view of jurisdiction is online businesses are subject to jurisdiction everywhere where the information is downloadable.

(B) The Gray Zone

Courts take a closer look at websites in the gray area between passive and interactive websites to determine whether a defendant targeted the forum with advertising, solicitation of orders, or other emblems of a forum presence. In *Williams v. Advertising Sex*, 2007 WL 2570182 (N.D. W.Va. 2007), the plaintiff filed suit after Advertising posted a link to another site. This link falsely said the plaintiff appeared in a sex tape on the other website. The federal court found Advertising's site allowed users to comment on the posted links, so it was not merely a "passive" site under the *Zippo.com* test.

Advertising Sex's website fell within the middle ground or gray area of the *Zippo.com* scale. The *Advertising Sex* court found no basis for personal jurisdiction given no evidence that the defendant targeted customers in West Virginia. "Personal jurisdiction is not found unless the defendant does 'something more' that shows it purposefully directed its activities toward the forum state." *Origin Instruments Corp. v. Adaptive Computer Sys. Inc.*, 1999 WL 76794 *2 (N.D. Tex. 1999).

§ 3.4 Emerging Case Law

No transnational sovereign devises uniform rules for Internet jurisdiction and the enforcement of online judgments. Most U.S. courts are mechanically applying traditional jurisdictional concepts forged for a bricks-and-mortar world. Hundreds of courts cite the *Zippo.com* court's interactivity test to support a finding that a website targeted the jurisdiction. The *Zippo.com* interactivity test is an inadequate test for determining purposeful availment during the second wave of cases where all but a few commercial websites are interactive.

Courts should not stretch the well-worn groves of doctrines unless they mesh well with the Internet. "There is nothing more revolting if the grounds upon which it was laid down have vanished long since, and the rule simply persists from blind imitation of the past." Oliver Wendell Holmes Jr., The *Path of the Law*, 10 HARV. L. REV. 457, 469 (1897). Courts, however, are mechanically extending traditional principles of personal jurisdiction rather than tailoring theories for the borderless Internet.

In *GTE New Media Services Inc. v. BellSouth Corp.*, 199 F.3d 1343 (D.C. 2000), the plaintiff filed a Sherman Antitrust Act complaint against the defendants alleging they were in a conspiracy to dominate the Internet directories market in the Washington, D.C., metropolitan area by diverting Internet users from GTE's website to the defendants' websites. The D.C. Circuit Court of Appeals found BellSouth lacked minimum contacts with the District of Columbia based solely upon the fact its residents could access defendants' Internet Yellow Pages from within the city.

The appellate court ruled GTE could conduct discovery in order to seek proof of sufficient contacts. The district court followed the *Zippo* "sliding scale" approach and finding the defendants' web-

sites fell into the uncertain gray zone finding jurisdiction based on the highly interactive nature and
commercial quality of the websites. The D.C. Circuit
Court reversed reasoning that jurisdiction based
solely on the maintenance of a passive website
would mean, "personal jurisdiction in Internet-related cases would almost always be found in any
forum in the country. Such a result would vitiate
long-held and inviolate principles of personal jurisdiction." *Id*. at 1350.

The court also reasoned personal jurisdiction
could not hinge solely on the ability of D.C. residents "to access the defendants' websites, for this
does not by itself show any persistent course of
conduct by the defendants in the District." *Id*. at
1349. The federal appeals court found no personal
jurisdiction reasoning "[a]ccess to a website reflects
nothing more than a telephone call. The mere receipt of telephone calls is not persistent conduct
within the meaning of the long-arm statute." *Id*. at
1349–50.

In *Instabook v. Instapublisher.com*, 469 F. Supp.
2d 1120 (M.D. Fla. 2006), the court jettisoned the
Zippo.com test in favor of a purposeful contacts
test. The court conceded the defendant's Instabook
websites would pass the interactive test of *Zip-
po.com* but noted interactivity is only one relevant
factor in determining online jurisdiction. *Id*. at
1125. Interactivity is not correlated with the reality
of whether an online company has purposefully
targeted the forum. In fact, the *Instabook* court
could not distinguish between an interactive web-

site and a toll-free-phone line. The court found no jurisdiction despite interactivity because the defendant's website sold products to only two Florida residents.

The court also found the defendant's website did not target or solicit Florida residents. Moreover, the Instabook's terms of services conditioned the use of its website on agreement to litigate in Tennessee. *Id.* at 1127. The court adopted a test based upon "purposeful contacts in order to insure non-residents have fair warning a particular activity may subject them to litigation within the forum." *Id.* In order to find jurisdiction, the court must find "something more" in gray zone cases than mere interactivity to support minimum contacts. Courts will typically consider the following factors in determining whether sufficient minimum contacts exist:

(1) website hits from forum residents, (2) the placement of cookies on computers within the forum, the number of listserv participants within the forum, (3) the administration or operation of a newsgroup accessible within the forum, and the number of participants from the forum; (4) the transmission of orders for products or services that were ordered over the Internet by forum residents, (5) the acceptance or processing of payments through credit cards, or electronic funds transfers, from forum residents, and (6) the placement of any hyperlinks to other Web sites active within the forum.

Proof of Personal Jurisdiction in the Internet Age, 59 AM. JUR. PROOF OF FACTS 3d 1 (2008).

The court in *ALS Scan v. Digital Services Consultants, Inc.*, 293 F.3d 707 (4th Cir. 2002) defined the meaning of "something more" than interactivity by following well established principles. ALS Scan, a Maryland-based adult entertainment website, filed suit against a Georgia ISP for enabling a third parties' misappropriation of its copyrighted photographs. The *ALS Scan* court found no personal jurisdiction because the ISP did not engage in continuous and systematic activities within the forum. In *ALS Scan*, the plaintiff argued Digital enabled Alternative Products' publication of the infringing photographs on the Internet caused ALS Scan injury in Maryland, thus supporting personal jurisdiction.

The *ALS Scan* court reasoned specific jurisdiction in the "Internet context may be based only on an out-of-state person's Internet activity directed at the forum and causing injury gives rise to a potential claim" in that forum. The *ALS Scan* court's approach was, a state may exercise judicial power over a person outside of the state when a person: (1) directs electronic activity into the state; (2) with the manifested intent of engaging in business or other interactions within the state; and (3) the activity creates in a person within the state, a potential cause of action cognizable in the state's courts. Benjamin Spencer contends the *Zippo.com* interactivity test conflicts with traditional due process analysis:

The difficulty here is the interactivity of a Web site actually bears no relationship to whether the defendant has purposefully availed itself of the forum state, particularly once the presumption of aimlessness is discarded. Rather, the conduct relevant to a purposeful availment analysis is which gives rise to the cause of action. Network-mediated contacts can give rise to several different types of claims: breach of contract claims; tort claims, including negligence, products liability, and intentional torts such as defamation or fraud, breach of implied warranty, etc.; and intellectual property claims such as patent, trademark, and copyright infringement. For none of these claims does the degree of interactivity of the Web sites—the medium through which contacts giving rise to the cause of action are mediated—determine whether those contacts will be credited for purposeful availment purposes under the Supreme Court's standards.

Benjamin Spencer, Jurisdiction *and the Internet*: *Returning to Traditional Principles to Analyze Network–Mediated Contacts,* 2006 U. ILL. L. REV. 71, 96. The trend is for courts to adopt a targeting analysis beyond the outmoded *Zippo.com* interactivity test. Michael Geist, *Is There a There There? Toward Greater Certainty for Internet Jurisdiction,* 16 BERKLEY TECH. L.J. 1345 (2001). (describing judicial trend towards targeting-based analysis that fits well with Internet architecture enabling jurisdictional picking and choosing).

In tort actions, the focus of minimum contacts is the "effects" or "brunt of the harm" test of *Calder v. Jones*, 465 U.S. 783 (1984). The effects test focuses on the nonresident defendant's committing a tort knowing it will cause harm to the plaintiff in their forum. A plaintiff must prove three elements to satisfy personal jurisdiction under the effects test: (1) the defendant committed an intentional tort, (2) creating harm to the plaintiff in a forum, which is the focal point of the harm, and (3) harm expressly aimed at the forum. In *Calder*, the U.S. Supreme Court upheld a California state court's finding it had personal jurisdiction over *The National Enquirer*, which had offices in Florida.

The tabloid reporter wrote a libelous article about Shirley Jones, who starred in *The Partridge Family*. The U.S. Supreme Court reasoned the tabloid knew the brunt of the harm would occur in California, a state where the tabloid had its largest circulation. The *Calder* Court reasoned California was the focal point for the brunt of the harm Shirley Jones suffered and jurisdiction "proper in California based on the "effects" of their Florida conduct in California." *Id.* at 789. Courts typically find sufficient minimum contracts in torts cases where the detrimental effects or injuries are expected in a foreign jurisdiction.

Courts apply the *effects test* to resolve personal jurisdiction in cybertort cases. In *Bochan v. La Fontaine,* 68 F. Supp. 2d 692 (E.D. Va. 1999), the court found defamatory statements made on the Internet about an individual known to be a Virginia citizen would satisfy due process. Bochan, a Virginia plaintiff, filed a lawsuit in the federal district of Virginia contending Texas and New Mexico residents defamed him in Virginia and elsewhere by posting libelous messages from Texas and New Mexico on an Internet newsgroup devoted to the JFK Assassination.

Journalists Ray and Mary La Fontaine, the plaintiffs, were Texas residents who authored *Oswald Talked: The New Evidence in the JFK Assassination.* Bochan bought the La Fontaines' book in Virginia and criticized the book on the Internet posting incendiary reviews. Their caustic review quoted from the LaFontaines' acknowledgments to their book: "[w]e thank Charlotte and Eugenia for putting up with weird parents." This posting provoked the La Fontaines to post responses to the newsgroup, which posted the allegedly defamatory review.

One inflammatory posting said the Bochan's should limit their interest to alt.sex.fetish.tinygirls and leave their children out of it. The Virginia federal court found the LaFontaines' conduct was within state's long arm statute requiring the defendant to cause a tortious injury by an act or omission within state. The court said the postings were made through the defendant's Virginia based America Online account and was within the realm of the long arm statute because the Virginia Internet account enabled the tortious act.

The plaintiff testified the defendant transmitted and stored his defamatory posting in Virginia. The *Bochan* court also noted a Virginia-based server transmitted the communications to servers around the world. These acts, according to the court, established a sufficient contact in Virginia. The *Bochan* court found Harris, another New Mexico defendant, had sufficient advertising and solicitation of business in Virginia to support personal jurisdiction. The court reasoned the defendants should have known the defamatory "effects" of their online communications in Virginia. Any AOL subscriber could be subject to personal jurisdiction everywhere for online activities under this expansive theory not adopted by many other courts.

§ 3.5   International Jurisdiction

The Internet is interconnected and transnational, challenging traditional sovereignty based upon geographic borders. The countries connected to the Internet have not agreed to cede their sovereignty in order to harmonize cyberjurisdictional rules. Instead, courts adapt their own national rules to determine jurisdiction. No other country has adopted the U.S. style minimum contacts approach to personal jurisdiction. The American approach to jurisdiction differs significantly from the bright-line rules found in most other countries connected to the Internet.

(A) Dow Jones & Co. v. Gutnick

In *Dow Jones & Company Inc. v. Gutnick*, HCA 56 (Austl. 2002), Gutnick sued Dow Jones, the publisher of the Barron's Digest. Barron's published an allegedly defamatory article about Joseph Gutnick's illegal stock transactions on the *Wall Street Journal* website. The article was stored on a computer server located in New Jersey and uploaded to the Dow Jones website where paid subscribers downloaded the article. The defendant's argument was that if any tort was committed it would have been in New Jersey not Australia.

The Australian High Court was asked to consider whether Gutnick's defamation action could be filed in Victoria, given the claim stemmed from an online article posted on the Internet by a U.S. based web server. The court held Gutnick's claim could be tried in Victoria since the allegedly defamatory article was downloaded and read there and where Gutnick suffered the brunt of the harm. *Dow Jones & Co. v. Gutnick*, HCA 56 (Austl. 2002). The High Court's view was Gutnick suffered harm in Victoria, which was the place of the tort. The *Gutnick* court also refused to adopt the American single publication rule in which a single edition of a newspaper, magazine, or television program gives rise to only one cause of action. A plaintiff must seek all damages in a single lawsuit and may not file further actions. Restatement (Second) Torts § 577.

If X posts a defamatory statement on a blog about Y, the single publication rule would dictate Y would be limited to only one lawsuit. In contrast, Y could file lawsuits in any jurisdiction where harm was felt under a multiple publication rule. A single posting of Internet content could potentially lead to multiple causes of action across the world. The *Gutnick* decision is disconcerting because of the potential liability facing content providers. The *Gutnick* case raises the specter of unlimited liability everywhere for any website publisher. Jurisdictions not following the single publication rule give the plaintiff the option to split causes of action to encompass each jurisdiction where harm is felt.

(B) Cross–Border Civil Procedure

The European Union enacted cross-border jurisdiction rules for all twenty-seven Member States. Europe's harmonized system of cross-border jurisdiction, a possible model for transnational Internet jurisdiction, has its roots in the unifying principles of the 1957 Rome Treaty. The European Commission, established in the 1950s by the E.U.'s founding treaty, is the only legal institution independent of national governments, which has the mission of representing the entire E.U.

(C) E.U.'s Brussels Regulation

Personal jurisdiction refers to the power of the court to preside over a defendant. Effective March 2002, the Brussels Regulation on jurisdiction and the recognition and enforcement of judgments in civil and commercial matters took effect throughout Europe replacing the Brussels Convention of 1968. The Brussels Regulation updates the law for all

Brussels Convention signatories including Denmark which had originally opted out. See, Council Reg (EC) 44/2001.

A federal district interpreted the Brussels Regulation as being "applicable 'even if the plaintiff is domiciled in a non-member country.' " *Gita Sports Ltd. v. SG Sensortechnik GmbH & Co. KG*, 560 F. Supp. 2d 432, 442 (W.D. N.C. 2008). An eBusiness directing its activities to a European consumer's home country will automatically be subject to jurisdiction because it has directed activities to that forum under Brussels Regulation, Article 15.

(1) Freedom to Choose

The Brussels Regulation lets the parties determine jurisdiction in advance in business-to-business transaction but not consumer transactions. The Regulation provides when "the parties, one or more of whom are domiciled in a Member State, have agreed a court of the courts of a Member State are to have jurisdiction to settle any disputes … that court shall have jurisdiction." *Id.* at Art. 23(1).

(2) Domicile as Default

A plaintiff may sue a defendant where they are domiciled. *Id.* at Art. 2. Plaintiffs may file actions against individuals in the Member State where their principal residence is located what Americans courts refer to as domicile. Article 60 establishes the domicile of a company or other entity in the place where it has its statutory seat, central administration, or principal place of business. *Id.* at Art. 60.

(3) Special Jurisdictional Rules

The general default rule for contracts is someone "domiciled in a Contracting State may, in another

Contracting State, be sued in matters relating to contract, in the courts for the place of performance of the obligation in question." *Id.* at Art. 5(1)(a). The European Commission devised a specialized rule for determining jurisdiction in sales of goods transactions. European courts base jurisdiction in sale of goods cases by the place of delivery often turning on shipping terms or other contractual terms. *Id.* at Art. (5)(1).

Courts determine jurisdiction in torts cases using a place of the harm test or *lex loci delicti* similar to the Restatement (Second) of Conflicts test used by courts in the United States. *Id.* at Art. 5. In many cybertorts cases, the place of the harm is more difficult to determine than in garden variety automobile negligence cases. The place of the harm test in a trade libel or data protection case is not likely a single jurisdiction. In online defamation or privacy cases, the place of the harm may be where the plaintiff feels the detrimental effects not confined to a single jurisdiction.

(4) Mandatory Consumer Rules

Articles 15–17 of the Brussels Regulation establishes mandatory consumer rules in business-to-consumer ("B2C") disputes because the consumer may try these contractual disputes within the courts of the consumer's country of domicile. A Swedish dentist purchasing a Volvo for his household use would be classified as a consumer. If a U.S. firm conducts B2C transactions in Europe, it is subject to jurisdiction in any of the twenty seven Member States, as courts will extend Brussels to protect their consumers. Article 15(3) provides in "matters relating to tort, delict, or *quasi-delict*, jurisdiction is in the Member State for the "place where the harmful event occurred or may occur." *Id.* at Art. 15(3). European courts will likely apply the consumer's "home court" if they file a lawsuit against a U.S. firm in a Member State of the E.U. National courts are likely to apply rules functionally equivalent to the Brussels Regulation even though the U.S. is not a Member State.

In *Air Canada v. United Kingdom* (1995) 20 EHRR 150, the European Court of Human Rights held the seizure of an aircraft carrying illegal drugs belonging to the Canadian applicant had not infringed Article 1 of the First Protocol of the European Convention on Human Rights. The court did not find it persuasive the applicant was a resident in Canada in making its decision. A second way the Brussels Regulation will apply is if U.S. companies have subsidiaries in Europe. Article 16(1) of the Brussels Regulation states "a consumer may bring proceedings against the other party to a contract either in the courts of the Member State in which that party is domiciled or in the courts for the place where the consumer is domiciled." *Id.* at Art. 16(1). Article 16(2) of the Brussels Regulation makes it clear the U.S. business may only sue "in the courts of the Member State in which the consumer is domiciled." *Id.* at Art. 16(1).

In addition, Article 17 of the Regulation makes the special consumer rules for cross-border civil procedure non-waivable. Companies cannot compel European consumers to waive the benefit of Brussels Regulation's mandatory home court rule. Thus, an online business has no ability to enforce a contractual term in which a consumer waives her right to sue in her own country or home court. While the Brussels Regulation does not address e-commerce transactions, European courts will stretch its principles to e-commerce transactions.

(5) Freedom of Contract

Article 23 of the Brussels Regulation allows parties in the Eurozone to choose which country's court will resolve their dispute. Article 23 of the Brussels Regulation gives the parties to a contract the right to depart from the default rules. *Id.* at Art. 23. However, this freedom is only for business-to-business contracts, since businesses may not side-step mandatory consumer rules.

§ 3.6 Parties' Choice of Law & Forum

(A) U.S. Parties' Contractual Choice

American courts broadly enforce choice of law and forum clauses unless "unreasonable and unjust." A parties' choice of law clause is an agreement to determine in advance what law applies in the event of litigation. In contrast, a party's choice of forum clause is a contractual provision predetermining the judicial or arbitral forum in the event of a dispute arising out of an Internet or web site agreement. Disney©, for example, requires all consumers to submit to jurisdiction in state or federal courts located in Los Angeles County, California. Nokia© requires all cell phone customers to submit claims to an arbitrator in Finland. The U.S. Supreme Court in *M/S Bremen v. Zapata Off–Shore Co.*, 407 U.S. 1 (1972) broadly validated forum selection clauses so long as they are not unreasonable. U.S. courts will dismiss claims brought in courts outside an agreed upon forum. Restatement (Third) of the Foreign Relations Law of the United States § 421 cmt. h, at 308 (1987) (action brought contrary to selected forum will generally be dismissed "unless the plaintiff shows the chosen forum is no longer available or could not be expected to grant him a fair hearing").

In *Carnival Cruise Lines, Inc. v. Shute*, 499 U.S. 585 (1991), the U.S. Supreme Court broadly validated choice of forum clauses in a consumer transaction. In *Shute,* a Washington State couple booked a cruise on the Florida-based cruise line. The cruise line sent Russell and Eulala Shute tickets with a printed contractual choice of law clause on the back designating courts in Florida as the agreed-upon *fora* for the resolution of disputes. Eulala Shute suffered personal injuries while the Carnival Cruise vessel was sailing off the Mexican coast. Upon their return, the Shutes filed suit in a Washington federal district court and the court dismissed for lack of personal jurisdiction. The Ninth Circuit reversed finding Carnival Cruise's advertising constituted sufficient minimum contacts in Washington. The U.S. Supreme Court reversed the Ninth Circuit ruling the consumers entered into a valid agreement to litigate in Florida.

Federal courts validate contractual choice of law and forum clauses in business-to-consumer transactions as well as in business-to-business transactions. In *Groff v. America Online, Inc.*, 1998 WL 307001 (R.I. 1998), for example, America Online operated an online computer service, which the defendant used to access and receive information from his personal computer. The court enforced the choice of forum clause finding it to be a reasonable contract term. The *Groff* court declared the plaintiff had the option to refuse the service offered by America Online. The court agreed with the provider the consumer "signed" the click through agreement by clicking "I agree" twice.

Terms of services available online are broadly enforceable unless the term is fraudulent, unconscionable or not conspicuous enough to give fair notice. In *Bowen v. YouTube, Inc.*, 2008 WL 1757578 (W.D. Wash. 2008), the court enforced YouTube's choice of law and forum clause. The court ruled the plaintiff agreed to YouTube.com's Terms of Use, which established jurisdiction in California. Courts broadly enforce these agreements so long as the visitor has online access to the terms.

In *Caspi v. Microsoft Network, L.L.C.*, 732 A.2d 528 (N.J. Super. Ct. App. Div. 1999), the court upheld Microsoft Network's forum selection clause finding the subscribers manifested assent to its terms. The *Caspi* court noted subscribers could review the browsewrap terms including the forum selection clause in a scrollable window and manifested assent by clicking "I Agree" or "I Don't Agree." The *Caspi* court noted New Jersey broadly enforces forum selection clauses and rejected the plaintiffs' argument the agreement was the result of fraud or "overwhelming bargaining power."

§ 3.7 Courts' Choice of Law

(A) U.S. Conflicts of Law

If the parties do not choose the law, the courts will apply conflicts of law principles to determine which law applies. Conflicts of law are inevitable in Internet cross-border transactions and courts resolve them by applying the following steps: (1) establish whether the laws at issue are substantive or procedural; (2) if substantive, categorize the laws as tort, property, or contract; and (3) look to the germane section of the Restatement (Second) of Conflict of Laws. "New rules for deciding conflicts of law might be necessary when contracts are negotiated, executed, and performed entirely in cyberspace." *Ulliman Schutte Cont., LLC v. Emerson Process Mgmt.*, 2006 WL 1102838 (D.D.C. 2006).

Courts have not developed new conflicts rules especially for cyberspace instead following the well-worn paths of the Restatement of Conflicts. A federal court applied traditional Michigan choice of law rules in determining Illinois law applied to a contract for the operation of an Internet website between the Detroit Tigers baseball team and an Illinois website. The court found Illinois to be the choice of law since the attorneys drafted the website contract and performed it there as opposed to Michigan. *Detroit Tigers, Inc. v. Ignite Sports Media, LLC.*, 203 F. Supp. 2d 789 (E.D. Mich. 2002).

Courts generally determine cross-border tort or delict cases based upon the place of the wrong or *lex loci delicti commissi*. Most courts have cast off these simplistic territorially based approaches in favor of multi-factorial tests considering public or state policies in addition to the situation of the parties. The history of U.S. conflicts of law arises out of multi-state transactions long before the rise of the Internet. In an online contract between a U.S. seller and a French buyer, for example, the court will choose between U.S. and French contract law.

(1) Significant Relationship in Contract Cases

No transnational Internet court has yet evolved to resolve cross-border conflicts of law in cyberspace. U.S. courts, like their foreign counterparts, revert to traditional principles in resolving conflicts of law in cyberspace cases. In the United States, many courts extend the principles of the Restatement (Second) of Conflicts to the Internet. In trade libel cases arising out of defamatory postings, a corporation's principal place of business will typically be the state with the closest relationship to the claim.

Courts determine where a contract was negotiated or formed to determine which jurisdiction's contract law to apply in contract interpretation disputes. Restatement (Second) of Conflict of Laws, § 188. The Restatement's factors key to the "most significant relationship" test include the: (1) place of contracting, (2) place of negotiation of the contract, (3) place of performance, (4) location of the subject matter of the contract, and (5) domicile, residence, nationality, place of incorporation and place of business of the parties. Few courts apply conflict of law principles to online activities but U.S. courts will likely turn to the Restatement for guidance.

(2) Significant Relationship Test for Torts

Many American courts apply a significant relationship test in torts cases. The rights and liabilities are determined by the local or state law which has the most "significant relationship" to the occurrence and the parties. It is difficult to apply the significant relationship to online defamation cases. The significant relationship test is multi-factorial examining: (1) places where the injury occurred; (2) places where conduct causing injury occurred; (3) domicile, residence, nationality, place of incorporation and place of business of parties; and (4) place where relationship between parties is centered. Restatement (Second) of Conflicts, § 145. The purposes, policies, and aims of local tort law are also critically important to determining which law to apply in a cross-border tort.

(B) European Union's Choice of Law Rules

The twenty-seven countries of the European Union ("E.U.") follow harmonized private international law rules. The E.U. enshrines freedom for the parties to choose the applicable law as cornerstone of business-to-business transactions. In contrast, the E.U. protects consumers with conflict rules favorable to the weaker party. The Rome I Regulation displaced the Rome I Convention of 1980 in 2005. Member States may refuse to opt-in to the new regulation and continue following the Rome I Convention. In 2006, the United Kingdom made the decision to opt out of the Rome I Regulation but reversed course in 2008. In June 2008, the European Commission replaced the Rome I Convention of 1980 with a Community–Wide Regulation, EC No. 593/2008.

(1) Scope of Rome I Regulation

The Rome I Regulation provides rules to determine which law applies to contracts with connections in more than one European Union Member State. Article 1 explains the scope of Rome I resolves conflict of law issues in contractual and commercial matters. Article 1 carves out exceptions from the scope of the Rome I Regulation, including questions involving the status or legal capacity of natural persons.

(2) "Business-to-Business Freedom of Contract

The Rome I Regulation permits parties in business-to-business ("B2B") transactions to choose what law should apply in the event of a dispute. Courts are to presume if parties specified a choice of forum or agreed to a jurisdiction clause, then they have chosen the law of that Member State. The parties' choice of law may not be divest the consumer of the protection of mandatory rules, a rule functionally equivalent to Brussels Regulation's mandatory rules. *Id.* at Art. 6. The Rome I Regulation instructs courts to determine the parties' contractual intent "with reasonable certainty by the terms of the contract or the circumstances of the case." Art. 3(1).

(3) Courts' Choice of Law

Rome I gives the parties in business-to-business commercial transactions the power to make their own choice as to the governing law. The provisions of Rome I come into play where the parties do not specify the governing law. In other words, if the parties do not choose the law, the court will apply the Rome I default, which is the "close connection" test. Article 4 of the Rome I Regulation mandates the law determined partially by substantive field of law as follows shall govern the contract:

(1) a contract of sale shall be governed by the law of the country in which the seller has his habitual residence;

(2) a contract for the provision of services shall be governed by the law of the country in which the service provider has his habitual residence;

(3) a contract of carriage shall be governed by the law of the country in which the carrier has his habitual residence;

(4) a contract relating to a right *in rem* or right of user in immovable property shall be governed by the law of the country in which the property is situated;

(5) the law of the country in which the person who transfers or assigns the rights has his habit-

ual residence shall govern a contract relating to intellectual or industrial property rights.

The remaining sub rules of Article 4 determine how a court shall choose the law for franchises and distributorships. In service contracts, for example, the law is "governed by the law of the country in which the party who is required to perform the service characterizing the contract has his habitual residence at the time of the conclusion of the contract." *Id.*

(4) **Mandatory Consumer Rules**

The Rome I Regulation adopted the consumer's home court rule, which means for consumer contracts the governing law is the place where a consumer has her "habitual residence." *Id.* at Art. 6. The special consumer rules apply only to natural persons who have their place of residence in European Commission Member States. Article 6 defines a consumer adopting the same definition used in the Brussels Regulation. A consumer "must be regarded as being outside his trade or profession with another person, the professional, acting in the exercise of his trade or profession." *Id.* Article 6 applies to anyone "direct[ing] such activities to that Member State or to several States." *Id.*

(C) **Rome II Governing Torts & Delicts**

The Rome II Regulation on the law establishes choice of law rules for cross-border international torts or *delicts*. The European Commission also approved Regulation (EC) No 864/2007 of 11 July 2007 on the law applicable to non-contractual obligations (Rome II) (OJ L199, 31/07/07). The principle of the *lex loci delicti commissi* or the place of the wrong *is* the basic rule for torts in Member States of the European Union. The Rome II Regulation works well for traditional torts such as automobile negligence, products liability, or medical malpractice. However, it is unclear where the place of the wrong is for online defamation. Presumably, a European court would determine the place of the wrong where the detrimental harm or injury occurred, which in most instances would be the plaintiff's country.

However, detrimental effects could be felt in multiple European Member States in trade libel cases. A website on the Internet making false statements about a company's business practices creates harm in multiple jurisdictions. Typically, Internet businesses may have a server in a different jurisdiction than their place of business. To date, no European court has interpreted the the "place of wrong" test in an Internet-related case.

§ 3.8 Enforcement of Judgments

Increasingly, the Internet creates dilemmas for courts in deciding which foreign judgments should be enforced where there are cultural and legal clases. The U.S. is not a party to a Convention or Treaty establishing cross-border reciprocal recognition of Internet-related judgments. The State Department describes four questions courts consider in determining the enforceability of foreign judgments whether: (1) the foreign court had jurisdiction, (2) the defendant was properly served with process, (3) the proceedings were vitiated by fraud, and (4) enforcement of judgments violates public policy where enforcement is sought. U.S. Department of State, *Enforcement of Judgments* (2008).

The U.S. State Department notes their procedures and documentary requirements for the enforcement of judgments vary significantly. While U.S. federal courts broadly enforce foreign judgments with few exceptions, many foreign courts do not reciprocally enforce judgments in favor of U.S. citizens. Germany, for example, refuses to enforce multi-million dollar punitive damages judgments against their citizens rendered in U.S. courts. No international convention or treaty requires the countries connected to the Internet to agree to the reciprocal enforcement of foreign judgments.

The U.S. Constitution's Full Faith and Credit Clause require U.S. courts to enforce out of state judgments so long as they find minimum contacts are satisfied. About half of the states have adopted the Uniform Foreign Judgments Act which provides, subject to certain exceptions, foreign judgments are "final, conclusive and enforceable" in the country where rendered are deemed conclusive between the parties and enforceable by U.S. courts. See, e.g., N.Y. C.P.L.R. §§ 5302, 5303. Courts need not defer to foreign court judgments made in contravention of public policy. Courts do not enforce foreign judgment repugnant to the state's public policy as in the Yahoo! case discussed in Chapter One. In *Sarl Louis Feraud Intern. v. Viewfinder,* 489 F.3d 474 (2d Cir. 2007), French clothing designers filed an action to enforce a French default judgment against Viewfinder, the operator of Internet website on which photographs of the French designers' products had been posted. The lower court held the enforcement of this French judgment would be repugnant to New York public policy because it would violate the website's First Amendment rights. The Second Circuit held a federal court did not complete the full analysis necessary in his ruling. The appeals court ruled the lower court must first determine the level of First Amendment protection required by New York public policy when the website engaged in the unauthorized use of intellectual property, and then it must determine whether French intellectual property law provided comparable protections.

(A) European Enforcement of Judgments

The Brussels Regulation governs the enforcement of judgments in addition to establishing European cross-border jurisdiction rules. Courts in the Member States reciprocally enforce judgments rendered in other Member States. The Brussels Regulation defines a "judgment" to mean any judgment given by a court or tribunal of a Member State, whatever the judgment may be called, including a decree, order, decision, or writ of execution. The Brussels Regulation does not permit courts to review the substance of a judgment except if the judgments are contrary to public policy.

(B) Enforcement of Arbitration Decrees

The 1958 New York Convention on the Recognition and Enforcement of Foreign Arbitral Awards is adopted by the U.S. and a vast majority of major U.S. trading partners. The New York Convention places *primary jurisdiction* over the arbitration award in the country which, or under the arbitration law of which, an award was made. Secondary jurisdiction is in the remainder of New York Convention signatory states. Courts in secondary jurisdiction countries have no power to annul or vacate an arbitral award. The Convention requires courts of Contracting States to give effect to an agreement to arbitrate when a panel determines a matter covered by an arbitration agreement. The New York Convention defines "arbitral awards" to mean not "only awards made by arbitrators appointed for each case but also those made by permanent arbitral bodies to which the parties have submitted." Art. 1(1). Article 2 of the Convention requires arbitration agreements to be in writing. Courts in the United States and other New York Convention countries must enforce arbitration agreements so long as they are in writing." *Id.* at Art. 2. The New York Convention also enforces awards made in other States, subject to specific limited exceptions. The Convention calls for broad enforceability of judgments rendered by arbitral tribunals.

(C) The Hague Convention Proposed Regime

On June 30, 2005, the Hague Convention on Choice of Court was proposed. This Convention applies to the recognition or enforcement of foreign judgments. *Id.* at Art. 1.3. The validation of "exclusive choice of court agreements" is the key provision of the Convention. The default is that courts will enforce the parties' agreement as to where a case should be decided. *Id.* at Art. 3. The Choice of Court Convention excludes consumer transactions defined as transactions for "personal, family, or household purposes." The Convention specifies several carve outs dealing in matters such as the status and capacity of natural persons, family law matters, bankruptcy, antitrust, and tort claims. *Id.* at Art. 2. The parties' choice of court does not determine intellectual property rights under the Convention. The Convention applies to court decisions, not arbitration proceedings.

Article 5 gives the chosen court jurisdiction to decide the matter "unless the agreement is null and void under the law of that State. *Id.* at Art. 5. The court shall dismiss an action filed in another court other than one agreed upon by the parties. *Id.* at Art. 6. Article 8 provides for recognition and enforcement of judgments in the chosen court.

The "Choice of Court" Convention displaced the Convention on Jurisdiction and Foreign Judgments in Civil and Commercial Matters. American companies and other Internet stakeholders opposed the U.S. becoming a signatory to the former Hague Convention. Stakeholders opposed the pro-consumer rules, which gave consumers a choice where to file suits in B2C transactions. The displaced convention would have set bright-line rules modeled on the European Commission's Brussels Convention governing jurisdiction and judgment in civil matters.

To date, no country has adopted The Hague Convention on Choice of Court.

§ 3.9 UNIDROIT Transnational Civil Procedure

The American Law Institute ("ALI") and UNIDROIT have drafted a promising proposal for new Principles and Rules of Transnational Civil Procedure. ALI, *ALI/UNIDROIT Principles* (2001). The Convention has yet to be finalized or adopted but does present the best model for harmonizing cross-border procedural rules. The model ALI/UNIDROIT statute proposes four bases for asserting transborder jurisdiction: (1) designation by mutual agreement of the parties; (2) in a defendant is subject to the compulsory judicial authority of that state, as determined by principles governing personal jurisdiction or by international convention to which the state is a party; or (3) where fixed property is located; or (4) in aid of the jurisdiction of another forum in which a Transnational Civil Proceeding is pending. *Id.* These rules reflect long-established principles in the U.S. as well as Europe.

CHAPTER FOUR

ELECTRONIC COMMERCE

§ 4.1 Overview of E–Commerce Law

Electronic commerce includes any consumer or commercial transaction conducted over the Internet for the sale, lease, or licensing of goods, services or for the transfer of software or other information. An online company monetizes its software by creating a portfolio of licensed products. In the law of real property, a "license" is a privilege to enter upon land of the possessor, but not a transfer of an interest in land. In the law of e-commerce, licensing is the chief method of transferring value. In contrast to a sale, licenses grant the licensee a contractual right to use or access software or other digital information. A software company's licensing efforts will also include copyrights, trademarks, patents, as well as access to trade secrets. In addition, an eBusiness will need to avoid infringing the IP portfolio's of third parties. Thus, an online company will need to obtain the rights to acquire licensed content including music, photographs, software, and streaming video and audio on its website.

§ 4.2 Sources of E–Commerce Law

(A) Online Sales Law

Article 2 of the Uniform Commercial Code applies to all "transactions in goods" whether sold in a "brick and mortar" store or on an online company's website. State legislatures enacted UCC Article 2 in the 1950s and 1960s decades before the rise of e-commerce. The American Law Institute ("ALI") and the National Conference of Commissioners on Uniform State Law ("NCCUSL") revised Article 2 to update sales law for the age of the Internet. Revised Article 2 envisions electronic means for parties to enter into contracts and communicate with their contracting partners. Presently, for example, Article 2 requires a signed writing for sales of goods $500 or greater. Revised Article 2 raises the statutory minimum to $5,000 and lets the parties to substitute an electronic record for a paper-based writing.

Currently, the UCC defines a signature or the term "signed" as "any symbol executed or adopted with the present intent to authenticate a writing." Revised Article 2 defines "authenticate" broadly to encompass any encrypted signature or other electronic records. Revised Article 2 provides needed infrastructure for e-commerce in its validation of online contracts by e-agents. Electronic events such as the transmittal of data messages, for example, may be "attributed to a person if it was the act of that person or its electronic agent." UCITA § 214(a). The parties may enter into an online contract with or without human review. As of January 2009, no U.S. jurisdiction has adopted Revised Article 2. Courts continue to stretch concepts of current UCC Article 2 to online contracts and licensing transactions.

(B) Electronic Data Interchange

Electronic data interchange ("EDI") is computer-to-computer interchange of strictly formatted messages by which goods are ordered, shipped and tracked computer-to-computer:

> An example of EDI is a set of interchanges between a buyer and a seller. Messages from buyer to seller could include, for example, request for quotation (RFQ), purchase order, receiving advice and payment advice; messages from seller to buyer could include, similarly, bid in response to RFQ, purchase order acknowledgment, shipping notice and invoice. These messages may simply provide information, e.g., receiving advice or shipping notice, or they may include data that may be interpreted as a legally binding obligation, e.g., bid in response to RFQ or purchase order.

National Institute of Standards, *EDI* (1996).

EDI saves money because the computer, and not an office staff, submits and processes orders, claims, and other routine tasks. EDI represents a significant advance over snail mail in transmitting business information. Under a more efficient approach, computer-to-computer transactions solve the problem of delay in supply chains. EDI has a lower rate of error than persons taking orders in a supply chain. Trading partners first enter into EDI master agreements to employ electronic messaging and computer-to-computer ordering of goods and services.

(C) Internet–Related Licenses

The World Wide Web is less than two decades old so it is not surprising online contracting practices are rapidly evolving. Software developers and other content creators routinely structure their contracts as licenses. This trend represents the displacement of the durable goods by an economy built upon the Internet, intellectual property, software, entertainment, and other information transfers. Internet-related licenses are permissions to use software, databases, intellectual property, or other content. A sale, in contrast, involves the passage of title to goods for a price. License agreements vary on the number of copies licensed, the method of distribution, the type of end user, or the form of a license agreement. Consumers are unable to negotiate mass-market licenses offered by vendors on a take it or leave it basis with identical terms of service or conditions of use. Apple Computer Inc.'s iTunes requires consumers to agree to a license agreement in order to download music.

Licensors, in contrast, tailor customized software to the user's specific needs. A software developer will typically restrict use of licenses through site or time limitations. Licensing is a more flexible contracting regime as compared to the law of sales because sellers have no control over the disposition of goods after title passes. In contrast, licensors never pass title and set the conditions for use of software, data, or other content. A LEXIS/NEXIS license, for example, is a license to electronically display, print, and download copyrighted materials from its databases. WESTLAW and LEXIS/NEXIS, for example, are subject to many terms. These legal research services do not permit law students to use their services for commercial purposes.

An online company, for example, has developed software for interactive advertisements and will enter into license agreements with portals such as Yahoo! or Google in order to reap the benefits of advertising with a popular portal. Website businesses seek partnerships with other online and brick and mortar companies, which mean contractual relationship for the purposes of software development, advertising, and online access.

Software may be licensed, leased, or sold. Licensing is the chief means of transferring value in the information-based economy. Software licensing allows far greater control than either sales or leases of goods. Location and use restrictions are necessary tools for software developers to realize their investment in developing intangible information assets.

(1) Mass–Market License

The term ''mass-market license'' refers to any standard form agreement whereby the user adheres to the terms and conditions set by the licensor without negotiation. A shrink-wrap agreement is when the licensee is contractually bound by cracking open the seal on a shrink-wrapped package. Mass-market licensors typically disclaim warranties, offering only the repair or replacement of the software disk or other media as the sole and exclusive remedy.

(2) Click Through Agreements

The typical "click through" website agreement requires end users to click on an icon, "I agree," which creates a contract where the user agrees to submit to all of the licensor's terms and conditions. A Dilbert cartoon lampoons these adhesion contracts by depicting a licensee who unwraps the shrink-wrap only to learn he has become Bill Gate's towel boy. In the cartoon, Dilbert states, "I didn't read all of the shrink-wrap license agreement on my new software until after I opened it. Apparently, I agreed to spend the rest of my life as a towel boy in Bill Gates's new mansion." Michael L. Rustad & Thomas H. Koenig, *The Tort of Negligent Enablement of Cybercrime*, 20 BERKELEY L.J. 1553, 1563 (2005). Standard-form agreements are adhesion contracts in which the licensee adheres to the terms of the stronger party.

(3) Shrinkwrap Agreements

Shrinkwrap is the plastic surrounding boxed software. The software license may have the caption "Limited Use License Agreement" printed on the package containing computer software. A typical mass-market license will state: "You have purchased and/or paid for a license to use the software only in accordance with the applicable terms and conditions in this agreement." Vendors often place notice of the license on the outside of the shrink-wrapped box containing the CD–ROM or DVD–ROM. Shrinkwrap agreements limit liability of the software vendor by disclaiming implied warranties and limiting remedies.

The typical Internet-related shrink-wrap or other mass-market license agreement do not provide warranties of any kind and foreclose any remedy by requiring the consumer to litigate in a forum of the vendor's choice often in a distant forum. The first paragraph of a shrink-wrap license usually provides the opening of the package constitutes acceptance of the license terms. The shrink-wrap license conditions access to and use of its software on acceptance of its terms and conditions. The licensor's purpose is to create a "reverse unilateral contract," which is structured so the customer who opens the plastic wrap and uses the software is bound to the one-sided terms of the shrink-wrap license. Mark A. Lemley, *Intellectual Property and Shrinkwrap Licenses*, 68 S. CAL. L. REV. 1239, 1241 (1995). Many shrinkwrap license agreements generally begin with a legal notice, disclaimer, or terms of use equating breaking shrinkwrap confirming the users' acceptance of the license terms. Standard form license agreements not only reallocate the risk of software failure to the licensee, but usually also bypass the first sale doctrine of federal copyright law.

(4) Clickstream & Browsewrap

The clickstream or browsewrap contract requires the user to click "yes" to signify acceptance to the license agreement. Christina L. Kunz et al., *Browse–Wrap Agreements: Validity of Implied Assent in Electronic Form Agreements*, 59 BUS. LAWYER 279 (2003). A browsewrap means Internet users may not use a website unless they agree to the site's terms of service though the agreement does not appear on the screen automatically. "So, for example, the term in its purest form includes an interface that presents a link at the bottom of the page to the terms and conditions. It also includes more ambiguous situations, such as where there is a statement that the purchase is governed by terms that are linked to the page" but requires no clicking of "a radio button acknowledging the terms." Ronald J. Mann & Travis Siebeneicher, *Just One Click: The Reality of Internet Retail Contracting*, 108 COLUM. L. REV. 984, 990 (2008). Four hundred and thirty nine out of five hundred of the largest Internet retailers used only browsewrap agreements versus other contracting practices. *Id.* at 998. The difference between a browsewrap and a clickwrap or clickstream agreement is a user must take some affirmative action such as clicking a button to proceed further in order to access content. Browseware binds the user when they merely browse the website.

§ 4.3 The Emerging Case Law of Standard Form Licenses

Online merchants typically offer consumers "take it-or-leave it" basis. A recent study of Internet businesses described diverse merchant channels running "along a spectrum ranging from virtual (no bricks-and-mortar operations, like Amazon.com) to catalog/call center (such as L.L.Bean) to branded manufacturer (such as Dell) to retail chain (such as Office Depot)." Ronald J. Mann & Travis J. Siebeneicher, *Just One Click: The Reality of Internet Retail Contracting*, 108 COLUM. L. REV. 984, 997 (2008). The authors found the typical online retailer "rarely designed interfaces to obtain assent to their posted terms, and the posted terms rarely include harsh pro-retailer terms." *Id.*

(A) Licensor's Unilateral Modifications

The case law tends to center on one-sided pro-licensor agreements beginning with *Step–Saver Data Sys. v. Wyse Technology*, 939 F.2d 91 (3d Cir. 1991). In *Step Saver*, the Third Circuit refused enforcement of TSL's box-top mass-market license entitled "Limited Use License Agreement" printed on a package containing the defendant's Multilink Advanced computer software. Step–Saver was a value-added retailer for IBM products licensing TSL's software. Step–Saver bought a program by TSL for use on the multi-user system, which it marketed as a turnkey solution for professional's offices such as lawyers and doctors. *Id.* at 93. Step–Saver began receiving complaints from its customers when the TSL software failed. Step–Saver referred the complaints to TSL, which was unable to solve the system integration problems.

Step–Saver argued TSL's box-top license agreements disclaiming all warranties and limiting remedies to return were not enforceable against the purchaser. TSL's shrink-wrap licenses said, "Opening this package indicates your acceptance of these terms and conditions." Step–Saver contended the contract was already formed when TSL agreed to ship the product and any limitations in the shrink-wrap agreement were unilateral proposals for modification and therefore not enforceable. Step–Saver contended the box top license was a material alteration falling out of the contract under a UCC § 2–207(2) battle of the forms analysis. TSL's position was that the box-top license was the final and complete expression of the parties' intent.

The Third Circuit agreed with Step–Saver holding that TSL's box top license was not enforceable because it was a unilateral modification or additional terms outside the parties' agreement. The Third Circuit agreed with Step–Saver the box top license was not part of the contract since the contract was already completed. The Third Circuit disagreed with TSL ruling its box-top form license disclaiming warranties and limiting remedies was a proposed term not part of the contract and classifiable as a unilateral modification. UCC § 2–209.

(B) Copyright Preemption

The Fifth Circuit in *Vault Corp. v. Quaid Software, Ltd.*, 847 F.2d 255 (5th Cir. 1988) affirmed a district court's finding a shrink-wrap license was an unenforceable contract of adhesion and Louisiana Software License Enforcement Act was preempted by the U.S. Copyright Act of 1976. The *Vault* court refused to enforce a contractual term that prohibited reverse engineering. The Fifth Circuit concluded that federal copyright law preempted Louisiana's Software License Enforcement Act, a statute validating anti-reverse engineering clauses. Before the mid–1990s, U.S. courts struck down many shrink-wrap agreements. The recent path of shrink-wrap law however, is to enforce standard form license practices.

(C) Enforceability of Rolling Contracts

In *ProCD v. Zeidenberg*, 86 F.3d 1447 (7th Cir. 1996), the Seventh Circuit upheld a shrink-wrap agreement in which the licensee paid first and was given the terms of agreement only after he paid. ProCD compiled a computer database called Select Phone consisting of more than 3,000 telephone directories. ProCD sought to protect its investment in the database by requiring licensees to enter into a licensing agreement limiting use and containing restrictions. Matthew Zeidenberg purchased a copy of ProCD's Select Phone in Madison, Wisconsin but chose to ignore the terms of the agreement, which had terms against transfers or assignments of rights. *Id. at* 1449. Zeidenberg formed a company to resell the information in ProCD's database. He charged its customers for access to the information in Select Phone and made the information available over the World Wide Web. ProCD filed a copyright infringement lawsuit seeking an injunction against Zeidenberg's further dissemination of its software because he exceeded the scope of the rights granted in the license.

The federal district court held ProCD's license agreements were unenforceable since the terms did not appear on the outside of the package and a customer could not be "bound by terms that were secret at the time of purchase." The Seventh Circuit disagreed ruling ProCD's license agreements were enforceable. The Seventh Circuit applied UCC Article 2 to the license agreement, noting the sales article allows contract formation in "any manner sufficient to show agreement." *Id. at* 1451. The *ProCD* court said in this mass-market license the licensor invited acceptance by silence.

The *ProCD* court found the licensee accepted the software "after having an opportunity to read the license at leisure." The court reasoned ProCD "extended an opportunity to reject if a buyer should find the license terms unsatisfactory." *Id. at* 1452. The court rejected the defendant's argument he had no choice but to adhere to ProCD's terms once he opened the package. The court also gave short shrift to Zeidenberg's argument shrink-wrap license agreements must be conspicuous to be enforced. The *ProCD* court also rejected the argument that the Copyright Act preempts software licenses. The court did not find the rights created by ProCD's license agreement to be the functional equivalent of any of the exclusive rights of the Copyright Act. *Id.* The court noted there were strong policy arguments for the validation of shrink-wrap and pointed to the benefits to consumers of these standard form licenses.

Judge Easterbrook, who authored *ProCD*, was also the author of another influential Seventh Circuit opinion on a mass market license agreement, *Hill v. Gateway 2000, Inc.*, 105 F.3d 1147 (7th Cir. 1997). In *Hill,* a husband and wife challenged an arbitration clause in Gateway's software license agreement included in a standard form contract shipped with their home computer. Gateway's long-time business practice was to send its computer system with a software license agreement included inside the box mailed to the customer. The Seventh Circuit said the "terms inside Gateway's box stand or fall together." *Id.* at 1148. The appeals court held Gateway's license agreement was enforceable because of the consumer's decision to keep the Gateway system beyond the 30–day period specified in the agreement. The *Hill* court reasoned Gateway gave the Hills notice so they would be subject to arbitration if they did not send the computer back to Gateway within the prescribed 30–day return period. The *Hill* court determined there was acceptance by silence and the entire mass-market agreement was binding including the arbitration clause. This is an example of a "rolling contract" where the consumer pays for the product and receives the terms in the packaging of the product when the shipper sends it a later point. A content analysis of mass-market license agreements concluded that only 44 out of the 500 largest Internet sellers required consumers to submit to arbitration. Ronald J. Mann & Travis Siebeneicher, *Just One Click: The Reality of Internet Retail Contracting*, 108 COLUM. L. REV. 984, 998 (2008). A federal district court struck down PayPal's arbitration clause in its standard user agreement as substantively unconscionable in *Comb v. PayPal Inc.*, 218 F. Supp. 2d 1165 (N.D. Cal. 2002). However, most courts broadly enforce similar choice of forum clauses. An Arkansas court upheld PayPal's revised terms of services agreement in *Burke v. E–Bay, Inc.*, 2007 WL 1219697 (W.D. Ark. 2007) (holding the user agreement providing a forum selection clause designating the forum of choice to Santa Clara County, California was not unconscionable).

(D) Licensor's Unilateral Modifications

In *Klocek v. Gateway, Inc.*, 104 F. Supp. 2d 1332 (D. Kan. 2000), the federal court refused to enforce Gateway's "shrink-wrap" license agreement included in the box containing the personal computers. The *Klocek* court found the shrink-wrap agreement was not enforceable since contract formation already occurred when Gateway charged the consumer's credit card and shipped the computer. The federal court therefore refused to enforce Gateway's arbitration clause as it was not part of the agreement between the consumer and the computer maker.

In *i.Lan Sys., Inc. v. NetScout Serv. Level Corp.*, 183 F. Supp. 2d 328 (D. Mass. 2002), a Massachusetts federal court upheld a clickwrap agreement under Article 2 of the Uniform Commercial Code, because plaintiff explicitly accepted the clickwrap license agreement when it explicitly clicked the box

stating "I agree" and implicitly accepted the click-
wrap agreement because its additional terms were
not material. The clickwrap license agreement may
be analyzed as either (1) forming a contract under
UCC § 2–204 or (2) adding terms to an existing
contract. The *i.Lan* court noted it was following the
ProCD line of cases broadly enforcing mass-market
licenses. The court's justification was the mass-
market licenses were consistent with the liberal
purposes of the UCC. The court found the licensee
implicitly accepted the clickwrap license agreement
because its additional terms were not material

(E) Notice & Opportunity to Read

Most U.S. courts broadly enforce mass-market
license agreements so long as the consumer has
notice, an opportunity to read, and does some act
manifesting assent. Courts will not enforce agreements where a licensor makes little effort to draw
attention to pro-licensor terms such as arbitration.
In *Specht v. Netscape Communications Corp.,* 306
F.3d 17, 32 (2d Cir. 2002), the Second Circuit refused to enforce Netscape's Smart Download software license agreement compelling arbitration. The
consumer filed suit under the Computer Fraud &
Abuse Act and Electronic Communications Privacy
Act charging Netscape with allegedly monitoring his
activities over the Internet. The consumer in *Specht*
downloaded free software while the license appeared only on a submerged screen. The court reasoned the consumer had insufficient notice because
she would need to scroll down to the bottom of the
page just to notice the license agreement. The court

refused to enforce the license agreement and compel arbitration.

In *Bragg v. LindenResearch, Inc.*, 487 F. Supp. 2d 593, 593 n. 4 (E.D. Pa. 2007), the owner of Second Life confiscated the plaintiff's virtual property and deported him from their virtual world. The plaintiff filed suit and Second Life filed a motion to compel arbitration. The *Linden Research* court found the arbitration agreement to be procedurally and substantively unconscionable. The Second Life's arbitration agreement was buried in a take-it-or-leave-it contract. The court found the provision's lack of mutuality, the costs of arbitration, the forum selection clause, and the confidentiality provision too one-sided to enforce.

§ 4.4 UETA

(A) Provisions

In July of 1999, NCCUSL approved the Uniform Electronic Transactions Act ("UETA") which is enacted in forty-six states as of January 2009. The purpose of UETA is to remove barriers to e-commerce, implement reasonable practices, and harmonize e-contracting procedural rules. UETA, § 6.

UETA adopted a non-regulatory approach to electronic signatures and writings. UETA validates electronic signatures and records in order to remove barriers to electronic commerce. UETA "applies to any electronic record or electronic signature created, generated, sent, communicated, received, or stored on or after the effective date" of the statute. *Id. at* § 4. A digital signature is an electronic identifier created by computer with the same legal validity as a handwritten signature. Digital signatures employ "public key cryptography," which incorporates an algorithm using two different but mathematically related "keys;" one for creating a digital signature or transforming data into a seemingly unintelligible form, and the another key for verifying a digital signature or returning the message to its original form.

UETA does not apply to any articles of the Uniform Commercial Code, wills, or trusts, UCITA or other state laws. *Id. at* § 3(b)–(d). If there is a conflict between UCC Article 2 governing sales and UETA, Article 2 holds the trump card. UETA defines the "electronic signature" as "an electronic sound, symbol, or process attached to or logically associated with a record, and executed or adopted by a person with the intent to sign the record." *Id.* at § 2(8). UETA does not require any party to use electronic signatures or records. *Id.* at § 5(a). UETA applies "only to transactions between parties, each of which has agreed to conduct transactions by electronic means." *Id.* at § 5(b). UETA provides "[a] record or signature may not be denied legal effect or enforceability solely because it is in electronic form." *Id.* at § 7. UETA legitimizes the concept of electronic contract, providing "[a] contract may not be denied legal effect or enforceability solely because an electronic record was used in its formation." *Id.* at § 7(b).

(B) Electronic Records

UETA provides the ground rules for what constitutes an electronic record. Electronic records must minimally be "capable of retention." *Id.* at § 8(a). An online communication that "inhibits the ability of the recipient to print or store the electronic record" is not accorded the legal status of a retained record. *Id.* For electronic contracts to be viable there must be some mechanism of attribution. Attribution of electronic contracts is necessary so the parties know each other's identity and authority to contract.

Passwords, for example, are a well-established attribution method. A WESTLAW user supplies a password authenticating the user's identity for each login. The attribution of messages between sender and receiver is a key feature of the infrastructure of online contracting. Attribution procedures also verify whether a message contains errors or alterations. Attribution procedures use algorithms or other codes, identifying words or numbers.

(C) Risk of Errors

UETA's method for allocating the risk of errors in electronic records places the risk of loss of a transmission error on the party failing to employ an agreed-upon security procedure. If both parties fail to use an agreed-upon security procedure, the rule does not apply. The party following reasonable security procedures will avoid the effect of the changed or erroneous electronic record only if the other party deviates upon the agreed-upon procedure. Persons entering into electronic contracts must be able to prevent and correct errors.

§ 4.5   E–Signature Act

The Electronic Signatures in Global and National Commerce Act ("E–Sign") of 2000 validated digital signatures and records. 15 U.S.C. § 7001. A court may not deny a contract's legal effect, validity, or enforceability merely because it is in electronic form. Courts may not deny the legal effect or the enforceability of contracts solely because the parties formed the contract through electronic signatures or electronic records. Internet-related contracts may take the form of sales, leases or the licensing of intellectual property. E–Sign validates electronic signatures to authenticate the identity of the sender of a message or the signer of a document, and possibly, to ensure the original content of the sent message or document is unchanged. Digital signatures can be automatically time-stamped and are more transportable than physical signatures.

Section 101(c) is a rule of consent requiring consumers affirmatively consents before receiving electronic communications in lieu of writings. The consent rule also gives consumers a prescribed method for withdrawing consent. Consumer disclosures are required if an electronic record is substituted for a paper-based record. *Id*. at 101(c)(1)(A), (D). Consumers may not be compelled to use electronic contracting and must consent to this method of entering into contracts. Consumers also have the right for the seller or services provider to make the record available on paper or in another electronic form. *Id*. at 101(c)(1)(B)(i)(ii). Congress took the unusual step of incorporating a saving clause, which defers to UETA where there is a conflict with E–Sign. The E–Sign Act preempts state law unless it is an "enactment or adoption of the Uniform Electronic Transactions Act ("UETA"). *Id.* at 102. The vast majority of U.S. states already enacted UETA by the time Congress passed the federal E–Sign in July of 2000.

§ 4.6 UCITA

The United States was the first post-industrial society to develop a specialized legal code for the licensing of software. In 1999, the National Commissioners on Uniform State Law ("NCCUSL") approved the Uniform Computer Information Transactions Act (UCITA). Nevertheless, as of September 30, 2006, only Maryland and Virginia have UCITA and future adoptions are unlikely. UCITA applies to a wide range of Internet-related contracts and is the single most comprehensive body of contract law for cyberspace. UCITA is a stand-alone state statute governing most Internet-related contracts. In the early 1990s, NCCUSL and the American Law Institute ("ALI") agreed to update the UCC to include software-licensing agreements.

(A) History

The sponsors of the Uniform Commercial Code initially proposed UCC Article 2B as a new article of the Uniform Commercial Code creating the first specialized law for software licensing. However, the American Law Institute, one of the UCC's co-sponsors withdrew its sponsorship of Article 2B. UCITA provides a legal infrastructure for standard form licenses, including access contracts, terms of service agreements, click-wrap agreements, shrink-wrap agreements, and website user agreements.

(B) Formation Rules

UCITA § 202 imports UCC Article 2's liberal contract formation rules for cyberspace transactions and other computer information contracts. The drafters define a signature to mean, "a mark made with the intent to authenticate." UCITA, like UCC Article 2, imports common law legal and equitable doctrines to supplement its provisions. However, UCITA § 204 developed specialized rules for the thorny problem of acceptance with varying terms. Under UCITA, the parties may use electronic agents to enter into contracts (offer and acceptance) without the benefit of human review. *Id.* at § 206. Electronic agents are automated means of initiating action or responding to electronic records without appraisal by human beings.

UCITA adapts the Restatement's concept of manifestation of assent to contract terms to apply to Internet or online contracts. UCITA fulfills the manifestation of assent as an affirmative act such as clicking a display button such as "I accept the terms of this agreement." One of the difficult policy issues is to decide what affirmative conduct constitutes assent. In a paper-based contract, a signature establishes the manifestation of assent. UCITA permits the manifestation of assent to be fulfilled by an affirmative act, such as clicking a display button such as "I accept the terms of this agreement." UCITA rejects the doctrine of acceptance by silence for standard form licenses. Courts enforce standard form contracts so long as the licensor meets two conditions: (1) the user has an opportunity to review the terms of the license, and (2) manifests assent after having an opportunity to review the terms. UCITA *broadly* validates click-wrap agreements giving the party an opportunity to review terms before assenting. The licensor can create a "safe harbor" proving manifestation of assent with a built-in double click requiring the user to confirm assent.

Simply clicking an "I accept" text or icon evidences a user's manifestation of assent. An increasing number of website vendors use a "double click" method, which asks the customer whether they are certain they accept the terms of the license. It is likely most visitors click through these icons without reading the license agreement before payment. UCITA provides mass-market licensees with a right to a refund if she has "no opportunity to review a mass-market license or a copy of it before becoming obligated to pay." *Id.* at § 210. A party adopts the terms of a shrink-wrap or click-wrap license if the customer has an opportunity to review the terms and manifest assent by some affirmative act. Software licenses typically limit all damages and provide an exclusive remedy. Some software licenses disallow reverse engineering or limit permissible uses. UCITA imparts contracting rules enabling the further expansion of electronic commerce.

UCITA updates the Statute of Frauds for online contracts by treating a "record" as a functional equivalent of "pen and paper" signatures. The drafters define records to mean information in-

scribed on a tangible medium. Records may also be
stored in an electronic or other medium retrievable
in perceivable form. UCITA allows computer-to-
computer transactions by substituting the concept
of an electronic record as the functional equivalent
of writing. UCITA provides essential legal infrastructure for many different forms of electronic
contracts. Section 201 of UCITA requires a writing
for license agreements which are $5000 or greater.
As with UCC Articles 2 and 2A, UCITA recognizes
several exceptions to the Statute of Fraud's writing
requirement: for example, a license agreement is
enforceable after completed performance, a court
admission, or a merchant licensor's failure to answer a confirming record. The United States is the
only country of the hundreds conducting E-Commerce to require a Statute of Frauds for the sale of
goods.

(C) Warranties

(1) Performance Warranties

UCITA permits licensors to exclude all implied
warranties so long as the language is clear, unam-
biguous, and conspicuous. Warranty limitations
must not be unconscionable nor violate fundamental public policies. UCITA divides warranties into
two types: warranties of authority (or non-infringement) and performance-based warranties of quality.
Section 401 parallels UCC § 2–312's warranty of
title. While title never passes with a license, the
licensor warrants it has the authority to transfer
software or other information the subject of the
license agreement. The warranty of non-infringe-

ment is equivalent to Article 2's warranty of title. As with Article 2, there are special merchant rules imposing a higher duty on professional licensors. A merchant licensor warrants that software is delivered free of claims of infringement or misappropriation. Section 401(b)(2) deals with intellectual property infringement claims.

UCITA's express warranty provisions for computer information transactions are substantially similar to UCC § 2–313. Affirmations of fact about computer software or information are express warranties to the extent they form the "basis of the bargain." Licensors create express warranties by making statements relating to software or other information in banner advertisements, sales literature, and advertisements. Website promotional materials, product descriptions, samples, or advertisements may create express warranties. Implied warranties of quality for computer information import UCC Article 2's concept of the implied warranty of merchantability to the licensing of information. Computer programs must be fit for their ordinary purpose.

A computer program need not be the most efficient but must be acceptable under general industry standards. Licensors must comply with implied warranties by adequately packaging, labeling, and producing multiple copies of an even kind, quality, and quantity. UCITA's implied warranty of system integration is the operative equivalent of UCC § 2–312's warranty of "fitness for a particular purpose." The systems integration warranty applies where the customer relies upon the software licensor's expertise to make computer information suitable for a particular computer system. An online company, for

example could be making a systems integration
warranty if it told a customer its software would
perform with Windows Vista platform. A licensor
creates a systems integration warranty if it warrants component subsystems function together.

(2) Information Content Warranties

UCITA, unlike Article 2, devises an implied warranty for informational content. This special warranty applies to merchant licensors or transfer information without exercising reasonable care. The
warranty for informational content does not arise
for published content or when the licensor is merely
acting as an information transfer conduit not providing editorial services.

(3) Disclaimers & Limitations

Just as in UCC Article 2, UCITA allows the
parties to disclaim or modify all implied warranties
by words or conduct. UCITA validates the universal
practice of the software industry in offering software or other computer information on an "as-is"
basis without warranties. In a business-to-business
case, a contractor made a computational error due
to software bug. The court found the software licensor disclaimed the warranties and followed UCC
Article 2's prescribed method for limiting remedies.
If a seller or licensor does not use the magic words
"sole and exclusive" or an equivalent, the buyer of
licensee will have all the default remedies as well as
the limited remedy. In *M.A. Mortenson Co., Inc. v.
Timberline Software Corp.*, 140 Wash.2d 568, 588
(2000), the construction contractor bought software

from the vendor in the past with similar disclaimers and limitations of remedy. The court upheld the disclaimers and limitations despite a software bug that caused the contractor to submit a bid resulting in a $2 million error.

The licensing agreement disclaiming warranties and limiting remedies appeared on the screen each time the licensee boots a program up on the screen. UCITA is a U.S. style-licensing regime favoring freedom of contract with few mandatory consumer rules. UCITA relies upon doctrines such as unconscionability and the failure of essential purpose to police contract terms. UCITA does not preempt other state and federal consumer protections applicable to software.

§ 4.7 Principles of Software Contracts

(A) History

The ALI withdrew its support from UCITA in 1999 but NCCUSL took over sponsoring UCITA as a stand-alone state statute. Maryland and Virginia adopted UCITA in 1999 but no other states have followed suit. In May of 2008, the ALI approved the Principles of the Law of Software Contracts ("Principles of Software Contracts") The American Law Institute, *Principles of the Law of Software Contracts* (Tentative Draft, March 24, 2008). The goal of the Principles is to provide guidance for courts and legislatures when addressing software contract issues. *Id.* at xix. "Courts can apply the Principles as definitive rules, as a 'gloss' on the common law or U.C.C. Article 2, or not at all, as they see fit."

Maureen O'Rourke, *Software Contracting*, SM088 ALI–ABA 27, American Law Institute–American Bar Association, CLE (June 7–8, 2008) (presenting discussion draft). The Principles are broadly classifiable as "soft law" much like a Restatement. The American Law Institute distilled the common law in developing Restatements of the Law. In contrast to UCITA or UCC Article 2, the Principles of Software are not self-executing and do not apply unless a court adopts them. *Id.* at xxi. The Principles offer courts a limited number of rules applicable to most software contracts. American Law Institute Reporters, *Memorandum to Principles of Software Contracts* (May 2008) at xix. Courts may also apply these rules by analogy to transactions outside the scope of the Principles.

(B) Scope

The Principles guide software law whether structured as licenses, transfers, assignments, or sales. The Principles resolve four issues: "(1) the nature of software transactions; (2) the acceptability of current practices of contract formation and the implications of these practices for determining governing terms; (3) the relationship between federal intellectual property law and private contracts governed by state law; and (4) the appropriateness of contract terms concerning quality, remedies, and other rights." *Id.*

Software contracts are often mixed sales, leases, and licenses. The Principles applies a predominant purpose test or what the Convention for the International Sale of Goods conceptualizes as the preponderant part test. If a manufacturer embeds software in goods or software is part of a mixed transaction, courts ask the question as to whether the goods aspect or software predominates. *Id.* at *xx*.

(C) Preliminary Concerns

Chapter 1 of the Principles consists of definitions, scope, and general terms such agreement, digital content, record, software, and standard forms. The Principles make it clear software contracts are governed by state law and trumped by federal intellectual property law under the Supremacy Clause of the U.S. Constitution. Any license agreement is unenforceable: "if it (a) conflicts with a mandatory rule of federal intellectual property law; or (b) conflicts impermissibly with the purposes and policies of federal intellectual property law; or (c) would constitute federal intellectual property misuse in an infringement proceeding." Principles of Software Contracts, § 109. Chapter 1 of the Principles addresses general principles of law such as unconscionability, choice of law, and choice of forum. The purpose of the Principles is to provide a legal infrastructure to guide courts when deciding cases involving software contracts.

(D) Formation

The case law on standard form contracts is rapidly evolving. The Principles broadly validate standard form contracts drawing in large part from UCITA's formation rules. The Principles also validate rolling contracts presented in a take-it-or-leave-it standard form. The Principles use the concept of electronic records as the operative equivalent of writing. Software license agreements or other transfers "may be formed in any manner sufficient to show agreement." *Id.* at § 2.01.

The drafters adopt a parol evidence rule with its rules of admissibility to reduce fraudulent assertions of the existence of license agreements and other transfers. Reporters' Memorandum, *Id.* at xxii. A license agreement does not fail for indefiniteness merely because the licensor does not specify all of the key terms. *Id.* at § 2.01(1). The Principles adopt a simple battle of the forms provision in which the contract consists in terms found in both terms and gap-fillers. § 2.01(2). Section 2.02 applies special rules for standard or mass-market transfers of generally available software. The transferee will be deemed to have adopted a standard form if the standard form is reasonable accessible before the transfer. The transferee must have access to the standard form before notice of payment. *Id.* at § 2.02(2).

(E) Unconscionability & Public Policy

The Principles guide courts to refuse to enforce license agreements if unconscionable or if enforcement would violate important public policies such as the First Amendment. Unconscionability is an issue for the court to determine rather than the jury. Typically, a court must find unfair bargaining (procedural unconscionability) as well an unfair bargain in fact (substantive unconscionability). A licensee must demonstrate that a contractual provision is overly harsh or one-sided so the result "shocks the conscience." Courts will typically look at the contract's purpose and circumstances in play when the contract was executed in making a determination about unconscionability. Software contracts are also subject to state and federal consumer protections as well as common law defenses.

(F) Warranties

Sections 3.02 through 3.07 import warranties concepts from UCC Article 2 and UCITA with some differences. The Principles, for example, replace the "basis of the bargain" test with an objective test focusing on whether the licensor's representations about software are sufficiently definite so a licensee or other transferee could reasonably rely upon it. If the transferor makes a statement constituting an affirmation of fact, promise, or description, the statement constitutes an express warranty, so long as a licensee, assignee, or licensee could reasonably rely on the statement. Express warranties survive unexpected disclaimers and the only way to disclaim them is not to make them.

Section 3.02 borrows much from UCITA and UCC Article 2 creating a licensee cause of action if delivered software fails to conform to the description in advertising or packaging. As with UCC Article 2, courts distinguish between puffery or seller's talk and statements more definite or specific constitute an enforceable express warranty. If a software licensor's employee demonstrates its software to a licensee, the software must conform to the demonstration. A licensor is potentially liable for express warranties to any transferee in the distributional chain, including intermediaries and end users. *Id.* at § 3.02(a). A licensor needs to make a decision whether to disclaim or limit the warranty of merchantability. Merchantable software means a licensor's software must pass without objection in the trade under the license agreement. Software must minimally "be fit for the ordinary purpose" and be "adequately packaged and labeled." *Id.* at 3.03.

If a software developer warrants its software will function with a given licensee's system, the company may be liable for the warranty of fitness for a particular purpose." A licensor will violate a fitness warranty if it selects software for the licensee's particular purpose. Section 3.04 requires the licensor know or have a reason to know of the licensee's particular purpose.

The Principles generally follow UCC Article 2 warranties except for the non-infringement warranty. UCC Article 2 imposes a strict liability for transferring goods infringing the patents or other intellectual property rights of third parties. Section 3.01 gives licensees and other transferees a lesser infringement warranty. A licensor is not liable for transferring software infringing the patents of others absent knowledge of the infringing content. Transferors do not give the non-infringement warranty when the transferee uses the software in a way contrary to the agreement. A licensor may disclaim or limit implied warranties. A software company makes a non-disclaimable warranty its software does not have hidden defects of which it is aware at the time of transfer. *Id.* at § 3.05(b).

(G) Performance Standards

The Principles drafters did not devise specialized rules for tender, acceptance, rejection, repudiation, and other performance-related issues easily imported from UCC Article 2 and the common law. Instead, the drafters developed rules not found in the common law tailored to the specific problems of software contracting. The Principles defines a breach as failure to perform without a legal excuse. *Id.* at § 3.11(a). UCITA classifies breaches into material and non-material. Section 701 of UCITA as well as the Restatement (Second) of Contracts also adopts a material breach standard determined by multiple factors such as the degree of harm or anticipated harm of the aggrieved party.

Courts may consider the behavior of the party as well as the covenant of good faith and fair dealing. A material breach signifies the end of the contract whereas a non-breaching party may recover for non-material breach and the contract is still in force. *Id.* at § 3.11. The Principles imported the concept of cure of breach from UCITA. Breaching parties have the right to cure where the time for performance has not yet expired. Software licensors often give licensees a period of acceptance testing during which time the licensor may cure defects.

(H) Remedies for Breach

The Principles enforce the parties' agreements as to remedies in the event of breach. The Principles

assume parties to software contracts will import
UCC Article 2 remedies such as the resale, market
price, or specific performance to software contracts.
Software licensors should provide a minimally adequate remedy. In the absence of agreement, the
drafters adopted the expectation theory of damages.
Reporter's Memorandum at xxii. The non-breaching
party is entitled to remedies for breach. The breach
of a software contract may constitute copyright
infringement as well as breach of contract.

The Reporters approve of the ability of a software
licensor to remove or disable software. However,
they do not adopt the remedy of automatic disablement. *Principles of Software Contracts*, *Id.* at 329.
Electronic self-help is controversial because of the
power it gives licensors over integral software in
enterprises. The Principles balance the interests of
licensors and licensees by permitting automated
disablement under certain delimited circumstances
but strictly prohibiting disablement as a self-help
remedy. *Id.* at 330. The Principles of Software Reporters note how parties frequently tailor their own
remedies with consequential damages exclusions.
Id. Limited remedies will fail of their essential
purpose making consequential damages limitations
unenforceable because they are unconscionable. *Id.*

§ 4.8   International Electronic Commerce

The Internet's blurring of national boundaries
creates a variety of new cyberlaw dilemmas. Europe
is unique because the twenty-seven countries of the
European Union enacted a *de facto* cross-border

regime governing electronic commerce. The European Commission has powers of initiative, implementation, management, and control, which allows it to formulate harmonized regulations. During the past decade, the Commission has approved Internet regulations such as the E–Commerce Directive, E–Signatures Directive, Distance Selling Directive, Data Protection Directive, Database Protection Directive, and the Copyright Directive. The European Union recognizes e-commerce does not flourish without borderless consumer protections.

(A) E.U. Consumer Protection

E.U. Regulations and Directives protect European consumers ordering goods and services over the Internet. The European Commission adopted many Regulations and Directives governing e-commerce. The chief online consumer protections cover: (1) advertising, (2) information provided before the conclusion of a contract, (3) conclusion of the contract and contractual obligations, (4) payment, and (5) guarantees. The central provision of E.U. Directives governing consumer transactions is that unfair contractual terms are unenforceable. Online businesses, including U.S. companies must give European consumers accurate pre-contract disclosures. Online sellers are required to give consumers confirmatory disclosures before the delivery of computer software or other e-commerce contracts. The seller's confirmation disclosure must explain the period in which a consumer can cancel the contract. Websites must give the consumer a right to cancel a distance contract.

A website seller must give European consumers a right of withdrawal period not shorter than seven working days. If an eBusiness accepts orders via its website or other instrumentality, it will have only 30 days to fill the order. An e-commerce seller must tell European consumers that they have the right to a refund payable within 30 days. Sellers may not require European consumers to waive consumer rights under the Distance Selling Directive or Unfair Contract Terms Directive or any other mandatory rule. Europe has a more comprehensive view of consumer rights in cyberspace than the U.S. piecemeal approach. Europe is to the United States as Mars is to Venus because of its mandatory consumer rules in contrast to the U.S. approach deferring to the free market.

(B) Unfair Online Advertising

The European Union adopted The Unfair Commercial Practices Directive ("UCP") on 11 May 2005. (Directive 2005/29/EC). The Directive regulates commercial practices from B2C replacing the Misleading Advertising Directive. See 84/450/EEC. The Directive prohibits misleading advertising distorting economic behavior. Directive 2005/29/EC, Art. 5.2(b). This includes misleading actions (Art. 6), misleading omissions (Art. 7), and aggressive commercial practices (Art. 8) on the advertiser's behalf.

(C) Distance Contracts

The European Commission enacted the Distance Selling Directive to give consumers the same rights as if they bought goods in person. The Distance

Selling Directive applies to home shopping including e-commerce teleshopping, and the use of the Internet. The Directive does not apply to the licensing of software for obvious reasons. If a consumer had a right to return defect-free software, the licensor would not have any paying customers. This Directive gives consumers minimum adequate information before their distance purchase. Sellers must give a consumer written confirmation. Consumers in the twenty-seven Member States have a right to cancel the contract for a minimum of seven days. Sellers may not penalize consumers for canceling a distance contract and may only be assessed the cost of returning the item. This cooling off period gives consumers an opportunity to inspect goods and reject them just as if they were in a brick and mortar shop. Consumers may also cancel the contract if the seller cannot deliver the goods or services within 30 days. These are non-waivable mandatory terms. Website suppliers must provide the European consumer with adequate disclosures concerning: (1) the seller's identity, (2) the goods, and services on offer, and (3) the contract and its obligations. 97/7/EC, Art. 4. In addition, the website must give accurate information concerning the online goods or services offered including: (1) the main characteristics of the goods or services, (2) the price . . . including all taxes, (3) delivery costs, (4) additional costs of communication, (5) the period for which the offer or the price remains valid, and (6) the minimum duration of contracts. 97/7/EC, Art. 4.1.

In addition, the Directive does not apply to goods bought at auctions. However, a 2004 German court applied the Directive to an eBay style auction despite the Directive's general exemption of auctions under German law. The German court ruled the eBay auction was not classifiable as an auction for purposes of the Directive's exemption because consumer rights are expansive. E.U.*Right to Revoke Distance Purchase Extends to Commercial eBay Auctions,* PIKE & FISCHER INTERNET LAW & REGULATION (Nov. 11, 2004).

(D) Unfair Consumer Contracts Directive

The Directive on Unfair Terms in Consumer Contracts (Directive 93/13/EEC, "Unfair Contract Terms Directive") applies broadly to e-commerce or Internet consumer transactions. Online contractual terms classified as unfair under the Directive are not binding on consumers. European consumer contracts are not enforceable unless drafted in plain and intelligible language. Courts are to interpret ambiguities in favor of consumers. *Id.* at Art. 5. "A term is unfair if, contrary to the requirements of good faith, it causes a significant imbalance in the parties' rights and obligations arising under the contract, to the detriment of the consumer." *Id.* at Art. 3. Unfair terms are to be determined at the conclusion of the contract. In contrast, U.S. courts broadly enforce contract terms disadvantaging consumers such as the disclaimer of all remedies, adverse choice of law and forum clauses, and limitation of meaningful remedies. "Even those firms without market power exploit the cognitive failures of their customers through the "shrouding" of terms and similar techniques." Ronald J. Mann & Travis Siebeneicher, *Just One Click: The Reality of Internet Retail Contracting*, 108 COLUM. L. REV. 984, 985 (2008).

(E) E–Commerce Directive

Member States are required to develop national legislation implementing the E–Commerce Directive. The E–Commerce Directive governs the activities of information society service providers ("ISSPs"). The European Union's Electronic Commerce Directive took effect on January 6, 2002. The Directive creates a legal framework for online service providers, commercial communications, electronic contracts, and limitations of liability of intermediary service providers. The Directive also covers issues such as the unsolicited commercial email and the prohibition of Internet-related surveillance. The E–Commerce Directive states an ISSP established within one European Member State need only comply with the laws of that state, even if the activities of the ISSP affect individuals from other Member States. (00/31/EC, Art. 3.1).

In other words, so long as the ISSP complies with the law of the country in which it is established, it is free to engage in electronic commerce throughout the European Union. The "country of origin principle," is the cornerstone of the E–Commerce Directive. The applicable law is the country of origin where the seller performed services. The country of origin principle is inapplicable to consumer transactions.

Member States must "ensure that service providers undertaking unsolicited commercial communications by electronic mail consult regularly and respect the opt-out registers in which natural persons not wishing to receive such commercial communications." *Id*. at Art. 7(2). Article 9 validates electronic or computer-to-computer contracts except for designated exceptions like real estate transfers or family law. *Id*. at Art. 9.

The Directive requires seller to give consumers disclosures before electronic contracting on how to conclude online contracts, as well as the means of correcting errors. Consumers must be able to store and retrieve contracts or they are unenforceable. *Id*. at Art. 10. Article 12 essentially immunizes ISSPs for conduit activities much like the DMCA's Section 512 discussed in Chapter 10. This liability limitation applies only if the ISSP does not initiate or modify the transmission. *Id*. The Directive immunizes an ISSP's caching and hosting activities in a functionally equivalent way to DMCA Section 512. *Id*. at Arts. 13–14. ISSPs have no duty to monitor their websites for illegal activities like the DMCA. Member States must develop legislation to inform the authorities of illegal activities. *Id*. at Art. 16. Member States are to develop legislation to encourage out of court settlements of disputes. *Id.* at Art. 17.

(F) E–Contracting Convention

The United Nations proposed UNCITRAL's E–Contracting Convention to bring certainty to cross-border e-commerce. In August of 2008, the ABA House of Delegates passed a resolution urging the U.S. Government to become a signatory of the E–Contracting Convention. This Convention like U.S. domestic laws such as E–Sign and UETA recognizes the validity of electronic records as the equivalent of statutory paper writings. Similarly, the Convention validates electronic signatures as fulfilling statutory signature requirements.

The E–Contracting Convention, shares common ground with E-Sign and UETA because it allows the parties to derogate or write around any provision. The Convention also sets default rules for the time and receipt of electronic communications. The Convention's receipt rule creates a rebuttable presumption of receipt. The Convention recognizes the enforceability of computer-to-computer contracts. The Convention also validates electronic authentication methods as the equivalent of hand-written signatures. The E–Contracting Convention applies to business-to-business transactions but not to consumer transactions in international commerce. The overarching purpose of the proposed convention will be to eliminate legal and functional barriers to cross-border e-commerce.

CHAPTER FIVE

TORTS IN CYBERSPACE

§ 5.1 Overview of Cybertorts

Cybertorts are civil actions to recover chiefly economic, reputational, or privacy-based damages arising from Internet communications such as email, blogs, or other Internet communications. The flexible nature of tort law is well suited to address Internet-related forms of injuries still evolving. Common law judges are working with traditional tort law principles to redress injuries in cyberspace. Internet torts are different from brick and mortar torts largely because the damages are chiefly reputational or economic as opposed to physical injuries. Torts in cyberspace arise in MySpace, email transmissions, web site postings, or software distribution, in contrast to traditional categories of injury such as automobile accidents, slip and fall mishaps, medical malpractice, or injuries due to dangerously defective products. In the United States, the common law of torts constitutes a method of private dispute resolution as a cost effective alternative to thick regulation. Europe and civil code countries in general tend to have a weak tort regime in the brick and mortar world as well as in cyberspace preferring top-down regulation.

§ 5.2 Intentional Torts against the Person

An intentional tort is committed where the defendant's has the desire to cause the consequences or it is substantially certain to occur. Intentional torts such as battery, assault, false imprisonment, or trespass to land are not likely to evolve in cyberspace. In contrast, the intentional infliction of emotional distress ("IIED") is commonly asserted as a cybertort. Justice Roger Traynor's landmark opinion in *State Rubbish Collectors Ass'n v. Siliznoff*, 240 P.2d 282 (Cal. 1952) recognized the right to be free from "serious, intentional, and unprivileged invasions of emotional and mental tranquility." *Id.* at 286. To succeed in an intentional infliction of emotional distress case, the plaintiff must establish: (1) extreme and outrageous conduct by the defendant with the intention of causing, or reckless disregard of the probability of causing, emotional distress, (2) the plaintiff's suffering severe or extreme emotional distress, and (3) actual and proximate causation of the emotional distress by the defendant's outrageous conduct. To qualify for IIED liability, defendant's conduct must be "so extreme as to exceed all bounds of that usually tolerated in a civilized community." Restatement (Second) of Torts, § 46. Unique to the intentional tort, is mere recklessness suffices in some jurisdictions.

Cybertorts committed in the workplace or on behalf of an employer presents special problems. The court in *Delfino v. Agilent Technologies, Inc.*, 52 Cal. Rptr. 3d 376 (Cal. App. 6 Dist. 2006) refused to hold a company vicariously liable for its employee's cyberthreats against his ex-employer using the Yahoo! pseudonymous user name, "crack_ smoking_ Jesus." One of the odious e-mails said:

> You can look forward to all your fingers getting broken, several kicks to the ribs and mouth, break some teeth, and a cracked head. Also, your car will be trashed and your computer destroyed. Maybe set your place on fire so you can be evicted. If your [expletive] is there, she'll take a little ride to the parts of San Jose where they don't speak [E]nglish … Die, [expletive]. You'll wish you had. *Id.* at 381.

The *Delfino* court extended Section 230 of the Communications Decency Act ("Section 230") to shield the employer for negligent and intentional infliction of emotional distress claims. The court classified the employer as a "provider or user of an interactive computer service" since it provided its employees with Internet access. The court reasoned even if Section 230 did not shield the ISP employer, the plaintiffs had not proven the elements of either the intentional or negligent infliction of emotional distress. The employer had no knowledge of the cyberthreats and placed his employee upon administrative leave, so it did not either authorize or ratify this misconduct. An employer will typically not be liable if the employee did something for his own purpose outside the scope of employment. A defendant is not liable for rude or intemperate language because IIED requires proof of egregious violations of social norms.

The First Amendment will trump IIED if the statements are classified as protected speech. A Texas court dismissed a Vice Principal's claims for IIED against students who created a fake MySpace website masquerading as the school official. The website contained the Vice President's name, photo, and place of employment, as well as made explicit and graphic sexual reference falsely describing her as a lesbian. The court first entered a summary judgment motion against the Vice Principal because the derogatory statements were not statements of fact. The court entered summary judgment on the plaintiff's intentional inflectional of emotional distress claim because this cause of action was based upon the same facts as the defamation claim. *Draker v. Schreiber*, 2008 WL 3457023 (Tex. App. Ct. 2008). Cybertort plaintiffs must demonstrate a defendant's extreme misconduct violating important social norms, which illustrates Lessig's point about how norms and the law interrelate.

§ 5.3   Negligence–Based Actions

(A) Internet–Related Negligence

Negligence-based lawsuits constitute more than 90% of torts committed in the brick and mortar world. Nevertheless, consumers have rarely prevailed in negligent Internet security cases because of the difficulty of proving a "present injury." Negligence is an act or omission by which the defendant violates a standard of care creating excessive preventable dangers. Courts have been unwilling to recognize new duties of care for cyberspace activities. Normally, courts carve out new duties to address new risks such as the development of medical malpractice and products liability in the 1960s. To prove negligence-based cybertorts, a plaintiff must prove by a preponderance of the evidence each element of negligence: duty, breach of duty, cause-in-fact, proximate cause, and damages. Duty is a legal obligation to conform to a reasonable person standard of care in order to protect others against unreasonable risks of harm. A breach of the duty of care is the failure of a defendant to conform to the standard of reasonable care. Courts construct tests for reasonable care such as whether the defendant has violated a statute, industry standard, or customary usage of trade. The Restatement (Second) of Torts adopts a risk/utility test to measure breach of the standard of care. Courts applying the risk/utility test first articulated in *United States v. Carroll Towing Co.,* 159 F.2d 169 (2d Cir. 1947) determine breach of the standard of care by weighing the defendant's burden of precautions against the expected costs of accidents or injuries if the precautions are not taken.

In cybertort cases, as in the brick and mortar world, negligence is determined by a finding of excessive preventable dangers. In *Remsburg v. Docusearch, Inc.,* 816 A.2d 1001 (N.H. 2003), the New Hampshire Supreme Court held an online data broker liable for providing personal data to a criminal who used the information to track down and murder a former high school classmate. The court held the Internet data broker owed a duty to the victim because a data broker sold her contact information foreseeably endangering her.

Cybertort negligence cases have been slow to develop. Relatively few courts have considered automobile negligence cases where drivers using mobile technologies for text messaging, blogging, or e-mail caused car accidents. Many states have enacted statutes banning the use of mobile devices while driving after reports of driver's text messaging at the time of accidents causing fatalities. A Los Angeles commuter train engineer was text messaging shortly before a collision with another train killing twenty-five persons. Similarly, courts are just beginning to hold a website or online company has a duty to implement reasonable security and inform users should a security breach occur. A federal court held MySpace had no duty to implement basic safety measures to prevent sexual predators from communicating with minors on its website. *Doe v. MySpace, Inc.*, 528 F.3d 413 (5th Cir. 2008). The court held MySpace was entitled to Section 230 immunity because it was a publisher of a third party's communications. The court held Section 230 shielded the ISP from the plaintiff's negligent security claim as well. The economic loss rule ("ELR") is another barrier blocking most computer security lawsuits. Courts must first determine as a question of law whether negligence has resulted in purely "economic loss" in which case the action is contractual, rather than a tort. Even if the plaintiff can prove the elements of negligent security, courts apply the

ELR where the breach of a duty merely restates a contractual obligation. The ELR is a barrier against recovery for lost proprietary data, trade secrets, and lost profits where there is a contractual nexus between the data handler and data "entruster." Negligent data security cases are discussed in Chapter Eight on Cybercrimes & Data Security.

(B) Professional Negligence

Professional negligence in American tort law is generally restricted to lawyers and doctors. No American court has recognized an action for computer or Internet security malpractice. Courts are just beginning to construct new duties for Internet security so it is unlikely computer malpractice will be a cognizable action.

§ 5.4   Business Torts in Cyberspace

Business torts typically arise out of online commercial or consumer contracts. Competitors may file Internet-related business torts and others injured by anti-competitive, predatory, or fraudulent business practices. Business torts include interference with contract, fraud, misrepresentation, trade libel, and the misappropriation of trade secrets. Companies seeking recovery for trade libel must prove the online defendant made disparaging, untrue statements made to influence potential purchasers. Online companies will find it difficult to prove damages in the typical anonymous trade libel case assuming they can locate the anonymous cybertortfeasor.

(A) Emerging Case Law

(1) Unfair Competition

Unfair competition occurs when the defendant makes representations deceiving the public such as palming off on the trademarks of others. Unfair competition also includes unfair commercial practices calculated to harm the business of another. The Utah Supreme Court upheld a state court's entering summary judgment against Overstock.com in its business tort lawsuit against Smartbargains for its use of Internet pop-up advertisements. Overstock filed a complaint against SmartBargains. Overstock contended the defendant's pop-ups appeared when its customers accessed Overstock's website. Overstock's complaint included counts for unfair competition, interference with contract, and interference with prospective economic relations in its use of Internet pop-up advertisements. *Overstock.com v. Smartbargains, Inc.*, 192 P.3d 858 (Utah 2008).

The Utah Supreme Court ruled Smartbargains' pop-ups did not constitute unfair competition because Overstock.com could not show the popups were either deceptive, infringed a trademark, passed off competitor's goods as those of online store, or were likely to cause consumer confusion. The court found no confusion because the pop-ups appeared in a separate and distinct window from the website and therefore did not deceive potential customers as to the source.

(2) Interference with Prospective Contract

Interference with prospective contractual relations requires the plaintiff to prove: (1) the defendant intentionally interfered with the plaintiff's existing or potential economic relations, (2) for an improper purpose or by improper means, (3) causing injury to the plaintiff. Plaintiffs deploy this tort in pop-up cases on the theory that these advertisements interfere with prospective economic relations. See e.g., *Overstock.com v. Smartbargains, Inc.*, 192 P.3d 858 (Utah 2008). A court did find interference with prospective contracts as well as breach of contract in a Pennsylvania case involving a Canadian website designer. *ConsulNet Computing, Inc. v. Moore*, 2007 WL 2702446 (E.D. Pa. 2007). The Canadian eBusiness designed websites for realtors and a competitor masqueraded as a potential customer. The realtor could use the websites to collect contact information and gain the business of website visitors. The defendant applied for membership masquerading as a RE/Max real estate broker interested in building a real estate website. His true purpose was to steal the plaintiff's copyrighted software code. The defendant cancelled his website membership after copying copyrighted code from the site and using the software to create a substantially similar real estate web-building service. To establish tortious interference with contract, a plaintiff must show: (1) the existence of a contract, (2) the wrongdoer's knowledge of the contract, (3) the wrongdoer's intentional procurement of the contract's breach, (4) the lack of justification, and (5) resulting damages. The jury found the defendant liable for the tort of interference with contract, breach of contract, and copyright infringement.

§ 5.5 Personal Property Torts

(A) Trespass to Chattels

Courts have adapted trespass to chattels to encompass injuries by spam e-mailers, computer hackers, and on-line auction sites. A *trespass to chattels* is intentionally interfering with possession of personal property causing injury. "A trespass to a chattel may be committed by intentionally (a) dispossessing another of the chattel, or (b) using or intermeddling with a chattel in the possession of another." Restatement (Second) of Torts, § 217. In trespass to chattels cases, the plaintiff is the person in possession of private property. Damages are a required element and found when the quality of value of personal property is diminished in some substantial way. Most cases involve concrete harm to a chattel, "actual impairment of its physical condition, quality, or value to the possessor as distinguished from the mere affront to [the owner's] dignity as possessor." *Id.* at § 218(b).

For most of the history of tort law, trespass to chattels was a tort adapted to an agricultural based economy. "In recent years, trespass to personal property, which had been largely relegated to a historical note in legal textbooks, has reemerged as a cause of action in Internet advertising and email cases." *Sotelo v. DirectRevenue, Inc.*, 384 F. Supp. 2d 1219, 1234 (N.D. Ill. 2005). Scrapers extracting data from websites without permission may commit trespass to chattels. "A scraper, also called a 'robot' or 'bot,' is nothing more than a computer program

that accesses information contained in a succession
of web pages stored on the accessed computer" *EF
Cultural Travel BV v. Zefer Corp.*, 318 F.3d 58, 60
(1st Cir. 2003).

(1) Spam Email

Internet service providers have been successful in
arguing that the eighteenth century tort of trespass
to chattels is well suited to address website intrusions by spyware, spam emailers, and web scrapers.
CompuServe, Inc. v. Cyber Promotions, Inc., 962
F.Supp. 1015 (S.D. Ohio 1997) was the first judicial
recognition that spammers were liable for trespass
to chattels. The court ruled Cyber Promotions' use
of the ISP's computer system exceeded consent and
constituted a trespass. The court based the trespass
claim on the defendant's bypassing CompuServe's
software programs to block out their spam. The
court also found Cyber Promotion's falsification of
point of origin information was proof it misused
CompuServe's computer network.

The court noted a plaintiff could sustain an action "for trespass to chattels, as opposed to an
action for conversion, without showing a substantial
interference with its right to possession of that
chattel." *Id.* at 1022. Conversion is cognizable when
one who owns and has right to possession of personal property proves that property is in unauthorized
possession of another who has acted to exclude
rights of owner. The *CompuServe* court held the
element of damage to the system could be established by the "multitudinous electronic mailings

demand the disk space and drain the processing power of plaintiff's computer equipment," and impose added inconvenience and Internet connection costs on CompuServe's customers. Under this logic, the personal property tort's physical contact element is satisfied by the mere reception of electrons. "Unwanted telephone callers would seem to be engaging in trespass to chattels; the telephone call sends signals to the instrument of the recipient. So, too, with fax machines that receives unwelcome transmissions." Dan J. Burk, *The Trouble With Trespass*, 3 J. SMALL & EMERGING BUS. L. 1 (1998).

The *CompuServe* case was followed soon after by *Hotmail Corp. v. Van$ Money Pie Inc.*, 1998 WL 388389 (N.D. Cal. 1998) holding Hotmail likely to prevail on its trespass to chattels claim against a spam emailer transmitting hundreds of thousands of commercial email to its subscribers. This flood of spam email violated Hotmail's terms of service agreement. The *Hotmail* court found Hotmail's email system was the personal property of the ISP and the spammer violated its Terms of Service by transmitting spam and pornography. The court found further the spammer defendants intentionally trespassed on Hotmail's property by knowingly and without authorization creating accounts and using them for purposes exceeding the limits of the Terms of Service. The court based damages upon evidence that the spammer's filled up Hotmail's computer storage space and interfered with its ability to serve its customers.

(2) Spiders or Bots as Trespassers

Computer software applications enable Internet bidders to submit bids. In *eBay Inc. v. Bidder's Edge, Inc.*, 100 F. Supp. 2d 1058 (N.D. Cal. 2000), eBay filed suit against Bidder's Edge, an aggregate auction website which enables consumers to do comparison shopping. EBay sought a preliminary injunction against Bidder's Edge for trespassing on its website (trespass to chattels) as well as a variety of other business torts including trade libel and interference with prospective advantage. Bidder's Edge's bots or spiders searched and copied files on bidding activity from eBay's website for use on its comparative or aggregate shopping auction site.

EBay sent BE a letter stating BE's spiders were unauthorized and contending its activities constituted civil trespass. EBay offered to license BE's activities but the parties could not agree on licensing terms. The eBay website used "robot exclusions headers" to detect and exclude BE's robots. These exclusion headers respond to the Internet Protocol ("IP") address of requesting computers. EBay's software enabled it monitor the extraordinary number of incoming requests from BE's IP address. EBay tried to block requests coming from BE's IP Address. EBay blocked 169 IP addresses it believed BE was using to query eBay's system. However, BE continued crawling on eBay's site using proxy servers evading eBay's filters which constituted trespass to chattels.

The *eBay* court found it unclear whether eBay's User Agreement included anti-bot or spider term at the time BE was searching and copying listings from eBay's website. BE's web crawlers exceeded the scope of any such consent when they began acting like robots making repeated queries. BE argued its robot activity constituted no more than 1.1% of eBay's requests. The eBay court ruled the "gravamen of the alleged irreparable harm is if BE is allowed to continue to crawl the eBay site, it may encourage frequent and unregulated crawling to the point that eBay's system will be irreparably harmed." *EBay Inc. v. Bidder's Edge, Inc.*, 100 F. Supp. 2d 1058, 1067 (N.D. Cal. 2000).

(3) The Substantiality of Damages

The central point of contention in most cybertrespass cases is the substantiality of damages. This issue arose in a trespass to chattels case in which the Intel Corporation filed suit against Ken Hamidi, an ex-employee. Hamidi created an anti-Intel website transmitting messages concerning Intel's employment practices to over 30,000 Intel employees six times. Intel demanded Hamidi stop sending the messages, but he refused and bypassed Intel's firewall that employed routers to filter and transfer information between Intel's internal network and the Internet. A firewall is software at the perimeter controlling access by examining packet headings to authenticate and identify users. Intel's packet filers use IP addresses to screen out unwanted traffic.

When Intel was unable to block or otherwise filter out the messages, it sent a letter demanding Hamidi stop sending the mass emails to current employees. After he refused to heed this warning, Intel sought injunctive relief based upon the tort actions of nuisance and trespass to chattels. Intel ultimately dropped its nuisance theory and claim for damages, and only sought injunctive relief. The Superior Court issued a preliminary injunction enjoining Hamidi from sending email messages to Intel employees. The California Court of Appeals upheld the injunction prohibiting Hamidi and his nonprofit organization from sending unsolicited email to Intel's employees. The appeals court found Intel was likely to prevail on its claim Hamidi trespassed onto Intel's computer system.

The California Supreme Court rejected Intel's trespass to chattels claim on the grounds it had proven no damages in *Intel Corp. v. Hamidi*, 71 P.3d 296 (Cal. 2003). The California Supreme Court found Hamidi's emails interfered but did not dispossess Intel of their computer system. The court found Intel's computer system was not even slowed by Hamidi's messages nor did he damage the physical quality or value of Intel's computer system. The court compared Hamidi's unwelcome emails to an unpleasant letter causing injury to the "recipient's mailbox, or the loss of privacy caused by an intrusive telephone call would be an injury to the recipient's telephone equipment." *Intel Corp. v. Hamidi*, 71 P.3d 296, 300 (Cal. 2003). The substantiality of damages was also issue in another case in which the court ruled a plaintiff failed to establish trespass to chattels because of the inconvenience of deleting the defendant's pop-up advertisements on several occasions. *DirecTV, Inc. v. Chin*, 2003 WL 22102144 (W.D. Tex. 2003).

(4) Spyware

In *Sotelo v. DirectRevenue*, L.L.C., 384 F. Supp. 2d 1219 (N.D. Ill. 2005), the plaintiff sued the defendant for surreptitiously installing spyware on its computers. Direct Revenue's spyware delivered advertisements to consumers' computer screens through the Internet. To induce consumers to view the ads, the company offered them popular software applications, such as screensavers or games, for free. When the consumer downloaded the free application, the applications installed another piece of software known as an "advertising client," which generated the pop-up ads. The ads may be discarded by clicking on an "X" in the upper right-hand corner of the box in which they appear. In *Sotelo*, the plaintiff claimed the spyware caused:

> computers to slow down, take up the bandwidth of the user's Internet connection, incur increased Internet-use charges, deplete a computer's memory, utilize pixels and screen-space on monitors, require more energy because slowed computers must be kept on for longer, and reduce a user's productivity while increasing their frustration.

Id. at 1230.

The *Sotelo* court refused to dismiss the plaintiff's trespass to chattels claim. The court found that the spam emailer caused an actionable injury. The court also refused to dismiss the plaintiff's Illinois Consumer Fraud Act and negligence claim that

Direct Revenue breached its duty not to harm its computers as well as a computer tampering claim.

(B) Conversion in Cyberspace

Conversion is a personal property tort that applied to identifiable corporeal chattels such as cows and horses not intangibles. Michael L. Rustad & Thomas H. Koenig, *Cybertorts and Legal Lag: An Empirical Analysis*, 13 S. CAL. INTERDISC. L.J. 77 (2003). Conversion is a personal property tort redressing a defendant's unlawful exercise of domain, control, or withholding possession of chattels. A plaintiff must prove four elements to prevail in a conversion action: (1) the defendant's unauthorized and wrongful assumption of control over the plaintiff's personal property, (2) the plaintiff's right in the property, (3) plaintiff's right to immediate possession, and the (4) plaintiff's demand for possession.

The distinction between trespass to chattels and conversion is a matter of degree. Conversion is an aggravated interference with personal property and the remedy is a forced sale for the full value of the chattel. In contrast, the remedy for trespass to chattels is compensation for the loss of value due to the defendant's interference. A plaintiff in a conversion case must also prove: "(1) the plaintiff has an immediate right to possession of the property converted, (2) the defendant's possession of the property was unauthorized, (3) the defendant acted to exclude the rights of the lawful owner of the property, (4) the property is specifically identifiable, and

(5) the defendant is obligated to return the property." *In re Cross Media Mktg. Corp. v. Nixon*, 2006 WL 2337177 *6 (S.D.N.Y. 2006). Finally, conversion is not cognizable in most jurisdictions unless the personal property owner makes a formal demand to the defendant for return of her property. No court has extended conversion to intellectual property misappropriation because federal or state statutes in most instances preempt this tort action.

(1) Conversion of Domain Names

In *Kremen v. Cohen*, 337 F.3d 1024 (9th Cir. 2003), ex-convict Stephen Cohen forged a letter to a domain name registrar, Network Solutions. In the letter, a confederate claimed he was the new contact person for Online Classifieds, Inc., the owner of the domain name, and requested Network Solutions to deregister sex.com. Network Solutions made no effort to determine the authenticity of the fake request and instead transferred the domain name, sex.com, to Cohen. *Kremen v. Cohen*, 337 F.3d 1024, 1027 (9th Cir. 2003). After Gary Kremen contacted Network Solutions some time later about the transfer of the domain name to Cohen, an administrator informed him it was too late to undo the transfer. Cohen went on to turn sex.com into a lucrative online porn empire.

Kremen filed suit against Cohen for hijacking sex.com. A federal court awarded him $40 million in compensatory damages and another $25 million in punitive damages. The defendant did not appear at trial and this award was uncollectible because Cohen fled the country. The court ordered Cohen, the primary wrongdoer, to disgorge profits gained in using the sex.com domain name and invoked a constructive trust over the ill-gotten gains. Cohen fled to Mexico hiding his ill-gotten gains in offshore locations beyond the reach of legal process.

Kremen next filed suit against Network Solutions for the tort of conversion. The district court concluded the letter to Network Solutions was a forgery directing the primary wrongdoer Cohen to return the domain name to Kremen. The district court, however, reasoned Network Solutions was not liable for conversion because domain names were not personal property because they were intangibles. The Ninth Circuit disagreed holding a defendant could convert a domain name despite its intangible nature. Cyberconversion cases are rarely successful because plaintiff must prove: (1) personal or property of a functional equivalent capable of precise definition, (2) exclusive possession or control, and (3) the putative owner must have exclusive rights in the personal property or equivalent.

(2) Data Theft & Conversion

Courts have held that intangible data can be converted as in a California court case where a defendant misappropriated the source code of an inventory control system from the plaintiff's laptop. *Ali v. Fasteners for Retail, Inc.*, 544 F. Supp. 2d 1064 (E.D. Calif. 2008). In *Fasteners for Retail*, the plaintiff was the inventor and patent owner of the "Smart Pusher" inventory control software. CVS

Pharmacy entered into a two-year non-disclosure agreement with Fasteners to keep any information regarding the software confidential. Fasteners contended a CVS employee loaned him a laptop computer to access his emails. The CVS employee made unauthorized copies of the emails without Fastener's knowledge or consent. Fasteners' emails contained software code and pricing information for the Smart Pusher software. The defendant copied the proprietary source code onto a CD/DVD–ROM. Fasteners sought recovery for conversion as well as trade secret misappropriation and other business torts. In another case, an insurance agent was successful in extending conversion when an insurer misappropriated business and personal information taken from his leased computer. *Thyroff v. Nationwide Mut. Ins. Co.*, 864 N.E.2d 1272 (N.Y. 2007). The *Thyroff* court held that a cause of action of conversion applies to intangible electronic records stored on a computer indistinguishable from printed documents. Conversion is keeping pace with the Internet in extending this personal property tort of conversion to intangible electronic records.

§ 5.6   Information–Based Torts

(A)   Cyberfraud

Consumer fraud is widespread on the Internet especially on online auction websites. A ''phishing'' con artist may send a consumer what appears to be an '' 'official' email message directing the person to a counterfeit site where they are encouraged to 'update their account.' '' Phishing enterprises are highly profitable even if a miniscule number of consumers respond with their credit card information. Online auction fraud is on the FTC's top ten swindles list in each annual report. EBay and other online auctions, however, have no responsibility for fraud committed by those using its service. Section 230 of the CDA, which courts have expanded beyond publisher's liability to encompass nearly every imaginable tort, shields online auction houses from most claims. The proprietors of an Internet ticket fraud scheme defrauded hundreds of American consumers by selling fake tickets for the 2008 Olympic Games. Fraud involves a false representation of a material fact, made intentionally, which induces reliance on a false representation, and resulting damage. To prevail in a fraud case, the plaintiff must prove the defendant made: (1) an intentional misrepresentation, (2) of a material fact or opinion, (3) intended to induce, and (4) did induce reasonable reliance causing, (5) the plaintiff to suffer economic losses. Fraud includes willfully deceiving another with intent to induce her to alter her position to her detriment.

The emblem of fraud is the deliberate suppression of a fact by one who is bound to disclose it or by the disclosure of information likely to mislead. The law of torts also recognizes negligent misrepresentation, which differs from intentional misrepresentation in the tort *scienter* requirement—negligent misrepresentation requires no intent to deceive. The plaintiff's *prima case* for negligent misrepresentation in an online business requiring proof: (1) the defendant failed to exercise reasonable care in obtaining or communicating information, (2) caused pecuniary loss to the plaintiff, (3) who justifiably relied on information supplied by the defendant. A company entering into a contract where it pays for each click to an advertiser will have an action for fraud if the online advertiser employs bots to click on the advertisements to boost their revenues.

In *Mazur v. EBay Inc.*, 2008 WL 618988 (N.D. Cal. 2008) the federal court ruled Section 230 of the CDA did not immunize eBay from liability for fraudulent misrepresentation with respect to its own statements regarding the safety, circumstances, and caliber of its live auctions. The plaintiff filed suit against eBay and a company called Hot Jewelry Auctions.com (HJA), which holds auctions via eBay's Live Auction service. The plaintiff contended HJA engaged in shill bidding—the practice of entering fake bids. The court found eBay's own statements were actionable where the statements falsely claimed live auctions were safe and involved carefully screened, reputable international auction houses.

EBay's assertion that live auctions were "safe" and involved "floor bidders" were affirmative misrepresentations not shielded by CDA Section 230. The court found Section 230 is a liability-limitation for third party torts and did not shield eBay for its own fraudulent misconduct. The court found eBay's statement created an expectation of safety regarding the procedures of their auctions. The court found eBay's representations went beyond traditional editorial discretion.

Some courts have held spam emailers who sent deceptive or false emails liable for intentional misrepresentation. In *Hotmail Corp. v. Van$ Money Pie, Inc.*, 1998 WL 388389 (N.D. Cal. 1998), the spam emailer falsified return addresses and inundated Hotmail with hundreds of thousands of misdirected responses. The ISP received complaints from subscribers because the spammer's messages bounced back to nonexistent or incorrect email addresses. The California court found the ISP was likely to prevail on its fraud and misrepresentation claim because the spammers fraudulently obtained many Hotmail accounts, promising to abide by the Terms of Service without any intention of doing so. The spammer suppressed the fact they created accounts solely to spam other Hotmail users. The spammer falsified emails to make it appear Hotmail's computers authorized the messages when these activities violated the ISP's terms of service. The *Hotmail* Court based the ISP's damages on the spammer's illicit use of storage space on Hotmail's computer system.

(B) Online Defamation

Defamation encompasses the twin torts of libel and slander. Internet-related defamation is libel injuring the plaintiff's reputation in the relevant online community. If a defamatory statement is actionable *per se,* then under common law principles the law *presumes* the defendant acted with common law malice and awards general damages. In contrast, if the defamation is not actionable *per se,* then at common law the plaintiff must plead and prove common law actual malice and special damages. Defamation law protects the reputation of the person defamed and thus communication to a third person is necessary to state a claim. Defamation is a common law tort action to redress statements impugning the reputation of another in the larger community. The general elements of an action for defamation are: (1) a false and defamatory statement concerning another; (2) some negligence, or greater fault, in publishing the statement; (3) publication to at least one-third person; (4) lack of privilege in publication; (5) special damages, unless actionable *per se*; and (6) some actual harm to warrant compensatory damages. Restatement (Second) of Torts, § 558. The emblem of defamation is that it subjects the plaintiff to hatred, contempt, or ridicule, or causes others to lose good will or confidence in that person. Defamatory communications "tends to harm the reputation of another as to lower him in the estimation of the community or deter third persons from associating or dealing with them." Restatement (Second) of Torts, § 559. One important question is how to determine whether the plaintiff's injury has been harmed in a significant segment of the online community. Courts have yet to determine the meaning of loss of online reputation in the relevant community of blogosphere, list-servs, or social network websites.

Online words clearly denigrating a person's reputation are defamatory on their face and actionable *per se.* Courts classify Internet postings as libelous rather than slander. Publication means the defendant posted the allegedly defamatory statement on a website or transmitted the statements in emails. The law of defamation requires factual statements, as opposed to mere opinions. In *Hammer v. Amazon.com*, 392 F. Supp. 2d 423 (E.D. N.Y. 2005), a self-published author filed a defamation lawsuit against Amazon.com in relation to unfavorable reviews of his books on their website. The court dismissed the action because the reviews were of pure opinion and therefore protected.

Several recent cases reflect the increased incidence of defamation lawsuits in blogospheres and peer networking websites such as MySpace. See, e.g., *Allstate Ins. Co. v. Cooper*, 2008 WL 1990785 (W.D. Pa. 2008) (reporting action by high school principal filed student against students for defamatory MySpace postings). Cisco was sued by two Texas patent litigators for allegedly defamatory statements made by a company employee on the ''Troll Tracker'' blog.

(1) State Action

The First Amendment does not regulate the conduct of private parties; a party may not allege a constitutional violation without alleging the conduct of a state actor. In other words, a party may not allege a constitutional violation without alleging the conduct of a state actor. *Hammer v. Amazon.com*, 392 F. Supp. 2d 423, 432 (E.D. N.Y. 2005).

(2) Publishers, Distributors, and Conduits

A *publisher* is liable for defamatory statements in their works and the plaintiff need not prove the publisher's knowledge of the defamatory content. In contrast, *distributors* are not liable for defamatory statements contained in materials unless they distribute without proof of actual knowledge of the defamatory statements. Distributors are subject to an intermediate standard between publishers and conduits. A distributor is only liable if they knew or had reason to know of the defamatory content of what they are disseminating. *Austin v. CrystalTech Web Hosting, Inc.*, 125 P.3d 389 (Ariz. Ct. App. 2005). *Conduits*, the third category of common carrier type defendants, are not liable for defamatory content since they have no ability to screen and control defamatory material.

(3) Emerging Case Law

Technocati uncovered 112 million blogs worldwide, not counting the estimated 72 million blogs in the Chinese blogosphere. Nigel Shadbolt & Tim Berners–Lee, *Web Science Emerges*, SCIENTIFIC AMERICAN (Oct. 2008) at 79 (citing Technocrati study). The potential for defamation lawsuits in the blogosphere is staggering. Online torts are not skyrocketing because of the broad immunity accorded ISPs under Section 230 of the CDA. One who repeats or otherwise republishes a defamatory statement is subject to liability just as the primary wrongdoer.

The California Supreme Court held an Internet user was not liable for republishing defamatory content because of the chilling impact on online speech. *Barrett v. Rosenthal*, 146 P.3d 510, 526 (Cal. 2006). The California Supreme Court reversed an intermediate court holding CDA Section 230 did not immunize a website because it was a distributor of libelous postings. The Internet raises complex substantive legal conflicts as to the meanings of community and reputation in the context of online defamation.

(4) Anonymous Online Defamation

Anonymous website postings make it difficult to pursue online libel lawsuits. Companies apply to courts to serve a *subpoena duces tecum* ("John Doe subpoena") directed to Internet service providers to unveil the identity of anonymous speakers. Compaq filed a John Doe subpoena against an ISP, ordering it to disclose the identity of anonymous posters whose false information depressed their stock price. A Seattle company filed a libel lawsuit against users of Yahoo! message boards who were unveiled with the help of John Doe subpoenas. Copyright owners sought John Doe subpoenas to unmask Verizon's customers who allegedly downloaded copyrighted music or video without authorization. A standard subpoena request will be for electronic files, email messages (with attachments), Instant Message communications, and/or other communication transmitted on a provider's service for a designated period.

Courts will not issue a *subpoena duces tecum* unless the ISP gives notice to the anonymous speaker and an opportunity to be heard. In a typical case, a plaintiff served subpoenas on four Internet service providers—America Online, Yahoo!, Microsoft, and Netscape—requesting them to produce any information, including emails, activity logs, and address books, in connection with thirteen Internet accounts. *Anderson v. Hale*, 2001 WL 503045 (N.D. Ill. 2001). The court applied a three-factor test to resolve the compelling interest/substantial relation inquiry: the relevance of the information sought, the need for information, and the extent of injury disclosure may cause to associational rights.

The *Anderson* court found the information sought was only marginally relevant to the litigation and the need for the information was slight. The court concluded reasoning the unveiling of anonymous Internet speakers' identities implicated their associational privilege. The court issued a protective order noting these persons demonstrated intent to remain anonymous by refraining from disclosing their identities with their email addresses. The difficulty of identifying and locating an online defamer often stymies Internet defamation lawsuits in the blogosphere.

Relatively few lawsuits for online defamation have arisen out of websites rating law professors, medical doctors, neighbors, and date sites such as DontDateHimGirl.com. The Internet has given estranged spouses a worldwide forum for online attacks. Millions of YouTube visitors watched a video in which a woman "attacked her ex-husband for everything from his alleged shortcoming in bed to what she couldn't stand about his family." Anita Hamilton, *Outsmart Your Haters*, TIME (Oct. 6, 2008) at 67. John Doe subpoenas to unveil anonymous tortfeasors raise troubling privacy issues when corporations use them to unmask whistle-blowers criticizing company ethics in online forums. Companies have misused subpoenas in order to stifle critics of their products and services. Courts issuing these subpoenas balance the rights of anonymous speakers against the right to vindicate tort rights and remedies.

(C) Constitutionalizing Defamation
(1) Public Officials

The Court in *New York Times v. Sullivan*, 376 U.S. 254 (1964) was the first to rule that a state defamation case violated the First Amendment of the U.S. Constitution. In *Sullivan*, the Montgomery, Alabama Police Commissioner filed a defamation suit after the New York Times published a full-page advertisement entitled "Heed Their Rising Voices" calling for support of Martin Luther King's peaceful protests. The paid *New York Times* advertisement included inaccuracies about the Montgomery, Alabama police actions directed against student civil rights demonstrators. The advertisement concluded with an appeal for funds for three purposes: (1) support of the student movement, (2) the struggle for the right-to-vote, and (3) the legal defense of Dr. Martin Luther King, Jr., leader of the movement, against a perjury indictment that was pending in Montgomery.

A Who's Who of the Civil Rights Movement added their signatures to the advertisement, The "Committee to Defend Martin Luther King and the Struggle for Freedom in the South." Under the Alabama tort law of the era, such inaccurate statements were "libelous *per se*," the legal injury being implied without proof of actual damages. The trial court held malice was presumed for purpose of the award of compensatory damages. The Alabama jury found for the police commissioner and awarded $500,000.

The *Sullivan* Court noted public questions were protected as a freedom of expression under the First Amendment. *Id.* at 269. The Court's ruling that a public official cannot recover damages for defamation absent proof of actual malice was necessary to encourage robust "debate on public issues." *Id.* at 270. After *Sullivan*, the Court required a public official to prove defamation by the rigorous malice standard as opposed to a lesser standard like negligence. If a plaintiff is a public official, she must show, by clear and convincing evidence the false and defamatory statement was made with actual malice: the defendant "knew the statement either was false or acted with reckless disregard as to the truth or falsity of the statement."

(2) Public Figures, Limited Public Figures

Public figures are plaintiffs who are famous or celebrities who have earned fame or notoriety. Limited public figures have injected themselves into some particular issue or public controversy. The

Court expanded the rules for public officials to public figures and limited public figures in *Curtis Publishing Co. v. Butts*, 388 U.S. 130 (1967).

(3) Online Defamation against Private Persons

In online defamation cases against ordinary private individuals, the plaintiff must prove: (1) a false and defamatory statement concerning another, (2) unprivileged publication to third party, (3) fault amounting to at least negligence on the publisher's part, and (4) either actionability of statement irrespective of special harm, or existence of special harm caused by publication.

(D) Privacy–Based Cybertorts

The right of privacy includes four distinct tort actions: (1) the right to be free from invasion into one's solitude or intrusion upon seclusion, (2) the right to be free from public disclosure of private facts, (3) the right to be free from placement in a false light, and (4) the right not to have one's identity appropriated for commercial purposes. Restatement (Second) of Torts § 652A (1965).

(1) Intrusion upon Seclusion

The most common Internet-related privacy tort is the intrusion upon seclusion. The plaintiff must satisfy two elements to prevail in an intrusion upon seclusion action: (1) an intentional intrusion, physically or otherwise, on another's solitude, seclusion, or private affairs or concerns that is (2) highly offensive to a reasonable person. Restatement (Second) of Torts, § 652. A plaintiff must prove she had an actual expectation of seclusion or solicitude objectively reasonable. The rise of the Internet and of email threatens privacy today just as the invention of the telephone or photography did in the early twentieth century. Eavesdropping, wiretapping, or intercepting email could qualify as an intrusion upon seclusion. Courts have been unreceptive to consumer lawsuits alleging spyware is an intrusion upon seclusion.

(2) Appropriation or Right of Publicity

The appropriation tort is an intellectual property right in protecting the value of one's name rather than one's name *per se*. *Id.* The right of publicity or appropriation is the only property-based privacy tort of the four privacy-based torts. The tort of commercial appropriation protects the "inherent right of every human being to control the commercial use of his or her identity." J. THOMAS MCCARTHY, THE RIGHTS OF PUBLICITY AND PRIVACY, § 1.2, 1–8 (1992). The right of publicity applies to "[o]ne who appropriates the commercial value of a person's identity by using without consent the person's name, likeness, or other indicia of identity for purposes of trade is subject to liability ..." Restatement (Third) of Unfair Competition § 46 (2005).

The common law elements of the tort of the right of publicity are: (1) the defendant's use of the plaintiff's identity, (2) the appropriation of plaintiff's name or likeness to defendant's advantage, commercially or otherwise, and (3) the plaintiff has not given the defendant consent. *C.B.C. Distribu-*

tion and Mktg., Inc. v. Major League Baseball Advanced Media, L.P., 505 F.3d 818 (8th Cir. 2007). In *C.B.C. Distribution*, CBC marketed fantasy sports leagues on the Internet as well as by regular mail and telephone. Fantasy league participants form teams by drafting players from various Major League Baseball teams and use the cumulative statistics of the teams' players in actual games to determine the fantasy team's success. *Id.* at 820–21.

The players were unable to prove the fantasy league exploited their identity without their consent and for the purpose of commercial gain. The Eighth Circuit ruled professional baseball players' "right of publicity" does not include personal statistics used in fantasy baseball leagues. CBC used "players' identities . . . for purposes of profit . . . and their identities [were] being used for commercial advantage" which satisfied the elements of right to publicity. *Id.* at 823.

The court, however, ultimately decided the company's right to free speech outweighed the players' right to publicity, because the "line between the informing and the entertaining is too elusive for the protection of that basic right." *Id.* The court cited the Restatement (Third) of Unfair Competition, § 47, cmt. c, that "[t]he right of publicity as recognized by statute and common law is fundamentally constrained by the public and constitutional interest in freedom of expression." *Id.* The tort of misappropriation is the unauthorized taking of another's name or likeness. This was the first form of invasion of privacy tort recognized by courts. There have been several cases where plaintiffs have sued for right of publicity based on their likenesses appearing on the Internet. The federal district court enjoined an adult entertainment website from distributing the video sex tape of Pamela Anderson Lee and musician Brett Michaels. *Michaels v. Internet Entertainment Group Inc.*, 5 F. Supp. 2d 823 (C.D. Cal. 1998).

The online pornography website posted a copy of the sex tape to its subscription website. The court enjoined the defendant website from displaying images of the sex tape, finding the site liable for copyright infringement and for infringing the celebrities' rights of privacy and publicity. Recently, the Ninth Circuit in *Perfect 10, Inc. v. CCBill LLC*, 488 F.3d 1102 (9th Cir. 2007) stretched Section 230 of the Communications Decency Act to immunize websites for claims based upon the right of publicity and other state intellectual property rights. In the *Perfect 10* case, the plaintiff charged a website with violating its models' rights of publicity when it allowed third parties to post infringing copyrighted images on the site. The gist of Perfect 10's right of privacy claim was the unauthorized commercial use of the models' names and images. The defendant website responded with a claim that Section 230 of the CDA immunized them from the claim and the Ninth Circuit agreed.

(3) Public Disclosure of Private Fact

In order to state a claim for public disclosure of private facts, the facts must not only be private, the matter revealed must be highly offensive to a reasonable person. Restatement (Second) of Torts § 652D. A California Appeals Court ruled a preliminary injunction prohibiting an ex-wife from posting "false and defamatory statements and/or confidential personal information" on the Internet was an unconstitutional prior restraint. *Evans v. Evans*, 76 Cal.Rptr.3d 859 (Ct. App. 2008). In a Maine case, the court considered a case in which a plaintiff filed a public disclosure of private facts case against a former classmate who published a book about their prolonged high school feud called, "Help Us Get Mia." The court rejected the plaintiff's claim for public disclosure for private facts finding many of the statements posted by the plaintiff on her My-Space page. *Sandler v. Calcagni*, 565 F.Supp.2d 184 (D. Me. 2008).

(4) False Light

The fourth privacy-based tort is "publicity which places the plaintiff in a false light in the public eye." One who gives publicity to a matter concerning another that places that other person in a false light if: (1) the other was placed would be highly offensive to reasonable person, and (2) had knowledge of or acted in reckless disregard as to falsity of publicized matter and false light in which other was placed. Restatement (Second) of Torts § 652C. False light is not a strict liability tort, and the defendant must have knowledge of or have acted in reckless disregard as to the falsity of the published facts to be liable.

§ 5.7 Products Liability

The term "products liability action" is broadly defined to include any action against a manufacturer or seller for recovery of damages or other relief for harm allegedly caused by a defective product, whether the action is based on strict products liability, negligence, misrepresentation, breach of express or implied warranty, or any other theory or combination of theories, and whether the relief sought is recovery of damages or any other legal or equitable relief, including a suit for: (1) injury, damage to or loss of real or personal property, (2) personal injury, (3) wrongful death, (4) economic loss, or (5) declaratory, injunctive, or other equitable relief.

Products liability has been slow to develop in cybertort cases. The Sixth Circuit rejected a products liability claim arising out of a Kentucky school shooting. The plaintiffs contended the school shooter "regularly played video games, watched movies, and viewed internet sites produced by the firms." *James v. Meow Media, Inc.*, 300 F.3d 683, 688 (6th Cir. 2002). The plaintiff contended the defendant's games desensitized the shooter to violence" and caused him to shoot classmates. "When dealing with ideas and images, courts have been willing to separate the sense in which the tangible containers of those ideas are products from their communicative element for purposes of strict liability." *Id.* at 701. Courts have generally been reluctant to classify Internet transmissions as "products" for purposes of products liability. Courts are hesitant to recognize new duties of care for digital data or information-based injuries. No U.S. court, for example, recognizes an action for digital product liability.

§ 5.8   Tort Immunities in Cyberspace

(A) Immunities in General

Immunity refers to the special favoritism the law accords designated categories of defendants, such as public entities, family members, charities, and other protected groups. The law of torts has historically recognized immunities such as spousal or parent/child immunities precluding lawsuits by family members against other family members. However, the trend has been the abolition or limitation of immunities since World War II.

(B) CDA Section 230

Section 230 of the Communications Decency Act of 1996 (CDA), immunizes providers of interactive computer services against liability arising from content created by third parties. "No provider of an interactive computer service shall be treated as the publisher or speaker of any information provided by another information content provider." 47 U.S.C. § 230(c). A defendant must establish three thing in order to claim immunity under the Communications Decency Act of 1996 ("CDA"): (1) the defendant is a provider or user of an interactive computer service, (2) the cause of action treats the defendant as a publisher or speaker of information, and (3) the information at issue is provided by another information content provider. Communications Decency Act of 1996, 47 U.S.C. § 230(c)(1).

Section 230(f)(3) defines "information content provider" as "any person or entity that is responsible, in whole or in part, for the creation or development of information provided through the Internet or any other interactive computer service." 47 U.S.C. § 230(f)(3). Section 230 also authorizes providers and users of interactive computer services to remove or restrict access to inappropriate materials without being subject to defamation liability. 47 U.S.C. § 230.

With section 230(c)(1), the so-called "Good Samaritan provision, Congress immunized providers for all claims stemming from their publication of information created by third parties." Over the past decade, courts have expanded the meaning of interactive computer services to encompass websites and search engines. Section 230 divests ISPs of immunity for content it creates or develops. "One need look no further than the face of the statute to see why. The CDA only immunizes information provided by another information content provider." *Anthony v. Yahoo! Inc.*, 421 F. Supp. 2d 1257, 1263 (N.D. Calif. 2006) (denying service provider's motion to dismiss the claims for fraud, negligent misrepresentation, and state unfair and deceptive trade practices act violations).

In *Anthony*, the plaintiff filed suit against Yahoo! contending the company sent "profiles of actual, legitimate former subscribers whose subscriptions had expired and who were no longer members of the service to current members of the service." *Id*. The court found Yahoo! potentially liable for misrepresentations or false profiles because they were a content provider as well as a service provider.

(C) Publisher's Immunity

Congress enacted Section 230 to protect the "infant industry" of online service providers, such as America Online™, CompuServe™, and Prodigy™, from tort liability arising out of postings by customers. Section 230 of the CDA immunizes Internet Service Providers (ISPs) for torts committed by subscribers and third parties. In *Stratton Oakmont, Inc. v. Prodigy Servs. Co.*, 1995 WL 323710 (N.Y. Sup. Ct. 1995) a New York court held the ISP potentially liable for a third party's posting on its service. The court found Prodigy was a publisher because it advertised itself as family friendly and filtered content on its service. The CDA expressly reversed the holding in Prodigy by immunizing providers for screening or blocking inappropriate content.

(D) Distributor Liability

Courts have long distinguished between primary publishers (i.e. newspapers or book publishers) and distributors (bookstores, libraries, or newsstands) in common law defamation lawsuits. A newspaper is a republisher with the same liability as the person who originally published it if it has notice of the defamatory content. Republishers are classified as primary publishers held to the same liability standard as the author of a defamatory work because of their active role in the publication. Distributors traditionally encompass mere conduits such as "telegraph and telephone companies, libraries, and news vendors." DAN B. DOBBS, THE LAW OF TORTS (2000) at 1123. Under the common law of defamation, distributors are not liable for content created by others unless "the distributor knows or should know of the defamatory content in the materials he distributes." *Id.*

A bookstore owner, for example, is not liable for defamatory statements if the store sold the books without actual knowledge of the statements. Similarly, websites and other online defendants are not liable for the defamatory postings of third parties absent proof of knowledge or notice of the objectionable materials. Distributors are liable if they fail to take action in removing libelous material as soon as they have notice or acquire knowledge of the allegedly defamatory material. In *Cubby v. CompuServe*, 776 F. Supp. 135 (S.D. N.Y. 1991), the Ohio federal court ruled the service provider was not liable for content posted on its bulletin board. The *Cubby* court held the service provider was merely a distributor akin to a bookstore, library, or newsstand and therefore was not liable for defamatory content. Section 230 adopted the *Cubby* court's view websites are distributors, not publishers.

Since the CDA, courts have bloated ISP immunity to include distributorship liability as well as every other information-related tort, including the invasion of privacy, and negligence. The result has been that ISPs have prevailed in nearly every tort-related case in the last decade. This broad immunity will likely protect eBay or any other website from liability for failing to detect or control third party wrongdoing on their systems.

(1) Failure to Remove Content

U.S. courts have ruled consistently service providers are not liable for ongoing torts (or crimes) committed by third parties on their services even after they have received notice from the victim. Courts have yet to recognize ISPs have a duty to remove content constituting ongoing torts or even crimes. "In fact, under the CDA, ISPs can apparently continue to host defamatory content that the original author wishes to have removed." Rebecca Tushnet, *Power Without Responsibility: Intermediaries and the First Amendment,* 76 GEO. WASH. L. REV. 986, 1002 (2008).

The leading case for "no liability" for failing to remove content is *Zeran v. America Online,* 129 F.3d 327 (4th Cir. 1997). In *Zeran,* the Fourth Circuit ruled a service provider was immunized from both publisher and distributor defamation lawsuits. Zeran sued AOL for failing to take down pseudonymous messages in his name advertising T-shirts with tasteless slogans related to the 1995 bombing of the Oklahoma City Federal Building.

The cruel online prankster instructed the public to call Zeran to order merchandise with tasteless slogans celebrating the bombing. *Id.* at 329. The messages listed Zeran's name and telephone number. An Oklahoma City radio announcer repeated some of these incendiary messages on the air. In the aftermath of the radio broadcast, Zeran was deluged with threatening calls and death threats but could not change his number because this was also his business number. Zeran filed suit against AOL contending it was negligent in failing to remove the defamatory messages promptly after receiving notice. AOL defended on grounds of Section 230 and the Fourth Circuit agreed reasoning it was Congress' intent to immunize providers from tort liability to maintain robust Internet communications. The Fourth Circuit became the first court to interpret Section 230 to include claims for distributor's liability as well as publisher's liability. The court reasoned:

> If computer service providers were subject to distributor liability, they would face potential liability each time they receive notice of a potentially defamatory statement-from any party, concerning any message.... Because service providers would be subject to liability only for the publication of information, and not for its removal, they would have a natural incentive simply to remove messages upon notification, whether the contents were defamatory or not.

Id. at 333.

The Fourth Circuit's ruling was the service providers are not liable for refusing to remove the defamatory postings of third parties even after receiving notice of illegal content. In *Austin v. CrystalTech Web Hosting, Inc.*, 125 P.3d 389 (Ariz. Ct. App. 2005), a plaintiff filed suit against a website hosting company that hosted the Bali Discovery Tour's website that published a defamatory article that the plaintiff was about to be criminally charged by Bali officials. The plaintiff sued CrystalTech after it refused to remove this objectionable story from the Bali Discovery website.

The court affirmed a lower court's summary judgment ruling against the plaintiff ruling Section 230 of the CDA immunized the defendant because it was classified as an interactive computer service. The plaintiff contended Section 230 only immunized publishers, not distributors. The Arizona Court of Appeals disagreed finding no liability for a website failing to remove material after notice. U.S. courts tend to immunize websites for any torts created by third parties on their services not the case throughout the world.

In contrast, the European Union's 2000 Electronic Commerce Directive adopted a notify and takedown policy not available to the plaintiff in *Zeran*. Under this European Directive, an ISP is liable for not removing illegal content after receiving actual notice. The European approach creates the possibility ISPs will remove content that should not be taken down. Another danger is ISPs will act preemptively removing content chilling expression. American courts have recognized no duty to remove content except under Section 512 of the Digital Millennium Copyright Act, discussed in Chapter 10.

(2) ISP's Sponsorship of Online Gossip

Commentator Matt Drudge made an allegedly defamatory statement about White House aide Sidney Blumenthal on his AOL-sponsored website, which subjected him to jurisdiction in the District of Columbia. In *Blumenthal*, Drudge issued a report on AOL that Blumenthal had a past of spousal abuse. Drudge later retracted the story and AOL published the retraction on its service. The plaintiffs contended AOL should be liable for the defamatory communication even though it conceded AOL was an interactive computer service. Zeran contended AOL's editorial role made it a content provider divesting it of its Section 230 immunity. AOL sponsored the site and paid Drudge $3,000 monthly royalty payments for his column. The court found AOL had no editorial role even though it had the right to edit, update, manage, or even remove objectionable content. AOL also advertised it hired Matt Drudge and was teaming up with his service in separate press releases. *Blumenthal v. Drudge*, 992 F.Supp. 44 (D. D.C. 1998). The court found no evidence AOL was exercising editorial control or jointly creating the Drudge Report. The federal court classified AOL as an interactive computer service reasoning a contrary ruling would result in too much liability.

(3) Liability for Third Parties' Illegal Activities

In *Chicago Lawyers Committee v. Craigslist, Inc.*, 519 F.3d 666 (7th Cir. 2008), the Seventh Circuit affirmed the federal district court's grant of summary judgment in favor of Craigslist because it concluded 47 U.S.C. § 230(c)(1) protected the provider from liability for the content of the housing ads. The *Craigslist* court rejected the plaintiff's argument the online service was liable merely because property owners posted for-sale ads on Craigslist's site that allegedly violated the Federal Housing Act, which prohibited discrimination based on race, sex, national origin, religion, color, and familial status.

The court observed Craigslist ads were discriminatory on their face with examples including " 'NO MINORITIES' and 'NO CHILDREN', along with multiple variations, bald or subtle." *Id.* at 668. The *Craigslist* court compared the online service to the classified pages of a newspaper or a common carrier. Neither a newspaper nor a common carrier is deemed to have made or published a "discriminatory advertisement, text message, or conversation that may pass over their networks." *Id.* at 668. The court said Section 230 "as a whole cannot be understood as a general prohibition of civil liability for website operators and other online content hosts." *Id.* at 669. The court wrote Section 230(c)(1) did not mention "immunity" and therefore did not shield websites from all civil liability.

The *Craigslist* court explained how difficult it was for the service to filter discriminatory content: "Statements such as 'red brick house with white trim' do not violate any law, and prospective buyers and renters would be worse off if Craigslist blocked descriptive statements." *Id.* "If Craigslist 'causes' the discriminatory notices, then so do phone companies and courier services." *Id.* at 671–672. The appeals court found Craigslist was neither a publisher nor speaker and was therefore immune under

Section 230 for discriminatory advertisements by third party posters.

(4) Non–Immunized Content Providers

Service providers are divested of their Section 230 immunity if they take on the role of content creation. In *Fair Housing Council of San Fernando Valley v. Roommates.Com, LLC*, 521 F.3d 1157 (9th Cir. 2008) the Ninth Circuit sitting *en banc* ruled by an 8–3 vote a roommate matching website was not immunized by Section 230 because it was a content creator. In the housing discrimination lawsuit, the plaintiff contended Roommates.com required users to answer discriminatory questions. As a condition of searching listings or posting housing openings, subscribers were required to answer questions disclosing their sex and sexual orientation. Roommates.com also asked whether they would bring children to a household. The site also encouraged subscribers to provide additional comments.

The court agreed the website operator designed the discriminatory registration process for locating roommates and was undoubtedly the "information content provider" with regard to the questions. The court reasoned websites could be both a service provider and content provider: only if it "passively displays content that is created entirely by third parties, then it is only a service provider with respect to that content." *Id.* at 1163.

The Ninth Circuit noted a website is a content provider for content "that it creates itself, or is responsible, in whole or in part for creating or

developing; the website is also a content provider."
Id. The court noted a "website may be immune
from liability for some of the content it displays to
the public but be subject to liability for other content." *Id.* The court found Roommates to be "forcing subscribers to answer them as a condition of
using its roommate location services." *Id.* However,
the website was entitled to immunity with regard to
additional comments posted by subscribers since it
provided no guidance and encouraged no discriminatory preferences.

(5) ISPs & Social Network Websites

A New Hampshire Jane Doe plaintiff filed suit
against Friendfinder, an adult networking site, for
defamatory third party postings under the screen
name "petra03755" which depicted her as a
"swinger." The anonymous poster created a false
defamatory profile of the Jane Doe plaintiff. The
federal district court granted Friend finder's motion
to dismiss the plaintiff's claims for invasion of privacy and defamation on grounds of the federal
immunity under Section 230 of the Communications Decency Act. The federal court ruled Friendfinder was an interactive service provider and said
an unrelated content provider provided the allegedly defamatory profile page. *Doe v. Friendfinder Network* Inc., 2008 WL 2001745 (D. N.H. 2008). The
court ruled Friendfinder was not transformed into a
content provider merely because it changed the
wording about the age of Jane Doe's profile from

age 40 or 41 to the "early forties." However, a website operator making extensive editorial modifications risks losing its Section 230 immunity.

(6) ISPs & Rights of Publicity

The Ninth Circuit held Matchmaker was not liable when an unidentified party posted a false online personal profile for a former Star Trek Actress on its service. *Carafano v. Metrosplash.com. Inc.,* 339 F.3d 1119, 1122 (9th Cir. 2003). In *Carafano*, a former Star Trek Actress was the victim of a cruel identity theft hoax perpetrated by an anonymous Matchmaker subscriber who created a fake matchmaking profile on the defendant's service. The anonymous tortfeasor included the plaintiff's photograph, home address and other personally identifiable information and she was deluged with sexually explicit emails, telephone calls, and faxes at her home. The Ninth Circuit held Section 230 immunized a website for the third party's postings on its dating service. The actress filed suit against Matchmaker charging it with a host of torts including defamation, right of publicity, invasion of privacy, and negligence. The Ninth Circuit held Matchmaker was insulated from all liability because it was an interactive computer service. Too much cybertort liability will chill expression and stifle innovation. However, courts have expanded the meaning of Section 230 to preclude nearly all tort lawsuits against ISPs, websites, and search engines. Courts have stretched 'interactive computer services,' to immunize web hosts, websites, search engines, and content creators. See, Michael L. Rustad and Thomas H. Koenig, *Rebooting Cybertort Law*, 80 WASH. L. REV. 355, 371 (2005).

§ 5.9 Secondary Tort Liability

Online companies face a substantial risk for secondary tort liability. Partners have joint and several liability for torts committed by the partnership, and the plaintiff may bring action against partners individually, and does not have to sue partnership first. The Restatement provides a party is liable for another's tort if the party "knows that the other's conduct constitutes a breach of duty and *gives substantial assistance* or encouragement to the other so to conduct himself." Restatement (Second) of Torts § 876(b) (1979). The common law doctrine of *respondeat superior* makes an employer liable for cybertorts and even punitive damages if the plaintiff shows the employee's action was committed within the scope of the employment.

§ 5.10 International Developments

What is defamatory in a foreign country may be protected expression in the United States. A unified set of rules is necessary to deal with Internet defamation. See generally, Barry J. Waldman, *A Unified Approach to Cyber–Libel: Defamation on the Internet: a Suggested Approach*, 6 RICH. J. L. & TECH. 9 (1999). In Internet defamation cases, international policies regarding tort law and the rights of free expression may be in conflict. Information posted on the Internet may be protected in North America, but may violate contemporary community standards in less developed countries.

The United States carved out special tort rules making it difficult for public officials, public figures, or limited public figure to sue for defamation. In *Carafano v. Metrosplash.com, Inc.*, 339 F.3d 1119 (9th Cir. 2003), a former Star Trek actress filed suit against an Internet dating service alleging she was defamed by a false posting filed by an anonymous subscriber. The court found the popular actress to be a "general purpose public figure" who needed to prove actual malice in her case.

A private figure need only prove the defendant acted negligently in most jurisdictions. In contrast, a public figure or official must prove the defendant acted with actual malice proven by the heightened standard of clear and convincing evidence to recover. A private figure may morph into a "limited purpose public figure" if a court determines she injected herself into "a public controversy." *Gertz v. Robert Welch, Inc.*, 418 U.S. 323, 351 (1974). These constitutional doctrines are not followed outside the United States. Due to stronger American protections for free speech, a "plaintiff with a transatlantic reputation in both the United States and the United Kingdom will find obvious advantages in bringing a defamation suit in the United Kingdom." Alexander Gigante, *Ice Patch on the Information Superhighway: Foreign Liability for Domestically Created Content*, 14 CARDOZO ARTS & ENT. L. J. 523, 525–26 (1996).

The Wall Street Journal, for example, was the defendant in a United Kingdom lawsuit over its

republication of an April Fool's Day prank press
release disseminated by Harrods Department Store
on its website and print editions. *Dow Jones & Co.,
Inc. v. Harrods, Ltd.*, 237 F. Supp. 2d 394 (S.D. N.Y.
2002) The English firm issued a mock press release
stating it planned to "float" its department store by
building a ship version of the store and offered to
sell shares in the venture. *Id.* at 400. Upon learning
the announcement had been a prank, the *Journal*
countered with a story stating: "If Harrods, the
British luxury retailer ever goes public, investors
would be wise to question its every disclosure." *Id.*
at 401.

Harrods and its owner, Al Fayed, filed a libel suit
in London's High Court of Justice. *Id.* at 402. Dow
Jones, the owner of *The Wall Street Journal*, sought
a declaratory judgment to preclude the plaintiffs
from pursuing their defamation claims. Dow Jones
alleged an action for defamation based on the Journal article "would be summarily dismissed under
federal and state constitutional law of any American jurisdiction because the publication comprised
only the author's non-actionable expression of opinion based on true statements." *Id.* The U.S. court
refused to grant Dow Jones preemptive relief
against Harrods' cause of action. *Id.* at 412.

It was not until 1994 any plaintiff prevailed in an
Internet tort case. In *Rindos v. Hardwick*, No.
940164 (Sup. Ct. W. Austl. March 31, 1994), The
University of Western Australia denied Dave Rindos
tenure. Gil Hardwick, a rival anthropologist, posted

a rabble rousing statement supporting the university's tenure decision and falsely accusing Rindos of being a pedophile. In addition, he stated that Rindos conducted anthropological research harming aboriginal peoples. Although the Australian court was the first to award damages in an Internet tort case, American courts have litigated the vast majority of cybertorts. Intentional torts dominate the U.S. cyberlitigation landscape with the most common actions being grounded on fraud, unfair competition, and business torts followed by personal property torts, including trespass to chattels or conversion and online defamation. Intentional torts dominate the U.S. cyberlitigation landscape with the most common actions grounded on fraud, unfair competition, and misappropriation (business torts) followed by personal property torts, including trespass to chattels or conversion and online defamation." *Id.* at 93. The principal finding of an empirical study was that Internet torts are nearly all classifiable as intentional torts as opposed to negligence and strict liability. Michael L. Rustad & Thomas H. Koenig, *Cybertorts and Legal Lag: An Empirical Analysis,* 13 S. CAL. INTERDISC. L.J. 77, 77–78 (2003). Classic tort doctrines are being applied successfully to constrain Internet wrongdoing. Tort remedies, such as punitive damages, teach even the most powerful actors "tort does not pay." However, the courts stretching of Section 230 of the CDA has created a tort safe harbor for powerful intermediaries. The downside of broad immunities that the ISP has less of an incentive to protect the consuming public.

CHAPTER SIX

CONSUMER REGULATION IN CYBERSPACE

§ 6.1 Overview of Consumer Protection

Consumer contracts are entered into for personal, family, or household purposes subject to state and federal mandatory consumer law. Daily reports of fraudulent online auctions, Nigerian money offers, deceptive work-at-home plans, and illegal pyramid schemes confirm the ubiquity of cyberspace fraud. Cyberspace poses greater consumer protection problems because businesses may have no physical location, no personal interaction, no customer service representation and no "bricks-and-mortar" business to receive a complaint. Consumer law is largely about giving consumers procedural protections, disclosures, remedies, and mandatory provisions. See generally, Michael L. Rustad, EVERYDAY CONSUMER LAW (2008). It is uniformly held that U.S. online businesses must comply with consumer laws governing Internet advertisements, the sale of securities, taxation, unfair and deceptive trade practices, pricing laws, and general state and federal consumer statutes. An online company must institute adequate policies, terms of service, and other related safeguards to ensure it does not violate state and federal consumer law. These policies apply in the clicks world just as in the bricks and mortar world.

This chapter will provide an overview of consumer protection regulation of Internet business activities. Counsel for a website must audit all consumer contracts defined as those entered into for personal, family, or household purposes. The European Union defines consumers as those persons entering into transactions outside their trade or profession. Internet regulation that constrains unfair and deceptive activities in virtual spaces may be challengeable on constitutional grounds. The interconnected nature of the Internet is both its greatest strength and its Achilles' heel. The Internet has spawned new classes of online injuries, such as online lotteries, pyramid schemes, Nigerian email swindles, spam email, and Trojan horse programs choking electronic commerce and bilking unwary consumers. The National Consumer League's Internet Fraud Watch warns online consumers to be wary of downloading digital images, music, or software because of the risk of viruses or malware.

§ 6.2   FTC as Cyberspace Constable

Congress created the Federal Trade Commission ("FTC") in 1914 to prevent unfair methods of competition in commerce. Congress amended the Federal Trade Commission Act to prohibit "unfair and deceptive acts or practices." The basic consumer protection statute enforced by the Commission is Section 5 of the FTCA, which sanctions "unfair or deceptive acts or practices in or affecting commerce, are ... declared unlawful." 15 U.S.C. § 45(a)(1).

The FTC administers many laws applicable to cyberspace activities including The Undertaking Spam, Spyware, and Fraud Enforcement With Enforcers Beyond Borders Act of 2006 ("Safe Web"). Safe Web amended Section 5 "unfair or deceptive acts or practices" to include "such acts or practices involving foreign commerce" causing reasonably foreseeable injury within the United States. § 45(a)(4)(A). The Safe Web statute immunizes Internet Service Providers and consumer reporting agencies from liability for voluntary disclosures to the Commission about suspected online fraud or deception. The FTC is also the chief enforcer of the Children's Online Privacy Protection Act and the Controlling the Assault of Non–Solicited Pornography and Marketing Act of 2003. The FTC has used its authority to pursue a variety of shady e-entrepreneurs for Internet based unfair and deceptive practices. The FTC filed suit against an Internet pornographer for unfair and deceptive billing practices. The pornographer billed telephone account holders for the adult entertainment service even if they did not actually use the service. *FTC v. Verity Intern.*, 124 F. Supp. 2d 193 (S.D. N.Y. 2000).

(A) Online Privacy

The Federal Trade Commission sanctions websites targeting consumers and misusing their personal identifying information. Any company collecting personally identifiable information from consumers must comply with four information practices: (1) Notice—Consumers are entitled to fair notice of what information a website collects and its overall information practices such as whether they disclose the information to other entities; (2) Choice—Websites are required to give consumers the choice of how to handle personal identifying information such as marketing back to consumers or disclosing data to other entities; (3) Access—The websites must give consumers reasonable access to the information a website has collected about them, as well as a reasonable opportunity to review information and correct inaccuracies or delete information; and (4) Security—Websites are required to take reasonable steps to protect the security of personal data.

In 2001, the FTC sued Toysmart.com, contesting the potential sale of Toysmart's customer list in the distribution of its bankruptcy estate. Toysmart allegedly collected personal customer information from website visitors, including consumers' names, addresses, billing information, shopping preferences and family profile information. Toysmart stopped its operation in May of 2000 and retained the services of a consultant to sell its business and assets. Under Section 5, the FTC argued Toysmart's proposed sale of customer lists and profiles was an "unfair or deceptive act." In addition, the FTC argued the proposed sale violated the Children's Online Privacy Protection Act. The FTC noted Toysmart represented it would "never" disclose, sell, or offer for sale customers' personal information. Before the federal bankruptcy court ruled, Toysmart entered into a settlement agreement with the FTC to protect the privacy of its customer list.

(B) Online Sales

The Federal Trade Commission's Consumer Sentinel uncovered online auction sites and retail schemes, and declared they are some of the leading sources of Internet fraud. The FTC's analysis of Consumer Sentinel data concludes the most pervasive online auction complaint is that the consumer did not receive the item they paid for online. Few Americans can resist a bargain for luxury goods such as Coach® purses, Mont Blanc® pens, or Gucci® jewelry. The most typical fraud is for the seller to secure payment and then deliver knockoffs or obvious fakes. E–Bay and other online auction houses typically disclaim responsibility for fraudulent sales transactions.

(C) Advertising

The FTC extends advertising regulations to the Internet. False and deceptive advertising will subject the online company to regulatory actions by the FTC. "Spyware software raises a host of privacy, security, and functionality issues for even the most savvy computer users. Installed on your computer without your consent, spyware monitors or controls your computer use." Federal Trade Commission, *Spyware* (2008). Spyware may be transmitted via pop-up ads and it redirects the user's computer to unwanted websites or records keystrokes. *Id.* In recent years, the FTC filed hundreds of enforcement actions against spyware companies installing software on a consumer's computer altering their browsers, homepage, or search capabilities without the user's consent or even knowledge. The FTC contends the use of spyware constitutes an unfair and deceptive trade practice under Section 5 of the FTC Act.

(D) Online Deceptive Practices

(1) Deceptive Pornographers

The FTC prohibits specific disreputable practices on the Internet. For example, the FTC prohibits the use of "negative option marketing," the practice through which a customer is charged for a product or service they never intended to purchase. Online scammers sometimes ship merchandise to consumers who have not requested it, forcing the recipient to either pay for the merchandise or return it at her own expense or inconvenience. *FTC v. Crescent Pub. Group, Inc.*, 129 F. Supp. 2d 311 (S.D. N.Y. 2001) (ordering injunction where consumers' credit cards were automatically charged for "free tour" of pornographic website).

(2) Nigerian Scams

'Nigerian Scams' "in which a purported third-world official or business representative typically offers to share his family's fortune with a consumer in return for help with circumventing his country's currency restrictions by moving assets outside his country to a safe banking haven" continue to victimize American consumers. FTC, *FTC Details Efforts to Halt Internet Scams* (2004). The consumer is instructed, "to set up a bank account in the scammer's name with a good-faith deposit that soon vanishes." *Id.* Many variants of the Nigerian money swindles are carried out on the Internet. One version involves an email purporting to be from a Nigerian banker offering the recipient the opportunity to earn hundreds of thousands of dollars if they send their banking information. Thousands of consumers fall victim to these fraudulent emails.

(3) Dot. Cons

The FTC asserts broad investigative and law enforcement authority through the Federal Trade Commission Act ("FTCA") to police fraud on the borderless Internet. The FTC has the statutory authority to initiate an enforcement action if it has the "reason to believe" a defendant has violated the FTCA. 15 U.S.C. § 45(b). The FTC has broad authority to prevent fraudulent, deceptive, and unfair business practices in the online marketplace. The FTC "e-cops" search the Internet for unfair or deceptive practices and often uncover victims of "dot cons." FTC's web-surfing enforcers have identified the top ten dot cons: (1) Internet Auctions, (2) Internet Access Services, (3) Credit Card Fraud, (4) International Modem Dialing, (5) Web Cramming, (6) Multilevel Marketing Plans/Pyramids, (7) Travel and Vacation Schemes, (8) Business Opportunities, (9) Investments, and (10) Health Care Products/Services. FTC, *Dot Cons* (2000).

(4) Mousetrappers

Mousetrapping uses malware to obstruct surfer's ability to either close the browser or go back to the previous page. In 2002, the FTC filed suit against a "cybersquatter" who was in the practice of "mouse-trapping" Internet users. The federal court found the defendant had violated the trademark rights of third parties by registering Internet domain names that are misspellings of legitimate domain names or that incorporated transposed or inverted words or phrases. *Federal Trade Commission v. John Zuccarini*, et al., 2002 WL 1378421 (E.D. Pa. 2002).

(5) Privacy

In August 2002, Microsoft Corporation settled Federal Trade Commission ("FTC") charges regarding the privacy and security of personal information collected from consumers through its "Passport" web services. The FTC found Microsoft could not substantiate its claim consumer purchases made with its Passport Wallet were secure. E–Businesses must substantiate any claims its makes about its goods and services on websites especially when these claims related to health, safety, or performance. Sellers must not make misleading or untruthful statements about their products and services. A website business needs evidence to substantiate claims about their software or hardware.

(6) Fraud

"A New York court has ordered the promoters of the "9/11 Freedom Tower" coin swindle to pay nearly $370,000 in penalties as well as to refund consumers $25,000" for its deceptive marketing and sale of its "Freedom Tower" Silver Dollar on its website. Consumeraffairs.com, '*Freedom Tower*' and '*American Mint*' *Coin Scams Halted* (Oct. 19, 2005).

The misleading advertisements claimed the coins were made of pure silver, but in fact, they were made of a cheap metal alloy minted with 1.4 cents worth of silver. Id. The ads also said the coins were made of pure silver bars recovered at Ground Zero; although the coins were made of very little silver and there was no evidence any came from the Ground Zero recovery operations. Id. The unsolicited merchandise claim arose out of its marketing practice of sending customer's unordered items and then threatening collection actions for the unpaid items. Id.

§ 6.3   Regulation of Online Spam

Spam is broadly defined as unsolicited bulk email ("UBE") or unsolicited commercial email ("UCE"). "Email's open architecture and low marginal costs thus combine to create a forgiving cost structure. A spammer can make money with as low as a 0.005% response rate, or even a 0.000005% response rate." Rebecca Bolin, *Opting Out of Spam: A Domain Level Do Not–Spam Registry*, 24 YALE L. & POL'Y REV. 399, 401 (2006). In a typical day, the average consumer has an email inbox full of offers to make fast money. "As self-proclaimed spam king bragged: "When you're sending out 250 million e-mails, even a blind squirrel will find a nut." *Id.*

The vast majority of states enacted anti-spam statutes in the late 1990s and early 2000s. Courts awarded AOL millions of dollars against spammers under Virginia's antispam statute. The Federal Trade Commission has successfully prosecuted scores of spammers on the grounds their activities

constituted unfair or deceptive trade practices
harming consumers.

(A) CAN–SPAM

Congress enacted the Controlling the Assault of
Non–Solicited Pornography and Marketing Act of
2003 ("CAN–SPAM"), 15 U.S.C. §§ 7701–7713.
CAN–SPAM prohibits false or misleading transmission information, deceptive headers, and requires
email to give an easy to use opt-out method. Commercial email must be labeled as an advertisement
and include the sender's physical postal address.
"Transactional or relationship messages"—based
on a preexisting relationship such as a bank-cus-
tomer relationship—are exempt from CAN–SPAM,
but the messages cannot be false or misleading."
Commercial emails using false or misleading headers, or violating CAN–SPAM's other provisions, are
subject to fines of up to $11,000 for each unsolicited
emailing. 15 U.S.C. § 7704. A federal court ordered
a California direct marketer to pay $3.4 million in
fines for spam sent to a school district.

Section 7 of the CAN–SPAM Act provides for
exclusive enforcement by the FTC and the Department of Justice. The FTC does not permit state
attorney generals to file anti-spam lawsuits if there
is a pending federal civil or administrative enforcement action. Furthermore, the new federal anti-
spam statute preempts all state anti-spam legislation, even those providing consumers with a cause
of action against commercial emailers.

Text messages are also subject to the rules. "The FCC has issued a rule under CAN–SPAM to regulate messages sent through Internet-to-phone technology, that is, messages sent to a cell phone but from an Internet address, for example, cellphone number@verizon.net." Gilbert, *No Place to Hide* (2007). CAN–SPAM needs consumers to give "prior express authorization" before a text message can be sent. *Id.* Commercial messages must identify the company and include an opt-out mechanism functioning for at least 30 days. If the consumer elects to unsubscribe from receiving more messages, the company must stop sending any other promotional messages within 10 days." *Id.* CAN–SPAM does not authorize private lawsuits by aggrieved consumers.

In *White Buffalo Ventures v. University of Texas at Austin,* 420 F.3d 366 (5th Cir. 2005), the Fifth Circuit considered a challenge by an unsolicited emailing company alleging the University of Texas' anti-spam policy violated the First Amendment. The University blocked email messages from an online service because they violated the university's anti-solicitation policies banning unwelcome bulk commercial emails. *Id.* at 368.

The federal appeals court rejected the online dating service's contention the federal CAN–SPAM preempted the university's anti-solicitation policy. CAN–SPAM "supersedes any statute, regulation, or rule . . . that expressly regulates the use of electronic mail to send commercial messages" to the extent, these rules prohibit "falsity or deception in any part of a commercial electronic mail messages." CAN–SPAM (8)(b). The court did not find CAN–SPAM expressly preempted the University policy but instead found a presumption against preemption. The court said CAN–SPAM "does not preclude a state entity like UT from using technological devices [such as] spam filters to conserve server space and safeguard the time and resources of its employees, students, and faculty." *Id.* at 372. The *White Buffalo* court also rejected the commercial emailer's claim its messages were protected as commercial speech. The Supreme Court in *Central Hudson Gas & Elec. Corp. v. Public Serv. Comm'n*, 447 U.S. 557, 561 (1980) defined commercial speech as "expression related solely to the economic interests of the speaker and its audience." The *White Buffalo* court also found the university anti-spam regulations passed the third prong because they promoted a substantial interest. The court held the University's policy in blocking email was no more extensive than what was necessary to secure the state's substantial interest in blocking unwanted spam.

§ 6.4 Federal Communications Commission Issues

(A) The Communications Act of 1934

The Federal Communications Commission ("FCC") is an independent United States' government agency established by the Communications Act of 1934, 47 U.S.C. § 151 et seq. The FCC regulates interstate and international communications through radio, television, wire, satellite, and cable. The FCC's jurisdiction covers the 50 states, the District of Columbia, and U.S. possessions. The 1934 Act combined previous statutes governing telephone voice service and radio broadcasting. The Telecommunications Act of 1996 amended and updated the 1934 Act with the goal of promoting competition in all communications sectors. Section 230 of The Communications Decency Act was part of the telecommunications reform. European regulators are amending the pan-European Telecoms Package in order to cut off broadband access to recidivist downloader's of illicit music or films.

(B) Regulation of VoIP

The Ninth Circuit in *Clark v. Time Warner Cable*, 523 F.3d 1110 (9th Cir. 2008) ruled the Federal Communications Commission ("FCC") has primary jurisdiction to consider a "slamming" claim. Slamming is when existing telephone service is canceled and replaced by the new provider's Voice over Internet Protocol ("VoIP") service without the user's consent. The Ninth Circuit held the FCC is the appropriate agency to define "slamming" violations and has the authority to regulate VoIP.

(C) Net Neutrality

The policy debate over "net neutrality" concerns what role the government should have in regulating broadband Internet providers transmitting and delivering Internet traffic over their networks. The major policy issue centers on what types and degrees of control the government should impose on broadband providers. Marc S. Martin, *Net Neutrality Update*, ABA Business Law Section, Cyberspace Committee Forum (Washington, D.C. 2007). The consumer interest in net neutrality is to prevent broadband providers from blocking or slowing traffic based upon content or the type of customer. Broadband providers point to the efficiency of tiered pricing depending upon customers and content. Network neutrality is more broadly "an environment or platform" permitting "minimum interference by the network or platform owner." Lawrence Lessig, *Hearing on The Future of the Internet. Testimony Before the U.S. Senate Committee on Commerce. Science & Transportation* (April 28, 2008) at 2. Professor Lessig drew upon American history to describe how the interests of the United States imposed limits on the freedom of infrastructure providers to enhance the public good.

The electricity grid signifies neutral network norms because electricity providers are not permitted to discriminate among users or applications for electricity. *Id.* at 5. The AT & T blocking of a Pearl Jam webcast, because one of the band members criticized President George W. Bush, is an example of how networks have the potential to censor speech. Network discrimination will have a chilling impact on Internet entrepreneurs and constrain new applications. Lawrence Lessig, *Hearing on The Future of the Internet. Testimony before the U.S. Senate Committee on Commerce. Science & Transportation* (April 28, 2008) at 8.

Lawrence Lessig notes the Post Office, which jump-started the development of newspapers and periodicals as well as overall economic development, prefigured the key communication infrastructure. Network owners "have the ability to, in effect open the Internet's letters to peek inside the packets and choose which go faster or which get blocked." *Id.* at 3. Congress should articulate network neutrality principles to ensure networks implement norms, to facilitate the qualities of abundance and neutrality. *Id.* at 4.

Regulatory policies should incentivize network providers to develop "broadband abundance" supporting a "wide range of economic and social activity." *Id.* at 6. In contrast, federal regulations allowed cable owners an "almost unlimited range of freedom" in determining pricing structures, which resulted in "significant price increases" and a "radical drop in independently produced television." *Id.* at 7.

Professor Lessig proposes that Congress direct the FCC to implement network neutrality. *Id.* at 9. He concludes Congress must act to ensure "both technical and legal control over innovation on the Internet." *Id.* at 10. The FCC is the chief federal agency concerned with net neutrality. The FCC has recently been investigating cases where Comcast and Cox Communications blocked the traffic of customers. Electronic Commerce & Law Report, *Network Neutrality Practices* (May 21, 2008).

The concept of network neutrality assumes a relative autonomy of users in controlling the content they view as well as applications they use on the Internet. *Id.* Network neutrality has been a hegemonic principle throughout the history of the Internet. The Internet has operated according to this neutrality principle since its earliest days. A telecommunications carrier violated network neutrality when they block Web traffic over their networks. *Id.* Network neutrality is the key to generative capacity in enabling innovation. "Fundamentally, net neutrality is about equal access to the Internet. Broadband carriers should not be able to discriminate against competing applications or content. Just as telephone companies are not permitted to tell consumers who they can call or what they can say, broadband carriers should not be allowed to use their market power to control activity online." Google, *A Guide to Network Neutrality* (2008).

§ 6.5 Antitrust Issues in Cyberspace

Antitrust laws ensure that new Internet technologies, products, and services are sold in a competitive marketplace. The Justice Department contends that free and open competition enforced by the antitrust law is the solution to net neutrality. Antitrust law includes state as well as federal statutes against anticompetitive mergers, collusions, and abuses of monopoly power. At the federal level, the Antitrust Divisions of the U.S. Department of Justice and the U.S. Federal Trade Commission are involved in enforcement levels. In 2007, the FTC made a decision not to challenge Google, Inc.'s proposed acquisition of Internet advertising server DoubleClick, Inc., concluding the proposed acquisition was unlikely to decrease competition in any relevant antitrust market.

In addition to federal enforcement, each state has an attorney general or equivalent, which is responsible for enforcement of state antitrust laws. Courts define antitrust violations as *per se* violations or fact-specific violations determined by the *rule of reason*. The *per se* rule of antitrust law applies to practices such as price fixing or bid rigging. The *per se* rule applies to agreements likely to harm competition with no procompetitive impact. The Justice Department and state attorney generals filed an antitrust suit against Microsoft. *United States v. Microsoft Corp.*, 253 F.3d 34 (D.C. Cir. 2001). The government charged Microsoft's integration of Internet Explorer in Windows created unprecedented network effects resulting in a monopoly. Furthermore, roughly nine in ten personal computers operated under that platform. The U.S. Justice Department settled its antitrust case with Microsoft. However, the European Union fined Microsoft hundreds of millions of euros for anti-competitive marketing practices.

(A) Monopolistic Power

Monopolies are harmful to consumers because firms abuse the power to control prices or exclude competition. The test for monopoly power is whether the defendant's market share excludes competition. Section 2 of the Sherman Antitrust Act makes it unlawful for a company to "monopolize." 15 U.S.C. § 2. A defendant is liable for monopolization if two elements are satisfied: (1) the possession of monopoly power in the relevant market, and (2) the willful acquisition or maintenance of that power as distinguished from natural growth. Monopolies alone do not trigger the Sherman Act. An online company engages in anticompetitive or exclusionary conduct violates Section 2 of the Sherman Act. Monopolists may defend themselves by demonstrating greater efficiency or enhanced consumer appeal. Once this is shown, the plaintiff must show the noncompetitive effect of the conduct outweighs the pro-competitive impact. *United States v. Microsoft Corp.*, 253 F.3d 34 (D.C. Cir. 2001).

(B) Tying Arrangements

A tying arrangement occurs when, through a contractual or technological requirement, a seller conditions the sale or lease of one product or service on the customer's agreement to take a second product or service. A "requirements tie-in" sale occurs when a seller requires customers who buy one product from the seller (e.g., a printer) also to purchase another product from the seller (e.g., ink cartridges). Such "tying" allows the seller to charge customers different amounts depending on their product usage, an anticompetitive practice. U.S. Department of Justice and Federal Trade Commission, *Antitrust Enforcement and Intellectual Property Rights; Promoting Innovation and Competition* (2007) at 10.

(C) Rule of Reason

The Department of Justice applies a rule of reason analysis to assess intellectual property licensing agreements. The FTC has broad authority to police antitrust and consumer protection policies. The

FTC defines "unfair" acts or practices as ones that "cause or [are] likely to cause substantial injury to consumers which [are] not reasonably avoidable by consumers themselves and not outweighed by countervailing benefits to consumers or to competition." Consumers sued Apple and AT&T in 2007 for engaging in anticompetitive conduct with iPhones. In July of 2008, Apple began selling new models of new iPhone without requiring an AT&T service contract.

§ 6.6   Online Securities Regulation

The Securities and Exchange Commission (SEC) has jurisdiction over the sale of securities subject to the registration requirements of the Securities Act of 1933. The SEC's Office of Internet Enforcement (OIE) administers the SEC's Enforcement Division's Internet program. Internet road shows or webcasts must comply with SEC regulations. The SEC, for example, protects consumers by policing web sites offering securities, soliciting securities transactions, or advertising investment services offshore. The SEC formulated proxy rules under the Securities Exchange Act of 1934 permitting issuers and other persons to furnish proxy materials to shareholders by posting them on an Internet website provided shareholders receive notice of the hard copy availability of the proxy materials. Issuers must make copies of the proxy materials available to shareholders on request, at no charge. SEC, Internet Availability of Proxy Materials, RIN 3235–AJ47 (March 30, 2007).

§ 6.7 Internet Payment Systems

On-line banking services are now well established permitting customers to pay bills, make payments, manage accounts, transfer funds, and even view images of cleared checks. Increasingly, Americans are doing much of their banking online rarely venturing into a brick and mortar bank. In addition to traditional banking systems, the Internet has created Internet-based alternative payment systems such as PayPal™ owned by eBay®. PayPal™ members can transfer money to other people or businesses for online auctions or purchases. In September of 2006, twenty-eight state Attorneys General settled with California-based PayPal™, in a complaint about inadequate disclosures about the funding source for each purchase given to customers about their service. PayPal™ was charged with withdrawing money from a consumer's bank account, even if users submitted their credit card information when signing up. The consumers registered complaints with their state attorney general after they learned money had been withdrawn from their bank accounts only when they received their monthly bank statements. This financial transaction conflicted with their intention to use a credit card as opposed to withdrawing money from their bank account. Other consumers complained PayPal™ placed a hold on funds held in the user's PayPal™ account. Still others were confused about how to use PayPal's in-house dispute resolution programs and chargeback features. The settlement requires PayPal to provide clear and conspicuous disclosures about the important terms and conditions before a consumer becomes a PayPal member.

§ 6.8 Internet Taxation

(A) Federal Tax Law

The Internet Tax Freedom Act imposed a "temporary moratorium on Internet-specific taxes" by states and localities to avoid "stunt[ing] the growth of electronic commerce." S. Rep. No. 105–184, at 1–2 (1998). Congress prohibited: (1) all state and local taxes on "Internet access" (unless grandfathered) and (2) all discriminatory taxes on "electronic commerce," including the provision of "Internet access." ITFA §§ 1101(a), 1105(3)

(B) State Internet Taxes

The U.S. Supreme Court ruled states could not compel businesses to pay a sales tax unless the company has a physical presence in the state. *Quill Corporation v. North Dakota*, 504 U.S. 298 (1992). Quill, a Delaware corporation with a physical presence in Illinois, California, and Georgia, sold $1 million in mail-order office supplies to 3,000 customers in North Dakota. North Dakota wanted to charge sales tax on this income. The Supreme Court held such a tax would not violate the Due Process Clause of the Constitution, because "Quill...purposefully directed its activities at North Dakota residents,...the magnitude of those contacts [were] more than sufficient for due process purposes, and...the use tax [was]related to the benefits Quill receives from access to the State." *Id.* at 308.

The Court, however, held the Commerce Clause does not allow individual states to interfere with interstate commerce when the "only connection with customers in the [taxing] State is by...mail. *Id.* at 315. Therefore, North Dakota could not impose its sales tax on Quill. Yet, twenty-one U.S. states have enacted state statutes agreeing to a Streamlined Sales and Use Tax Agreement (SSU-TA). The SSUTA is a statute encouraging Internet and catalog businesses to gather and remit sales taxes on purchases by the residents of that state. O'Connell, *Washington State Streamlined Sales and Use Tax* (2008). "The tax is voluntary at least for the businesses involved." *Id.* The physical stores are operating at a competitive disadvantage to Internet and Catalogue sellers who are not collecting or paying taxes.

The city of Chicago, Illinois filed suit against eBay and its subsidiary StubHub for failing to collect that city's amusement taxes on concert and sporting event tickets sold through the Websites. EBay takes the position the city's amusement tax is inapplicable to the Internet reselling of sports and entertainment tickets. SiliconValley.com, Chicago *Sues eBay Over Concert Ticket Sales,* May 20, 2008). The city of Chicago has also filed suit against Hotel.com for failing to remit city hotel taxes. *Id.* New York already compels online retailers to collect sales taxes on goods sold over the Net to New York residents even though they do not have a physical presence in that state. Utah-based Overstock.com challenged the constitutionality of the New York statute. Reuters, *Overstock.com Sues N.Y. Over Internet Tax* (May 30, 2008).

§ 6.9   State Consumer Protection

The states play a critical role in protecting consumers in cyberspace. The mission of a state attorney general is to protect consumers injured by unfair and deceptive practices. State attorneys general are the chief legal officers of the state and the chief constables for cyberspace state enforcement. Each state has a "Little FTC" statute punishing defendants for unfair or deceptive trade practices. A state deceptive trade practice act has three elements: (1) the business is engaged in trade or commerce; (2) the business has committed unfair or deceptive acts or practices in the trade or commerce in which they are engaged; and (3) the consumer proves a financial injury and is seeking damages. The phrase "unfair or deceptive practices" applies to a wide range of practices in online sales or services.

The Washington State Attorney General filed a claim against Movieland.com for its abusive use of pop-up ads. The consumer was given a trial period of the service, and then was bombarded with pop-ups appeared at least hourly and subjected the consumer to a 40 second payment demand that would not close. These annoying messages could not be easily removed until the consumer paid $19.95 to $100.00. The court ruled Movieland.com's scheme was an unfair and deceptive method of generating online revenue.

Washington is one of the few states to have an anti-spyware amendment to its computer crime statute. Washington imposes fines up to $2 million for deceptive practices such as planting software appearing whenever a consumer launches an Internet browser. This anti-spyware statute also makes it unlawful to use deceptive means to harvest personally identifiable information or to record keystrokes made by a consumer and transfer information to a business.

§ 6.10   Commerce Clause Challenges

The Internet raises difficult issues in determining the power of states to prescribe conduct outside its borders. The Commerce Clause of the U.S. Constitution gives the federal government the power to regulate commerce. The Commerce Clause, U.S. Const. Art. I, § 8, cl. 3, contains an express authorization for Congress to "regulate Commerce with foreign Nations, and among the several States." The Court has long recognized the so-called Dormant Commerce Clause, which prevents states from regulating or taxing to discriminate or materially burden interstate commerce. The idea behind this "negative" Dormant Commerce Clause is to prevent local authorities from burdening Interstate commerce activities. The district court in *American Libraries Association v. Pataki,* 969 F.Supp. 160 (S.D. N.Y. 1997) traced the Dormant Commerce Clause back to Justice Johnson's 1824 concurring opinion in *Gibbons v. Ogden,* 22 U.S. 1 (1824) where the issue was whether New York could restrain the navigation of out-of-state steamboats in its waters.

The *Pataki* court noted how the Commerce Clause prohibits state regulations that discriminate or unduly burden interstate commerce, even if they are facially nondiscriminatory. A "dormant" or "negative" aspect of this grant of power is a state's power to impinge on interstate commerce may be limited in some situations. *Quill Corp. v. North Dakota*, 504 U.S. 298 (1992). State regulations are evaluated under a balancing test, which requires a court to uphold a state regulation serving an important public interest, unless the benefits of the regulation are outweighed by the burden placed on interstate commerce. The U.S. Supreme Court ruled the Commerce Clause of the U.S. Constitution prohibits state regulations attempting to govern conduct "that takes place wholly outside of the State's borders, whether or not the commerce has effects within the State." *Healy v. Beer Institute Inc.*, 491 U.S. 324, 336 (1989).

In *Beer Institute*, Connecticut enacted a statute requiring out-of-state beer shippers to affirm their posted prices for products sold to Connecticut wholesalers are, as of the moment of posting, no higher than the prices at which those products are sold in bordering New England states. A brewers' trade association as well as major producers and importers of beer challenged the statute under the Commerce Clause.

The district court upheld the statute but the Second Circuit reversed holding the statute violated the Commerce Clause by controlling the prices at which out-of-state shippers could sell beer in other States. The U.S. Supreme Court ruled the beer statute had the practical effect of controlling commercial activity wholly outside Connecticut. The statute violated the Commerce Clause because it imposed a regulatory scheme on out of state beer shippers, requiring them to take into account their Connecticut prices, in setting prices out of state. The Court also found the statute violated the Commerce Clause on its face and discriminated against interstate commerce. It applied only to brewers and shippers engaged in interstate commerce, not solely Connecticut sales, and because it was not justified by, a valid purpose unrelated to economic protectionism.

In the 2005 case of *Granholm v. Heald*, 544 U.S. 460 (2005), the U.S. Supreme Court struck down Michigan and New York statutes permitting in-state wineries, but not out-of-state wineries, from shipping alcohol to customers on the grounds the statutes violated the Dormant Commerce Clause. Michigan and New York argued their statutes were valid exercises of state power under the Twenty–First Amendment, which ended federal Prohibition but left it to the states to regulate alcohol importation. The U.S. Supreme Court accepted certiorari because of a split between the Sixth and Second Circuits as to whether the respective statutes violated the Commerce Clause. The U.S. Supreme Court held both states' laws violated the dormant commerce clause because the regulations favored in-state wineries at the expense of out-of-state wineries and that the Twenty–First Amendment did not authorize this discrimination.

The Court reasoned the ability to sell wine over the Internet helped make direct shipments an attractive sales channel for the small wineries. The state laws at issue permitted local wineries to make direct sales to in-state consumers on terms not available to out-of-state wineries, yet they violated the Commerce Clause. The Court ruled the states did not establish a legitimate purpose to justify their discriminatory treatment.

CHAPTER SEVEN

INTERNET–RELATED PRIVACY

§ 7.1 Overview of Online Privacy

Companies have new legal obligations to protect data as transborder data flows go global on the Internet. An eBusiness must ensure it processes consumer's personal information fairly and lawfully. A 24/7 website must provide adequate disclosures about data. Pharmaceutical manufacturer Eli Lilly and Co. inadvertently released the email addresses of 669 medical patients who had registered at its website to receive messages regarding health-related matters, such as reminders to take certain medications. *Lilly Privacy Violation Charges Are Settled*, N.Y. TIMES (Jan. 19, 2002) at C3. Eli Lilly settled with the states, but no individual plaintiff received a monetary award. This chapter covers Internet-related privacy regulations. Privacy-based cybertorts are covered in Chapter Five.

§ 7.2 Online Privacy Issues

(A) Search Engine Profiles

The World Wide Web has had a profound impact on privacy. It is now impossible to imagine a workplace without bandwidth, browsers, and bytes. The term "googling" is part of the cultural lexicon and users routinely "google" prospective employees, dates, or neighbors. Search engines have the power to track a user's website visits, topics researched or browser history.

(B) Cookies

"A piece of data that a Website—or a third party that was commissioned or approved by the website—saves on users' computers' hard drives and retrieves when the users revisit that Website. Some cookies may use a unique identifier links to information such as login or registration data, online "shopping cart" selections, user preferences, Websites a user has visited, etc." Anti–Spyware Coalition: *Definitions and Supporting Documents*, www. antispywarecoalition.org/documents/20051027 definitions.pdf (last visited on June 1, 2008).

(C) Online Profiling

Online profiling is the practice of targeting advertisements to website visitors based upon an analysis of their online movements. A website visitor who visits a senior citizen's chat room may soon receive advertisements for funerals, walkers, or Viagra. Internet advertisers favored a self-regulatory framework for curbing potential abuses of online profiling. Even though self-control is the best form of control, it is not likely to address the problem of misuse and abuse of profiling by unscrupulous actors.

(D) Spyware

Spyware also includes "adware" and other programs secretly installed on computers without their permission or knowledge. Spyware causes pop ups, banner advertisements, and other nuisance ads. It "also includes 'adware, keyloggers, Trojans, hijackers, dialers, viruses, spam, and general ad serving.' " *Federal Trade Comm'n v. MaxTheater, Inc.*, 2005 WL 3724918 (E.D. Wash. 2005). Adware is a subset of 'spyware' because it collects "information to display targeted advertisements." *Federal Trade Comm'n v. Seismic Entertain. Prods. Inc.*, 2004 WL 2403124 (D.N.H. 2004). Adware is a revenue generating form of spyware. *Wells Fargo & Co. v. WhenU.com, Inc*, 293 F. Supp. 2d 734 (E.D. Mich. 2003).

Adware targets "certain executable applications whose primary purpose is to deliver advertising content potentially in a manner or context that may be unexpected and unwanted by users. Many adware applications also perform tracking functions, and therefore may also be categorized as Tracking Technologies." Anti–Spyware Coalition: *Definitions and Supporting Documents* (2008). Spware is "software that gathers information about a computer's use and transmits that information to someone else, appropriates the computer's resources, or alters the functions of existing applications on the computer, all without the computer user's knowledge or consent." *Federal Trade Comm'n v. Seismic Entertain. Prods. Inc.,* 2004 WL 2403124 (D.N.H. 2004). In *Seismic*, the defendants downloaded spyware and adware to consumers' computers without their knowledge or consent. The spyware used exploit code to alter consumer's homepages and deliver adware, a practice enjoined by the FTC.

§ 7.3   Email Monitoring of Employees

The email system is an efficient means for forwarding documents, including pornographic or obscene messages, and it is a common practice to forward off-color jokes or other objectionable materials to multiple recipients. The simple act of an employee forwarding these jokes may unwittingly expose a company to a discrimination lawsuit under Title VII of the Civil Rights Act of 1964 and state discrimination laws as well as cybertort litigation. Employers not only email or surf the web but also contribute to blogs or participate in social networks such as Facebook or MySpace while at work. Employees in the private sector have no recourse if they are terminated for blogging about a private employer. Public employees, in contrast, may be protected by the First Amendment's qualified immunity if they are blogging about matters of "public concern."

An information technology company has many reasons for electronic surveillance or monitoring of email or Internet usage of its employees to prevent its employees' from committing torts or crimes, misappropriating trade secrets of the company, or preventing lawsuits for discrimination or harassment, or other online torts. American employees monitor email or Internet usage without notice to their employees with impunity, whereas European companies are liable for violations of human rights for the same policy by the European Court of Human Rights.

(A) Public Employees

The Fourth Amendment of the U.S. Constitution gives the "right of the people to be secure in their persons, houses, papers, and effects, against unreasonable searches and seizures." U.S. Constit. amend. IV. The U.S. Constitution does not constrain foreign law enforcement officers monitoring Internet activities. The Fourth Amendment applies to governmental actions where the intrusion infringes on the plaintiff's reasonable expectation of privacy that is the legally protectable interest. Courts compel the plaintiff to prove that she had a subjective as well as an objective expectation of privacy in the place searched.

(B) Reasonable Expectation of Privacy

In *Katz v. United States*, 389 U.S. 347 (1967), federal law enforcement officers attached an electronic eavesdropping device to a telephone booth in order to listen to conversations of a suspected illegal gambler. The Court ruled in any Fourth Amendment case, the issue would be whether the defendant had a "reasonable expectation of privacy." The *Katz* Court held the Fourth Amendment protected people, not places, and that the defendant in *Katz* had a reasonable expectation of privacy when he shut the door on the telephone booth. The Court rejected the government's argument that it did not violate Katz's constitutional rights since it committed no trespass in its electronic surveillance.

A public employee has a reasonable expectation of privacy in her workplace computer but the employer may also have a legitimate right of access as well. The Fourth Amendment is inapplicable to private employees. Courts apply a balancing test to determine whether a public employer's intrusions on the constitutionally protected privacy interests of government employees is justified by the employer's legitimate purposes. *O'Connor v. Ortega*, 480 U.S. 709 (1987) (holding a psychiatrist employed in a state hospital had a reasonable expectation of privacy in his office and was entitled to Fourth Amendment protection with respect to the search of his office by hospital officials). Whether a defendant has, a constitutionally protected reasonable expectation of privacy involves two questions: (1) whether a defendant is able to establish an actual, subjective expectation of privacy with respect to the place being searched or items being seized, and (2) whether that expectation of privacy is one which society recognizes as reasonable.

(C) United States v. Slanina

The Fourth Amendment's requirement of probable cause for the issuance of a search warrant "safeguards an individual's interest in the privacy of his home and possessions against the unjustified intrusion of the police." *Steagald v. United States*, 451 U.S. 204, 213 (1981). The Fifth Circuit upheld the denial of a motion to suppress evidence arising out of the search of a Texas fire marshal's office computer containing images of child pornography from a newsgroup titled "alt.erotica.xxx.preteen."

Slanina v. United States, 283 F.3d 670 (5th Cir. 2002).

Investigators uncovered child pornography on each of the defendant's hard drives, and all together, these hard drives contained thousands of files with such images. *Id*. at 675. "The zip disk from Slanina's office contained more than one hundred files of child pornography." *Id*. The court found the defendant exhibited a subjective expectation of privacy in images of child pornography by storing them in containers away from plain view. "To limit access to his computer files, he installed passwords, thereby making it more difficult for another person to get past the screen saver and reboot his computer." *Id*.

The federal appeals court found the supervisor's search of Slanina's computer was reasonable under the standard established in *O'Connor v. Ortega,* 480 U.S. 709 (1987). The supervisor who conducted the search in Slanina already discovered the titles of child pornography newsgroups suggesting the presence of child pornography on his computer. The court found the supervisor justified in conducting an investigation into his employee's use of pornography because access to pornography violated city policy. The supervisor had a justification for conducting a full investigation to determine the extent of its employee's violations and therefore committed constitutional violations. *Id*. at 680.

(D) Leventhal v. Knapek

The Fourth Amendment does not apply to a search unless the governmental intrusion infringes the plaintiff's reasonable expectation of privacy. In *Leventhal v. Knapek*, 266 F.3d 64 (2d Cir. 2001), a government employee had a reasonable expectation of privacy where there was no evidence a state agency had either "a general practice of routinely conducting searches of office computers or had placed [employee] on notice he should have no expectation of privacy in the contents of his office computer." *Id.* at 73–74. However, the court concluded the agency's investigatory search did not violate his Fourth Amendment rights because the employee's privacy interest was outweighed by the government's legitimate purpose in conducting the search. In *Leventhal*, the agency's investigation revealed the employee was misusing his government-issued computer and this supported the search.

(E) Smyth v. Pillsbury

Smyth v. Pillsbury Co., 914 F.Supp. 97 (E.D. Pa. 1996) was the first reported case where an employee challenged email monitoring and review of an employee's emails and Internet usage on grounds of intrusion upon seclusion. In *Smyth*, a federal court held a company's interest in preventing inappropriate email activity on its own system outweighed any employee privacy interest. Pillsbury maintained an email system to enable communications with its employees. The company previously assured its employees that email communications could not intercepted. *Id.* at 98. Smyth, a regional operations manager, sent a combustible email attacking management to his supervisor that, threatened to 'kill the backstabbing bastards.' " *Id.* at

98–99, n.1. Pillsbury terminated Smyth's employment for "inappropriate and unprofessional comments over defendant's email system." *Id.* at 98–99.

The *Smyth* court ruled the employee had no expectation of privacy in online messages and in any case the employer's reading of these messages was not a "substantial and highly offensive" invasion of his privacy. The court reasoned Pillsbury's right to prevent unprofessional and illegal activity outweighed any privacy interest of its employee in email comments. The court ruled Smyth's termination did not violate a public policy based upon right of privacy.

(F) Garrity v. John Hancock

John Hancock terminated two long-time female employees for forwarding sexually explicit emails from Internet joke websites and from other third parties in violation of its Internet usage policy. *Garrity v. John Hancock Mut. Life Ins. Co.*, 2002 WL 974676 (D. Mass. 2002). One of their co-employees complained to management after receiving a forwarded email from the plaintiffs. John Hancock promptly began an investigation of the plaintiffs' email folders, as well as the folders of those with whom the plaintiffs emailed on a regular basis.

The *Garrity* court found the plaintiffs' off color email violated the insurer's email policy. The ex-employees disputed the insurer's characterization of the emails in question as sexually explicit or in any way in violation of the policy language. The Massachusetts federal court dismissed the plaintiffs' privacy-based actions since they had no reasonable expectation of privacy in emails transmitted on their employer's computer system. Further, the court said the interest of the employer to take affirmative steps against harassment outweighed the plaintiffs' privacy interest.

§ 7.4 Federal Statutory Developments
(A) COPPA

Congress enacted The Children's Online Privacy Protection Act ("COPPA") to prevent children from revealing personally identifiable information without their parents' consent. 15 U.S.C. §§ 6501 et. seq. The FTC's COPPA rules, were effective on April 21, 2000 codified at 16 C.F.R. § 312. The FTC mandates that the site operator obtain parental consent and give conspicuous notice of their information practices. 16 C.F.R. §§ 312.4, 312.5 (2008). A website must get verifiable parental consent before collecting a child's personal data. Parents have a right to review personal information provided by a child and delete the information or have it deleted. *Id.* at § 312.6. A website may not condition a child's participation in the website on the collection of personal information. *Id.* at § 312.7. A child's parents must be given the opportunity to restrain further use or collection of information. *Id.* at § 312.5.

A website must have reasonable security to protect the confidentiality, security, and integrity of personal information collected from children. *Id.* at

§ 312.8. The FTC's COPPA Rule provides websites with a safe harbor for sites so long as they comply with approved self-regulatory guideline formulated by marketing or online industries. *Id.* at § 312.10(a). At a minimum, the self-regulatory guidelines must subject operators to the same or greater protections for children as contained in Sections 312.2 through 312.9 of the FTC's COPPA Rule. *Id.* at § 312.10(b). A website is not entitled to the safe harbor unless it requires operators to comply with the guidelines. The site is required to conduct "periodic reviews of subject operators' information practices." *Id.* at § 312.10(3)–(4).

The website operator must first make a threshold determination of whether the website or online service is directed to children under 13. The test is whether an operator of a commercial website or online service is directed to children under the age of 13. The FTC states the website must comply with COPPA if the operator has a "general audience web side and actual knowledge that they are collecting personal information from children." *Id.*

The FTC developed a multi-factorial test to determine whether a given website targets children. The most important factors include the subject matter (visual or audio content), the age of models on the site, the age of the actual or intended audience and "whether a site uses animated characters or other child-oriented features." *Id.* The Commission defines an entity an "operator" depending on who owns, controls, and pays for the collection of information. If COPPA applies, the operator must link to a notice of its information practices on the home-page of the website or online service. This notice must extend to each area where it collects personal information from children. The FTC requires the link to be clear and prominent. Personal information is defined to include: (1) an individuals' first and last name, (2) home or other physical address, (3) an email address or other online contact information, (4) a telephone number, (5) a Social Security number, (6) a persistent identifier such as a code, and (7) any other information concerning the child or the parents of that child the operator collects online from the child. *Id.* at § 312.2(2)(a)–(g).

Personal information may be collected directly from a child or passively through devices such as cookies. A cookie is a set of data that a website server gives to a browser the first time the user visits the site updated with each return visit. The remote server saves the information the cookie contains about the user and the user's browser does the same, as a text file stored in the Netscape or Explorer system folder. A New York federal district court found no cause of action in favor of Internet users whose personal information such as names, email addresses, telephone numbers, searches performed and the defendant's cookies were systematically collecting other personal information. The court dismissed all federal and state claims finding it implausible website visitors did not consent to the use of cookies. *In re Doubleclick Privacy Litigation*, 154 F. Supp. 2d 497 (S.D. N.Y. 2001). In May of 2008, the Texas Attorney General settled the first

COPPA action filed by a state attorney general. TheDollPalace.com was charged with violating COPPA in unlawfully collecting personal information from children without obtaining parental consent. DollPalace.com, a site for cartoon dolls, conditioned website access on children completing a ten page questionnaires about them and their friends. The Texas Attorney General found the parental consent feature of sites as easily circumvented. Children were participating in interactive chat rooms and forums without their parents' knowledge.

(B) HIPAA's Online Privacy Rules

Congress enacted HIPAA to allay the increasing public concern about the threat to privacy posed by interconnected electronic information systems: (1) to protect and enhance the rights of consumers by providing them access to their health information and controlling the inappropriate use of that information; (2) to improve the quality of health care in the U.S. by restoring trust in the health care system among consumers, health care professionals, and the multitude of organizations and persons committed to the delivery of care; and (3) to improve the efficiency and effectiveness of health care delivery by creating a national framework for health privacy protection building on efforts by states, health systems, and individual organization and persons. Standards for Privacy of Individually Identifiable Health Information, 65 Fed. Reg. 82,-462, 82, 463 (Dec. 28, 2000) (codified at 45 C.F.R. pts. 160, 164).

The Health Insurance Portability & Accountability Act of 1996 ("HIPAA") applies to health information created or maintained by health care providers who engage in certain electronic transactions, health plans, and health care clearinghouses. The purpose of the HIPAA standards is to provide enhanced protections for individually identifiable health information. HIPPA prohibits a person from knowingly using your "unique health identifier" or wrongfully obtaining "identifiable health information relating to individual "or disclosing" individually identifiable health information to another person" 42 U.S.C. § 1320d–6.

Online health providers will need to comply with information security requirements to comply with HIPAA. Section 501 of HIPAA requires each institution to protect the security and confidentiality of personal information. Fines range from $25,000 for multiple violations of the same standard in a calendar year to fines up to $250,000. The criminal penalty for egregious violations of HIPPA is up to 10 years in prison. This sanction requires proof beyond a reasonable doubt of the defendant's knowing misuse of a consumer's individually verifiable health information.

(C) Gramm–Leach–Bliley Act

President Clinton signed the Gramm–Leach–Bliley Act ("GLBA") on November 12, 1999. Subtitle A of Title V of the GLBA on the "Disclosure of Nonpublic Personal Information" applies to many Internet transactions. The GLBA's purpose is to give consumers control over their financial information. The GLBA gives consumers the choice as to whether to disclose their financial information and whether to share it with third parties. The GLBA gives the Federal Trade Commission the power to enforce the financial privacy rules. The GLBA defines financial institutions to mean "any institution the business of which is engaging in financial activities as described in § 4(k) of the Bank Holding Company Act of 1956." If a company is "significantly engaged" in providing financial products or services to consumers must comply with the privacy provisions of Subtitle A of Title V of the Gramm–Leach–Bliley Act, 15 U.S.C. §§ 6801–6809.

The GLBA mandates financial institutions to disclose to all of their customers the institution's privacy policies and practices with respect to information shared with both affiliated and non-affiliated third parties. The GLBA prohibits financial institutions from disclosing nonpublic personal information about customers to nonaffiliated third parties without adequate disclosure. Financial institutions must give customers an opt-out procedure if they do not wish their financial information to be shared with third parties. The FTC promulgated the GLBA Final Rules governing financial institutions.488 Subtitle A of Title V of the Gramm–Leach–Bliley Act is entitled "Disclosure of Nonpublic Personal Information (Title V).

SEC's Regulation S–P ("S–P") implements the privacy rules of the GLBA. Section 504 requires the SEC and other federal agencies to adopt rules, which implement notice requirements and restrictions on sharing a consumer's information. S–P requires brokers, dealers, investment companies, and investment advisers to provide notice of their privacy policy and to protect the privacy of customer information. Financial institutions must provide individuals with statutorily prescribed disclosures in initial as well as annual privacy notices. The GLBA regulation also specifies the affiliates and nonaffiliated third parties to which personal information may be disclosed. Financial institutions were required to post privacy notices and institute safeguards by July 1, 2001.

Congress' intent in enacting the GLBA was to provide consumers with access and control over private financial information maintained by banks and other institutions and the opportunity to correct any errors. S–P dictates online companies provide customers with a clear and conspicuous notice of their privacy policies and practices. To comply with S–P, companies must not disclose personal information about a consumer to nonaffiliated third parties unless the institution provides certain information to the consumer and the consumer has not opted out of the disclosure. The online company needs to provide annual notices to its customers, post its privacy notice on its website, and offer its customers the option of opting out of disclosures.

§ 7.5   State Regulation of Online Privacy

California's 2004 online privacy statute applies to any operator of website or online service collecting personally identifiable information through the Internet about individual consumers residing in California who are Internet users. An online company will be in violation of California law unless it "conspicuously posts its privacy policy on its website. Calif. Bus. & Prof. §§ 22575–22579. If a company operates an online service, it must comply with the statute in making its privacy policy available to California Internet users. Online companies have 30 days after being notified of noncompliance to post their online privacy policies in compliance with the statute.

California mandates every online company's policy to: (1) complete an audit of each category of personally identifiable information collected or shared with third parties or other entities on the Internet about website visitors, (2) give consumers notice if there is a process for reviewing and revising their personally identifiable information, and (3) describe the process by which the operator notifies consumers as to any material change in their privacy policy. The California statute gives online companies several ways of complying with the statutory requirement of conspicuous posting of its online policy. First, the company may post its privacy page on its homepage. Second, it is also permissible for a website to post an icon that hyperlinks to a web page on which the actual privacy policy. The icon must be on the homepage or "the first significant page after entering the website, and if the icon contains the word 'privacy.' " *Id.* A company must use a color that contrasts with the background color of the web page or is otherwise distinguishable. Finally, a website operator may include a text link hyperlinking to a web page on which the actual privacy policy is posted so long as the text link is located on its homepage. The text link must include the word "privacy" and be written in capital letters equal to or greater in size than the surrounding text. The California online privacy statute determines conspicuousness by the standard of the reasonable person.

§ 7.6 Third–Party Disclosure of Private Information

In *Bartnicki v. Vopper*, 532 U.S. 514 (2001), the U.S. Supreme Court held a journalist had an absolute First Amendment privilege for broadcasting a private recording surreptitiously intercepted by an unknown person. Bartnicki was the teacher's union chief negotiator in a contentious labor dispute with a high school. A third party intercepted his cell phone conversation with the union president. At one point in the cell phone conversation, the Union President thundered: "If they're not going to move for three percent, we're gonna have to go to their homes ... To blow off their front porches..." *Id.* at 524.

A journalist obtained a taped copy of this cell phone statement after an unknown third party left a copy in his defendant's mailbox. *Id.* at 525. The Court held the journalist was not liable for violation of the ECPA for broadcasting the taped conversation. The court commented, "[t]he normal method of deterring unlawful conduct is to impose an appropriate punishment on the person who engages in it." *Id.* at 529–30. The Court noted it would be unusual to punish a law-abiding journalist for the criminal act of an anonymous third party interceptor. *Id.*

The *Bartnicki* Court held the First Amendment prohibited imposition of civil liability on defendant for his "repeated intentional disclosure of an illegally intercepted cellular telephone conversation" concerning matter of public concern. This case "has significant implications for Internet law because of the vast opportunities for republication of information enabled by the Internet." Mark Lemley et al., SOFTWARE AND INTERNET LAW 955 (3rd 2006).

§ 7.7 **International Online Privacy**

The Organization for Economic Cooperation and Development ("OECD") proposed an action plan for electronic commerce at a 1998 Ottawa Ministerial Conference. The OECD Privacy Guidelines were incorporated into the Directive on Data Protection the went into effect in October 1998.

In order to bridge these different privacy approaches and provide a streamlined means for U.S. organizations to comply with the Directive, the U.S. Department of Commerce in consultation with the European Commission developed a 'Safe Harbor' framework. A website business will qualify for the FTC's safe harbor if it implements consumer awareness, choice, data security, data integrity, and consumer control over personally identifiable data on its website, which are norms inconsistent with the Data Protection Directive.

In a more recent international agreement, the United States government and European regulators agreed to permit the Bush Administration to gather data on European travelers. After 9/11, the United States Government sought "passenger data held by airlines flying out of Europe and by a consortium, known as Swift, which tracks global bank transfers. Several E.U. countries objected, citing privacy laws." Reuters, *U.S. and E.U. Near Private Data Deal: Report,* WASHINGTON POST (June 28, 2008). Online activities are increasingly likely to be subject to European privacy regulations in the interconnected world of the Internet. The U.S. must also consider privacy regulations of individual nations. The Swedish Data Protection Act, for example, prohibits companies from harvesting names, addresses, and other personal information from its website without prior consent. Companies will need to examine the data protection laws and practices of many countries to ensure they will not be sued in a distant forum. American based companies doing business online are subject to E.U. privacy regulations.

Counsel for 24/7 companies must determine what personally identifiable information is collected and how long to keep it. If a website business processes information, The European Union Directive on Data Protection will classify it as a service provider. Article 25 of the Data Protection Directive forbids the transfer of personal data to countries not providing "adequate protection." The European Directive on Data Privacy became effective on October

25, 1998. The European Commission negotiated a safe harbor with the United States' Department of Commerce that obliges companies to certify their compliance with the Data Protection Directive.

(A) Data Protection Directive

The Council of Europe adopted the European Convention on Human Rights (ECHR) in 1950. Article 8 of the ECHR treats the right to respect for his private and family life, his home, and his correspondence as basic rights. The Data Protection Directive of October 1995 commands any E.U. company to comply with specific rules for processing and transferring European consumer data. Each E.U. Member States must enact legislation fulfilling the six legal grounds defined in the Directive are consent, contract, legal obligation, vital interest of the data subject or the balance between the legitimate interests of the people controlling the data and the people on whom data is held (i.e., data subjects).

The Data Protection Directive gives data subjects control over the collection, transmission, or use of personal information. The Directive gives data subjects the right to be notified of all uses and disclosures about how their personal data is collected and processed. An Internet business must procure explicit consent as to the collection of personal data concerning race, ethnicity, or political opinions.

The European Union's Data Protection Directive demands data handlers protect personal information with adequate security. Data subjects have the right to get copies of information collected as well as the right to correct or delete personal data. It is important to obtain consent from the data subject before entering in to the contract. *Id*. at Art. 7. Data handlers may not transfer data to other countries without "adequate level of protection." *Id*. at Art. 25.

The Data Protection Directive requirement clashed with free expression in a case originating in the Göta Court of Appeal in Sweden. The court asked the E.U. Advocate General to gives its opinion about a case in which a Swedish church member, Bodil Magret Lindqvist, established a homepage on the Internet posting information about parishioners classified as personal data on the Directive. Mrs. Lindqvist was fined 4,000 Swedish crowns for violating Sweden's Data Protection Directive by transferring personal data to third countries without authorization. Sweden's authority for electronic personal data. Mrs. Lindqvist reported a church member suffered a foot injury and was on a part-time medical leave in an online church bulletin. Even though Mrs. Lindqvist promptly removed the homepage after a church member complained about it, the Swedish government charged her with processing sensitive data without receiving prior written notification. The European Court of Justice agreed with the Swedish government that Mrs. Lindqvist was processing personal data by loading information on the Church homepage. Case C/101/01 *Criminal Proceedings Against Bodil Lindqvist.*

(B) U.S. Safe Harbor

The European Community achieved greater harmonization of data protection when the European

Commission approved the Data Protection Directive, which expects each of the twenty-seven Member States to enact national legislation protecting "the fundamental rights and freedoms of natural persons, and in particular their right to privacy with respect to the processing of personal data." Council Directive 95/46, Art. 1. Article 25 of the European Commission's Directive on Data Protection prohibits the transfer of personal data to non-European Union not implementing adequate security. The U.S. Department of Commerce in consultation with the European Commission developed a safe harbor program for U.S. companies.

The U.S. Department of Commerce's Safe Harbor is voluntary. Companies may join a self-regulatory privacy program by developing their own self-regulatory privacy policies. Companies seeking a safe harbor must adhere to the seven principles first formulated by the OECD and embodied in the Data Protection Directive: (1) notice, (2) choice, (3) onward transfer; (4) security, (5) data integrity, (6) access, and (7) enforcement. Companies joining the safe harbor are subject to Federal Trade Commission enforcement under Section 5 of the Federal Trade Commission Act prohibiting unfair and deceptive acts or another law or regulation prohibiting such acts.

(C) Directive on Privacy & E–Communications

In 2002, the Directive on Privacy and Electronic Communication, which targets specific privacy issues relating to electronic communications, expanded the general principles in the Data Protection Directive. The Data Base Directive specifically states the confidentiality of communications prohibits the practice of interception or surveillance of private communications such as email over computer networks. This is an extension of the protection already recognized for private phone calls.

CHAPTER EIGHT

CYBERCRIMES & DATA SECURITY

§ 8.1 Overview of Cybercrimes

Cybercrime respects no national borders and is often difficult to detect because criminals leave no traditional crime scene. The first part of this chapter investigates the evolving law of cybercrimes concerning computer hacking, viruses, economic espionage, trade secret misappropriation, intellectual property theft, and cyber terrorism. Online companies typically are not liable for the cybercrimes of their employees unless they directed or otherwise ratified online postings or email transmissions constituting crimes. The second part of this chapter examines the rapidly evolving duty to implement reasonable security.

Cybercrime may be broadly defined to encompass any violation of criminal law perpetrated online or using the Internet as an instrumentality. The U.S. Justice Department indicted a Brazilian cybercriminal, Leni de Abreu Neto, for participating in a conspiracy with a 19–year–old man from the Netherlands, Nordin Nasiri, "to use, maintain, lease and sell an illegal botnet." A botnet is a network of computers infected with malicious software, known as "bot code." The malevolent bot code exploits vulnerabilities of the Internet, searching for other computers to infect. The botnet sold was a network of 100,000 computers infected with malware used to transmit spam email, disable computers, and launch denial of service attacks. This example underscores many features of cybercrime, the most obvious being the ease of committing crimes across international borders. Internet crimes are difficult to prosecute because there are no geographical borders and no "traditional crime scene." Despite difficulties, during the 2007 fiscal year alone, the Justice Department charged 2,470 defendants with identity theft, and successfully prosecuted an online hack/pump/dump scheme perpetrated by an online brokerage house.

(A) Computer Fraud & Abuse Act (CFAA)
(1) Overview

The Computer Fraud & Abuse Act ("CFAA") is the principal criminal statute addressing Internet-related computer crime. The CFAA makes it a crime to access a protected computer and get information "without authorized access," or in a way exceeding authorized access. 18 U.S.C. § 1030(a). The CFAA provides any person who "knowingly causes the transmission of a program, information, code, or command, and as a result of such conduct, intentionally causes damage without authorization, to a protected computer," shall be subject to certain sanctions and punishments. 18 U.S.C. § 1030(a)(5)(A)(i). The CFAA's civil action compels proof at least one person suffered damage aggregating in at least $5,000 in value in any one year period. 18 U.S.C. § 1030(a)(5)(B)(i). The CFAA, in both criminal or civil actions, applies to computers connected to the Internet. Congress defines "protected computer" broadly to mean computers:

> exclusively for the use of a financial institution or the United States Government, or, in the case of a computer not exclusively for such use, used by or for a financial institution or the United States Government and the conduct constituting the offense affects that use by or for the financial institution or the Government" or a computer "used in interstate or foreign commerce or communication, including a computer located outside the United States is used in a manner that affects interstate or foreign commerce or communication of the United States.

18 U.S.C. § 1030(e)(2).

(2) Elements of CFAA Crime

The first time in world history a court mentioned the Internet was a 1990 CFAA case in which a first year Cornell University computer science student released a worm or virus infecting hundreds of educational and military computers. In *United States v. Morris*, 928 F.2d 504 (2d Cir. 1991), Morris, was convicted of accessing a federal interest without authorization as his malware exploited bugs to infect computers in both an email program (sendmail) and a finger demon program providing information about the users of computers. The computer replicated and reinfected computers exponen-

tially causing machines to crash or become "cata-
tonic." The Second Circuit upheld Morris's CFAA
conviction finding he was without authority to
transmit his worm to protected computers. In order
to violate the CFAA, "it is necessary defendant do
more than merely access computers and view data."
United States v. Ivanov, 175 F. Supp. 2d 367, 372
(D. Conn. 2001) (citing 18 U.S.C. § 1030(a)(4)). The
defendant must knowingly obtain, alter, or cause
the transmission of information with the intent to
defraud.

The CFAA also punishes conduct committed "in
furtherance of any criminal or tortious act in violation of the . . . laws of the United States or of any
State." 18 U.S.C. § 1030(c)(2)(B)(ii). The first criminal prosecution for a cybertort was filed in 2008. A
prosecutor charged a homemaker with violating the
Computer Fraud and Abuse Act for masquerading
as a teenage boy and stalking a 13–year–old girl
inducing her to commit suicide. The 48–year–old
defendant, in order to revenge a slight to her own
daughter, masqueraded as a 16–year–old boy by
setting up a MySpace® website account and stalking the decedent. The older woman "proceeded to
make romantic overtures to Meier, only to cut them
off suddenly four weeks later with the callous statement that 'the world would be a better place without you.' " Calvin Ross, *Policing the Net* (2008).

The young girl hung herself as a result of the
cyberbullying. *Id.* The government charged the middle-aged woman and her unnamed co-conspirators
with "knowingly agreeing with each other to inten-

tionally access a computer used in interstate and foreign commerce without authorization and in excess of authorized access, and by means of an interstate communication, obtains information from that computer to further a tortious act, namely, intentional infliction of emotion distress." *Id.* The courts will generally not permit CFAA charges to go forward without proof of the defendant's criminal online activities. The Interstate Stalking Act includes imprisonment or fines, but no private right of recovery so intentional torts are the only possible recourse for victims. See 18 U.S.C. § 2261(b). Congress defined the crime as where the defendant "exceeds authorized access," such as accessing "a computer with authorization and [using] such access to get or alter information in the computer that the accesser is not entitled so to obtain or alter." 18 U.S.C. § 1030(e)(6).

The CFAA sanctions the trafficking of computer passwords or similar identifiers to allow unauthorized access of computer files. *Id.* at § 1030(a)(6). The use of a computer to "extort from any person, firm, association, educational institution, financial institution, government entity, or other legal entity, any money or other thing of value," is also a violation of the CFAA. *Id.* at 1030(7). The CFAA punishes criminal attempts as well as acts causing damage to a computer and unauthorized access to nonpublic computers with a fine or imprisonment of one year or both. Addtionally, a repeat offenders may be fined or imprisoned for up to five years. The

CFAA punishes "threatening national defense or foreign relations by a fine ... or imprisonment for not more than ten years or both. *Id.* at § 1030(C)(1). Repeat offenders endangering the national defense or foreign relations may receive a fine or imprisonment "for not more than twenty years or both ... after a conviction for another offense." *Id.*

The CFAA requires proof the defendant caused a minimum of a $5,000 loss over a one-year period by knowingly causing the transmission of a program, information, code, or command. 18 U.S.C. § 1030(a)(4). "Damage" is defined as "any impairment to the integrity or availability of data, a program, a system, or information that ... causes loss aggregating at least $5,000 in value during any 1–year period to one or more individuals ..." 18 U.S.C. § 1030(e)(8). The CFAA's civil action defines "loss" to mean any "reasonable cost to any victim, including the cost of responding to an offense, conducting a damage assessment, and restoring the data, program, system, or information to its condition prior to the offense, and any revenue lost, cost incurred, or other consequential damages incurred because of interruption of service." 18 U.S.C. § 1030(e)(f).

Many of the Internet-related CFAA cases arise out of private litigation. The CFAA's civil action provision allows private litigants to file civil damages lawsuits against defendants that:

knowingly and with intent to defraud, accesses a protected computer without authorization, or exceeds authorized access, and by means of such conduct furthers the intended fraud and obtains anything of value may be liable in a civil action to any person who as a result suffers loss to 1 or more persons during any 1–year period aggregating at least $5,000 in value.

18 U.S.C. § 1030(a)(4), (a)(5)(B)(i), (g).

The Computer Fraud and Abuse Act prohibit any person from knowingly causing the transmission of information, which intentionally causes damage, without authorization, to a protected computer. 18 U.S.C. § 1030. In *Hotmail Corp. v. Van$ Money Pie, Inc.*, 1998 WL 388389 *5 (N.D. Cal. 1998), the defendant was a spam emailer that knowingly falsified return email addresses so they included many false Hotmail addresses.

The *Hotmail* court found a violation of the CFAA because the spammer set up accounts with the intention of collecting never-to-be-read consumer complaints and "bouncing back" emails. Moreover, the defendants knowingly caused this false information to be transmitted to thousands of email recipients. In a similar case, the *America Online, Inc. v. LCGM, Inc.*, 46 F. Supp. 2d 444 (E.D. Va. 1998) court held commercial spam emailers who sent unauthorized and unsolicited bulk emails to AOL's subscribers violated the CFAA because they had violated the service provider's terms of services in harvesting email addresses and transmitting them through AOL.

The First Circuit held a tour company operator's use of a software scraper, to extract data from its competitor's website, exceeded authorized access violating the Computer Fraud and Abuse Act ("CFAA"). *EF Cultural Travel BV v. Explorica, Inc.*, 274 F.3d 577 (1st Cir. 2001). Explorica's software scraper program "sought information through the Internet. Unlike other robots, however, the scraper focused solely on EF's website, using information that other robots would not have." *Id.* at 579.

The plaintiff accused Explorica and its executives with violating the civil law provisions of CFAA. The plaintiff claimed Explorica used spiders or robots to extract pricing information from its travel website. Explorica first copied EF's pricing information by scanning and keying in information from its brochures and other printed materials. Explorica's computer consultant then ran the scraper software program twice, retrieving all of EF's tour prices and downloading "the equivalent of eight telephone directories of information." *Id.* at 580. The consultant developed a spreadsheet to systematically undercut all of EF's prices. *Id.* The consultant sent more than 30,000 inquiries to EF's website recording the pricing information into a spreadsheet. The First Circuit held the defendant's "scraping" of the tour company's travel codes constituted use that "exceeded authorized access" within the meaning of the CFAA. The federal appeals court also found the plaintiff's payment of consultant fees to assess the effect on its website was compensable "loss" under CFAA.

§ 8.2   Cross–Border Cybercrime Enforcement

Countries connected to the global Internet may not embrace free expression or other constitutionally based legal norms. China, for example, recently ordered ISPs to monitor private emails and impose legal sanctions for illegal postings appearing on websites they host. China is a leading venue for the producers of badware, such as spyware, that tracks computer users' clickstream. A Stopbadware.org report studying 200,000 websites uncovered "ten network blocks that contain the largest number of badware sites and six of the ten originated in China." Berkman Center for Internet & Society, *China Hosts Majority of Badware Sites* (June 24, 2008). The United States is responsible for about one in five badware sites.

In August of 2008, a federal grand jury indicted eleven defendants located in Eastern Europe, China, and the United States for exploiting vulnerabilities in many U.S. retail companies, including TJX. The cybercriminals were located in a global network and stole more than 40 million credit card numbers. The U.S. grand jury charged the defendants with an international conspiracy to commit unlawful access to TJX and many computer systems, in violation of the Computer Fraud and Abuse, Act, 18 U.S.C. § 1030. The codefendants were also charged with federal wire fraud (18 U.S.C. § 1343), credit and debit card fraud (18 U.S.C. § 1029), identity theft (18 U.S.C. § 1028A), and money laundering in violation of 18 U.S.C. § 1956.

(A) Detrimental Effects

The Internet creates a legitimation crisis for sovereignty because the Internet is extraterritorial by definition. In criminal jurisdiction cases, U.S. courts stretch the detrimental effects test developed under *Strassheim v. Milton Daily*, 221 U.S. 280 (1911) to the Internet. The detrimental effects test should not be confused with the *Calder* effects test used in personal jurisdiction cases discussed in Chapter Three. In *Strassheim*, the U.S. Supreme Court held acts done outside a jurisdiction, but intended to produce and producing detrimental effects within it, warranted the exercise of criminal jurisdiction. The *Strassheim* three-part test asks: (1) Was the defendant's act outside the state? (2) Was the act intended to produce detrimental effects within the state? (3) Was the defendant's act the actual cause of detrimental effects within the state? Historically, minimum contacts have had no place in determining whether a state may assert criminal personal jurisdiction over a foreign defendant. It is clear U.S. courts will not extend the minimum contacts framework to Internet-related criminal cases.

A Russian extortionate hacker was indicted in the United States on charges of conspiracy, computer fraud and related activity, extortion and possession of unauthorized access devices. *United States v. Ivanov*, 175 F. Supp. 2d 367 (D. Conn. 2001). Ivanov "hacked" into the Online Information Bureau, Inc. ("OIB") computer system and stole key passwords to control the company's entire network. Ivanov sent OIB a series of unsolicited emails indicating he had obtained the "root" passwords for OIB's computer system, which enabled it to manipulate, extract, and delete all data in the company's system.

Ivanov next threatened OIB with the destruction of its computer systems including its merchant account database demanding $10,000 for "helping" OIB secure its system. OIB rejected this offer and contacted federal law enforcement. Ivanov was charged with violation of the Computer Fraud and Abuse Act and other federal criminal statutes. Ivanov moved to dismiss his indictment because he could not be charged with committing crimes in the U.S. while residing in Russia. However, the *Ivanov* court reasoned a defendant, while residing in Russia, had gained root access to a business's computers in Connecticut and therefore obtained access to a business's intangible property, for purposes of the Computer Fraud and Abuse Act. The court ruled Ivanov's online ransom email was classifiable as a detrimental effect experienced in Connecticut and a sufficient basis for personal jurisdiction. The detrimental effects doctrine holds a defendant accountable as if he were present in the jurisdiction where the harm occurred.

(B) Cybercrime Convention

The Cybercrime Convention concluded in Budapest in 2001 is an international treaty to improve cooperation between nation states in the fight against cybercrime. Articles 2–4 compels signatory states to enact national legislation addressing computer crimes such as illegal access, illegal interception, and data interference. Article 5 criminalizes the creation or transmission of computer viruses or malware and expects states to enact legislation adopting the doctrine of corporate liability for cybercrimes. Articles 7 and 8 of the Convention criminalizes computer-related forgery and fraud. Article 9 constitutes an agreement to criminalize the production and distribution of child pornography. In Articles 10 and 11, the signatories agreed to criminalize copyright infringement, as well as aiding and abetting computer crimes.

Article 17 of the Convention also treats computer crime as an extraditable offense and calls for mutual assistance in the investigation and prosecution of computer crimes. Article 24 provides mechanisms for obtaining an "expeditious preservation of data" on a computer system or server in another territory. Parties must promptly disclose traffic data and may refuse a request only if compliance would threaten sovereign immunity security, the public order, or other essential interests.

Article 23 of the Convention obliges signatories to cooperate in criminal investigations "to the widest extent possible." The Convention recognizes the need for a mechanism allowing law enforcement to investigate offenses and get evidence quickly and efficiently, while remaining aware of each nation's sovereignty and constitutional and human rights.

The Cybercrime Convention does not demand "dual criminality" as a condition for mutual assistance consistently throughout the treaty. Dual criminality is the reciprocal criminalization of a specific crime by both countries.

§ 8.3 Electronic Communications Privacy Act

The ECPA or The Wiretap Act, 18 U.S.C. §§ 2510–2522, was enacted in 1968 to address the interception of wire and oral communications. In 1986, Congress updated the Federal Wiretap Act and enacted the Electronic Communications Privacy Act ("ECPA"). Title I of the ECPA amended the Wiretap Act to address the interception of electronic communications. Title II of the ECPA created the Stored Communications Act ("SCA"), 18 U.S.C. §§ 2701–2711 to address access to stored wire and electronic communications and transactional records. The SCA prohibits electronic communication services ("ECS") from knowingly divulging the contents of a communication while in electronic storage by that service. 18 U.S.C §§ 2701–2712. The ECPA extended the Wiretap Act to include new technologies, such as electronic communication. 18 U.S.C. § 2701–2711. The ECPA states:

It shall not be unlawful . . . to intercept or access an electronic communication made through an electronic communication system that is configured so that such electronic communication is readily accessible to the general public.

18 U.S.C. § 2511(2)(g)(i).

Congress defined "intercept" to mean "the aural or other acquisition of the contents of any wire, electronic, or oral communication through the use of any electronic, mechanical, or other device." 18 U.S.C. § 2510(4). The term "electronic communication," means "transient electronic storage that is intrinsic to the communication process for such communications." 18 U.S.C. § 2510(12) Title I of the Wiretap Act sanctions three types of activities: (1) intercepting or endeavoring to intercept electronic communications, (2) disclosing or endeavoring to disclose unlawfully intercepted information, and (3) using the content of unlawfully intercepted information. 18 U.S.C. § 2511. The ECPA requires proof the defendant's interception is intentional, which means the person committing the interception has to know or have reason to know the information has been illegally intercepted. *Id.* at § 2511(1).

Within the Act, Congress also created a private action which authorizes plaintiffs to seek monetary damages against a person who "intentionally intercepts, endeavors to intercept, or procures any other person to intercept or endeavor to intercept, any wire, oral, or electronic communication." 18 U.S.C. § 2511(1)(a). The First Circuit in *United States v. Councilman*, 418 F.3d 67, 79 (1st Cir. 2005) held email messages no longer in transit could not be intercepted as defined by the ECPA. In *Councilman*, the defendant was in a dual role of book dealer and an email service provider. The defendant created software redirecting incoming emails from

Amazon.com to customers of the defendant's company. Federal prosecutors charged the defendant with conspiring to intercept electronic communications under 18 U.S.C. § 2511. The First Circuit dismissed the indictment against Councilman, reasoning he copied incoming emails from Amazon already in storage. By definition, a message in storage cannot be intercepted. Email waiting to be delivered is classified as being in electronic storage. The court ruled emails already in storage (opened or unopened) could not be intercepted but were subject to the Stored Communications Act.

§ 8.4 ECPA Developments

(A) Consent

The ECPA allows service providers or anyone else to intercept and disclose an electronic communication where either the sender or recipient of the message has effectively consented to disclosure, explicitly or implicitly. Consent, as defined by the ECPA, also encompasses implied consent, which in the context of email monitoring is an employer's prior notice it will monitor Internet usage and email. 18 U.S.C. § 2511(2)(c)–(d). The ECPA prohibits employers from intercepting email messages, but the Act does not apply if an employee consents to email monitoring. *Id*. at § 2511(2)(d).

(B) Ordinary Course Exception

The ECPA contains an ordinary course of business exception applies to "any electronic, mechanical, or other device." 18 U.S.C. § 2510(5). If an ISP acquires the contents of information in the ordinary course of business, it is not classifiable as an interception under the ECPA.

(C) The Patriot Act & Government Disclosures

Section 2709 was originally enacted as part of Title II, the Stored Communications Act, of the ECPA in 1986, and amended in 1993 and 1996. "Shortly after the terrorist attacks of September 11, 2001, however, Congress again amended § 2709 by means of Title V, Section 505 of the Uniting and Strengthening America by Providing Appropriate Tools Required to Intercept and Obstruct Terrorism Act of 2001 ("USA PATRIOT Act")." *Doe v. Gonzales*, 449 F.3d 415 (2d. Cir. 2006). The USA Patriot Act amended the ECPA to list crimes for which investigators may get a wiretap order for wire communications. 18 U.S.C. § 2516(1) (explaining procedures for government interception of electronic communications to combat terrorism). The USA Patriot Act permits federal government agents to intercept email and monitor other Internet activities.

Congress authorized the Federal Bureau of Investigation to issue National Security Letters ("NSLs") to wire or electronic communication service providers, which allowed the FBI to gain access to subscriber information relevant to authorized terrorism investigations. A NSL is defined as an administrative subpoena that allows the Federal Bureau of Investigation to gain access to, among other things, subscriber information, or electronic communication transactional records held by Internet service providers when this information is relevant to international terrorism or clandestine intelligence activities. 18 U.S.C. § 2709(a).

The ECPA may order service providers to disclose stored communications and transaction records including the name, telephone or instrument number and other subscriber information confirming identity including temporary network addresses. 18 U.S.C. § 2703. The ECPA requires the government to show facts, capable of articulation, illustrating reasonable grounds relevant to a criminal investigation to support orders for service providers to turn over customer information. The subscriber whose information is turned over to the government has no reasonable expectation of privacy and is thus not protected under the Fourth Amendment of the U.S. Constitution. *United States v. Perrine*, 518 F.3d 1196, 1204 (10th Cir. 2008).

(D) Email Communications

The term 'electronic communication' is intended to cover email as well as a broad range of communication activities. More specifically, electronic communications are all communications do not constitute wire or oral communications. Providers of wire or electronic communications services may monitor their services to ensure adequate services. Another exception again refers to the "ordinary course of business" exception. In certain circumstances, employers may be allowed to monitor their employees' email. To meet the ordinary course of business exception, the employer has to show: (i) the device used to intercept the electronic communication, and (ii) the device is used by the employer within the ordinary course of the business. However, the employer is only allowed to intercept long enough to determine the nature of the communication. If the communication is personal, the employer must stop intercepting the communications further.

(E) Stored Communications Act

The Stored Communications Act (SCA) punishes those who do not have authority to access an electronic communications service facility and thereby obtains access to a wire or electronic communication in electronic storage. 18 U.S.C. § 2701(a). Another provision bars electronic communications service providers from divulging to any person or entity the contents of a communication while held in their electronic storage. 18 U.S.C. § 2702. The SCA created a service provider exception, permitting a provider to divulge an electronic communication to a person employed or authorized or whose facilities are used to forward such communication to its destination, § 2702(b)(4), or as may be necessarily incident to the rendition of the service or to the protection of the rights or property of the provider of that service. 18 U.S.C. § 2702(b)(5).

(F) ECPA Civil Actions

The civil action provision of the ECPA is an example of a "private attorney general" statute allows private litigants to file a suit fulfilling a public interest in addition to receiving private damages. Congress has enacted scores of private attorney general statutes in diverse fields.

(1) Konop v. Hawaiian Airlines, Inc.

In *Konop v. Hawaiian Airlines, Inc.*, 236 F.3d 1035 (9th Cir. 2001), a Hawaiian airlines pilot sued his employer for violation of the SCA claiming the airline had viewed his secure website without his consent. Konop "created and maintained a website where he posted bulletins critical of his employer, its officers, and the incumbent union, Air Line Pilots Association." *Id.* at 850–51. The Hawaiian Airline's manager secured the password of non-management employees and used their passwords to access the pilot's website. The SCA exempts from liability, "conduct authorized by a user of [the electronic communication service] with respect to a communication intended for that user." 18 U.S.C. § 2701(c)(2). While the airlines manager had the consent of the two non-management employees to use their passwords, there was no evidence either of those employees had ever been "users" of the pilot's website. *Id.* at 873.

Later that day, the pilot received word the Hawaiian Airlines Vice President was upset by the contents of the website. The pilot believed the company official secretly obtained the contents of his website and was unauthorized to access his website. *Id.* The Ninth Circuit affirmed the lower court's ruling the airline did not violate the Wiretap Act because the pilot's website was not intercepted during transmission, but rather while it was in electronic storage. The court reasoned "that for a website such as Konop's to be 'intercepted' in violation of the Wiretap Act, it must be acquired during transmission, not while it is in electronic storage." *Id.* at 878.

However, the court held the airline did violate the Stored Communications Act because the two pilots who shared their log-in information were not "users" of the website at the time they authorized the airline officer to use their names. A transfer of information from a website owner to an Internet user, which involves a web server sending a copy of a document to the user's computer for viewing, constitutes an "electronic communication" within the meaning of the Wiretap Act, 18 U.S.C. § 2510(12).

(2) Bohach v. City of Reno

In *Bohach v. City of Reno,* 932 F.Supp. 1232 (D. Nev. 1996), two police officers were the subjects of an internal investigation by the city and sought an injunction pursuant to the ECPA, to prevent disclosure of the contents of electronic messages sent between them. The *Bohach* court held the police department could retrieve pager text messages saved on the department's computer system without violating Title II of the ECPA or the privacy rights of the officers. *Id.* at 1232. The *Bohach* court reasoned the department was " 'the provider' of the 'electronic communications service' " *Id.* at 1236. The court classified stored transmissions of a paging system as storage, irrespective of whether the storage of paging messages was classifiable as temporary, intermediate, or merely incidental "to its impending 'electronic transmission,' or more permanent storage for backup purposes." *Id.*

(3) McVeigh v. Cohen

In *McVeigh v. Cohen*, 983 F.Supp. 215 (D.D.C. 1998), the U.S. Navy discharged Timothy McVeigh (no relation to the Oklahoma City bomber) after learning of his sexual orientation from an email transmitted through America Online. A civilian Navy volunteer, received an email message through the America Online Service ("AOL") stating it was from the alias "boysrch" signed by a "Tim" in the email text. The volunteer searched through the "member profile directory" and learned the screen name "boysrch" was, in fact, a gay male living in Honolulu, Hawaii and working for the military. A Navy investigator learned the AOL profile belonged to McVeigh.

The court found the Navy's investigation violated the ECPA because it sought McVeigh's profile from AOL without a warrant, subpoena, or court order. The court found AOL, as well as the Navy, violated the ECPA. The court ordered the Navy suppress the information about McVeigh's homosexuality it discovered in its illegal request to AOL. The court enjoined the Navy from discharging McVeigh and compared its actions to George Orwell's "Big Brother" in his novel, 1984.

(4) *In re* Pharmatrak

Congress enacted the Electronic Communications Privacy Act ("ECPA") to protect against the disclosure of customer information except in limited circumstances. Pharmatrak sold a NETcompare service permitting pharmaceutical companies to study website traffic and usage of consumers visiting their websites to learn about their drugs and to get rebates. Pharmatrak "collected certain information meant to permit the pharmaceutical companies to do intra-industry comparisons of website traffic and usage." *Id.* at 12. Pharmatrak's pharmaceutical company customers "were emphatic that they did not want personal or identifying data about their website users to be collected." *Id.*

Pharmatrak assured the companies data collection on individual users would not occur. Pharmatrak, nevertheless, collected user identifying information primarily because one of Pharmatrak's clients had employed the "get" method to transmit information entered by users. When the "get" method was used, information entered by users into the online form was appended to the next URL. Thus, NETcompare, which routinely recorded the full URLs of the web pages accessed by a user before and after visiting a client pharmaceutical company's website, also recorded personal information appended to the next URL. *Id.*

In *In re Pharmatrak, Inc.*, 329 F.3d 9 (1st Cir. 2003), the users of a web monitoring corporation and certain pharmaceutical corporations contended Pharmatrak secretly intercepted and accessed their personal information through the use of "cookies" in violation of the ECPA. Pharmatrak invoked a statutory exception under the ECPA claiming, among other things, they had received the consent of those companies. The First Circuit recognized consent was one of the statutory exceptions to ECPA liability. *Id.* at 19.

The plaintiffs filed a class action against Pharmatrak and the pharmaceutical companies asserting they violated the ECPA by intercepting electronic communications without their consent. *Id.* The First Circuit reversed a Massachusetts federal district court's granting of summary judgment in favor of Pharmatrak. The court found Pharmatrak "intercepted" electronic communications between Internet users and pharmaceutical companies within the meaning of the ECPA. The court also held the lower court had incorrectly interpreted the "consent" exception to the ECPA and remanded the case, in particular the issue of intentional requirement, for further proceedings. *Id.* at 3. The court ruled Pharmatrak had the burden to prove it had the consent of users.

§ 8.5 Economic Espionage Act

The Economic Espionage Act ("EEA") was enacted to punish and deter state-sponsored espionage to protect our nation's competitiveness. The EEA criminalizes the misappropriation or theft of trade secrets and confidential information. The federal statute provides criminal and civil penalties for the theft of trade secrets, 18 U.S.C. §§ 1831, 1832. To qualify for trade secret protection, the owner must "have taken reasonable measures to keep such information secret; and the information derives independent economic value, actual or potential from not being generally known to, and not being readily ascertainable through proper means by the public." *Id.* at § 1839.

The EEA criminalizes stealing or appropriating trade secrets whether by "fraud, artifice, or deception." *Id.* at § 1831(a). Economic espionage includes (1) theft benefitting foreign governments or entities (§ 1831) and (2) the "theft of trade secrets that benefit any person but the true owner" (§ 1832). Section 1831 of the EEA covers misappropriation by foreign governments or their agents, which is punishable by fines up to $500,000 or imprisonment of up to fifteen years. Offending organizations may be subject to fines of up to $10,000,000.

Section 1832 covers misappropriation intended to benefit persons and corporations. Persons are subject to fines and up to 10 years of imprisonment, while organizations are subject to fines of up to $5,000,000. The EEA criminalizes a person who "copies, duplicates, sketches, draws, photographs, downloads, uploads, alter, destroys, photocopies, replicates, transmits, delivers, sends, mails, communicates or conveys a trade secret." *Id.*

§ 8.6　Data Security

(A)　Internet Security

Tens of millions of Americans are victimized by negligent computer security yet courts have been slow to carve out a duty of care to implement reasonable computer security. Companies are increasingly sending data containing the personally identifiable information of millions of Americans to back office operations in India, China, and the Philippines, a practice known as business process outsourcing ("BPO"). While companies may assign non-core operations to BPOs, they will be unable to relocate their legal responsibility to maintain reasonable data security. No court has recognized a duty of American companies to ensure data is protected by BPOs often located in developing countries.

(B) Negligent Enablement of Cybercrime

The first generation of negligent enablement lawsuits is beginning to evolve. In 2008, a New York consumer filed suit against Lending Tree claiming a security breach in their website resulted in him receiving a higher credit card interest rates. He also alleged the security breach was causally connected to a rejected loan application with another lender. Several statutes already give the state attorneys general or federal officials the right to seek penalties against any company failing to disclose security breaches when consumer data has been compromised. However, notification statutes give the victims of data theft a private cause of action for data theft. The economic loss rule, present injury requirement, and the lack of a judicially created duty to secure data limits defendants liability for negligent data handling. An Internet website with lax computer security, enabling the theft of consumers' personally identifiable information such as credit card numbers, could be liable for facilitating the data heist. Courts are just beginning to hold data intermediaries such as software licensors, financial service companies, and other defendants liable for inadequate computer security enables the theft of data.

Negligent security policy is at the heart of recent data theft disasters involving identity fraud and the misappropriation of electronic information. The largest Internet-related data heist in history targeted TJX. The Massachusetts retail company reported in January of 2007 hackers compromised at least 45.7 million credit cards through a breach of its computer system. A consumers' lawsuit contended TJX failed to maintain adequate computer data security. The Justice Department indicted 11 defendants for illegally installing programs to capture card numbers, passwords and account information and transmitting the data to servers in the United States and Eastern Europe.

The government charged the hackers with many federal crimes including the Computer Fraud and Abuse Act, the Electronic Communications Privacy Act, as well as statutes governing money laundering, credit card theft, identity theft, and conspiracy. The injured credit card holders filed a civil action against TJX for conversion on the theory TJX enabled the hackers by failing to secure its computer system. The Massachusetts federal court dismissed the conversion count ruling, "conversion relates to interference with tangible rather than intangible property," such as electronic records. *In re TJX*

Companies Retail Sec. Breach Litigation, 527 F. Supp. 2d 209, 212 (D. Mass. 2007).

The *TJX* court rejected the New York case *Thyroff v. Nationwide Mutual Insurance Co.*, 864 N.E.2d 1272 (N.Y. App. Div. 2007) which decided electronically stored documents could be converted if deleted or misappropriated. To the New York court, data stored on electronic media was no different from the theft of printed documents and was therefore subject to a claim of conversion. The *TJX* court, however, reasoned the *Thyroff* case was not applicable because it related only to data "indistinguishable from printed documents." *Id.* at 214. Plaintiffs in data theft cases often propose a credit monitoring remedy analogous to medical monitoring sometimes ordered in toxic torts cases.

In identity theft cases, courts have been slow to recognize present and future monitoring for identity theft as compensable damages. Data theft cases filed by consumers are often unsuccessful because of the problem of establishing damages. Courts do not treat a consumer's risk of being an identity theft victim because of a data breach as compensable damages. To prevail in a negligent computer security case against companies such as TJX, the plaintiff must prove: (1) a duty of care owed by TJX to the consumer class of victims; (2) TJX's computer security fell below the applicable standard of care amounting to a breach of that duty; (3) an injury or loss; (4) cause in fact; and (5) proximate, or legal, cause. Negligent security cases by consumers have failed chiefly because consumers are unable to show actual damages. Courts have been reluctant to construct a duty to maintain reasonable computer security.

(C) Negligence *Per Se*

A company's failure to secure financial data, which results in injury to a consumer, will violate the Gramm–Leach–Bliley Act ("GLBA") if the company has not implemented a comprehensive information security program. In the future, consumers can use other Internet security statutes to argue a company's actions are negligent *per se*. Negligence *per se* is a particularly powerful tool in the hands of a plaintiff because the statutory violation satisfies both the duty of care as well as the breach of the standard of care. However, some jurisdictions treat the statutory violation as only some evidence of the breach as opposed to a presumption of breach. In jurisdictions where the statutory violation is a presumed breach, negligence *per se* is the practical equivalent of strict liability. The plaintiff will prevail by showing the statutory breach so long as the defendant produces no evidence of an excuse. No plaintiff has successfully employed a negligence *per se* argument in a computer security case. It is arguable Congress did not intend to provide private plaintiffs with a cause of action when it enacted the GLBA. In the absence of a statutorily defined duty to maintain adequate computer security, injured consumers will likely turn to the common law of negligence.

(D) Premises Liability

Courts have yet to expand premises liability theories to inadequate Internet security lawsuits. To prevail in a premises liability lawsuit, a plaintiff must establish: (1) the defendant owed a duty to protect the injured crime victim; (2) the defendant breached that duty; and (3) the breach of the duty was a proximate cause of the criminal act and the victim's injuries. Premises liability began in the early 1970s as courts increasingly held property owners liable for the failure to provide reasonable security to protect their tenants.

The property owner's duty to minimize the risk of crimes to tenants has served as a viable legal theory. However, courts have yet to find data intermediaries liable for the foreseeable cybercrimes of third persons as in premises liability actions. The Fifth Circuit rejected a plaintiff's claim that the law of premises liability for owners of real property applied to a website. In *Doe v. MySpace, Inc.*, 528 F.3d 413 (5th Cir. 2008), the plaintiff contended MySpace was liable under a premises liability theory for failing to prevent sexual predators from harming minors using its services. A Texas federal court dismissed the claim against MySpace, for enabling a sexual assault committed by a nineteen-year-old man on a fourteen-year-old girl he met online. The young girl misrepresented her age claiming she was 18 years old when creating her My Space profile. The nineteen-year-old MySpace member contacted her and sexually assaulted her.

The Fifth Circuit affirmed the federal district court's finding Section 230 of the CDA immunized MySpace for liability. *Doe v. MySpace, Inc.*, 528 F.3d 413 (5th Cir. 2008). The court applied Section

230 despite this immunity applies to publisher's liability rather than negligence. The court found the law of premises liability "germane to owners of real property," was inapplicable "to publishers and Internet service providers operating in the virtual world of cyberspace." *Id.* at 418. The court refused to divest MySpace of its Section 230 immunity despite its role in constructing profiles. The more actively an ISP edits or participates in the construction of content, the more likely a court will divest it of its Section 230 immunity. Courts are reluctant to recognize new tort duties to maintain adequate computer security to protect users from third party crimes.

(F) Data Breach Notification

The majority of U.S. states require companies to inform its customers their personal data has been stolen or compromised. The duty to disclose encompasses a trend to impose greater legal duties to safeguard customer data. A growing number of state and federal statutes already require companies to tell customers of data theft. The duty to disclose may be extended to a general duty to secure their computer systems and to safeguard customer data. Private consumers have no private cause of action in the event a company fails to incorporate cost-justified precautions to secure their computer systems. The E.U. Commission proposed a Directive requiring notification of security breaches by service providers. Internet security is just beginning to evolve as a legal duty worldwide.

CHAPTER NINE

CONTENT REGULATION

§ 9.1 Overview of Internet Regulations

The borderless Internet is constrained by many conflicting content regulations constraining speech. Without overstatement, the Internet has revolutionized free speech in the United States. The study of Internet regulation encompasses content regulation and is relevant to e-commerce activities. Madeleine Schachter & Joel Kurtz, LAW OF INTERNET SPEECH (2008). Companies face the inevitable task of complying with content regulations throughout the world. Courts in the United States have had little difficulty in determining the Internet is an instrumentality of interstate commerce. *American Libraries Association v. Pataki*, 969 F.Supp. 160 (S.D. N.Y. 1997). This chapter focuses on the state regulation of speech as well as economic activities may affect an online business.

§ 9.2 Internet Speech Regulations

(A) Communications Decency Act

Congress enacted the Communications Decency Act of 1996 ("CDA") to criminalize sending or displaying patently offensive messages on the Internet to persons under 18 years of age. In *Reno v.*

ACLU, 521 U.S. 844, 868–870 (1997), the court applied strict scrutiny to strike down provisions of the CDA as overly broad and vague. "Sexually explicit material on the Internet includes text, pictures, and chat and 'extends from the modestly titillating to the hardest-core.'" *Id.* at 853. To satisfy strict scrutiny, the government must not only prove it had a compelling interest, but also show the CDA was necessary to further that interest.

(B) Child Online Protection Act

The Child Online Protection Act ("COPA") is a federal statute enacted to "protect minors from 'harmful material' measured by 'contemporary community standards' knowingly posted on the World Wide Web for commercial purposes." Congress passed COPA after the U.S. Supreme Court struck down, on First Amendment grounds, the Communications Decency Act in *American Civil Liberties Union v. Reno*, 521 U.S. 844 (1997). COPA applies only to material displayed on the World Wide Web, covers only communications made for commercial purposes, and restricts only "material that is harmful to minors." 47 U.S.C. § 231(a)(1). COPA prohibits knowingly making any material harmful to minors available to them for commercial purposes. Under COPA, 'harmful material' is measured by 'contemporary community standards.' The Court in *Ashcroft v. ACLU*, 535 U.S. 564 (2002) found COPA's reliance on "community standards" to identify what material "is harmful to minors" does not by itself render the statute substantially overbroad.

The *Ashcroft v. ACLU* Court, however, did not decide whether COPA suffers from substantial overbreadth for reasons other than its use of community standards, whether the statute is unconstitutionally vague, or whether the statute survives strict scrutiny. However, in July of 2008, the Third Circuit considered these issues holding COPA violated the First and Fifth Amendments because it was overbroad and vague.

The Third Circuit again struck down COPA because it was not narrowly tailored to advance government's compelling interest in protecting minors from exposure to sexually explicit material, and thus violated the First Amendment. *American Civil Liberties Union v. Mukasey*, 534 F.3d 181 (3d Cir. 2008). The *Mukasey* court acknowledged the government had a compelling interest in protecting minors but concluded Congress burdened too much protected speech for adults. Moreover, COPA also defined the terms "minor" and "for commercial purposes" too broadly. The court rejected the government's argument COPA's affirmative defense saved the statute permitting publishers to show use of age-verification measures. The court observed these technologies placed an unreasonable burden on publishers. The court also found software filters screening out objectionable content were as effective as COPA. The court concluded COPA could not withstand strict scrutiny because it was both vague and overbroad.

(C) Children's Internet Protection Act

Congress enacted The Children's Internet Protection Act ("CIPA") in 1999 requiring public libraries to install software to block obscene or pornographic images as a condition of receiving federal funds. In *United States v. American Library Ass'n*, 539 U.S. 194 (2003), the Court upheld CIPA and reasoned CIPA did not violate the First Amendment because the purpose of the software was to block obscene or pornographic images and to prevent minors from obtaining access to harmful material. The Court ruled the federal assistance programs for helping libraries secure Internet access was a valid statutory purpose.

(D) Children's Pornography Prevention Act

The Children's Online Protection Act ("COPPA") is a federal statute enacted to "protect minors from 'harmful material' measured by 'contemporary community standards' knowingly posted on the World Wide Web for commercial purposes." *American Civil Liberties Union v. Reno*, 217 F.3d 162, 165 (3d Cir. 2000). Congress passed COPPA after the U.S. Supreme Court struck down, on First Amendment grounds, the Communications Decency Act in *American Civil Liberties Union v. Reno*, 521 U.S. 844 (1997). COPPA applies only to material displayed on the World Wide Web, covers only communications made for commercial purposes, and restricts only "material that is harmful to minors." 47 U.S.C. § 231(a)(1). COPPA prohibits knowingly making available any material harmful to minors for commercial purposes. Under COPPA, "harmful material" is measured by "contemporary community standards." The Court in *Ashcroft v. ACLU*, 535 U.S. 564 (2002) found COPPA's reliance on "community standards" to identify what material "is harmful to minors" does not by itself render the statute substantially overbroad.

(E) The PROTECT Act of 2003

After the Court's decision in *Free Speech Coalition*, "Congress went back to the drawing board and produced legislation with the unlikely title of the Prosecutorial Remedies and Other Tools to end the Exploitation of Children Today (Protect Act of 2003)" *United States v. Williams*, 128 S.Ct. 1830, 1836 (2008). The PROTECT Act criminally sanctions the advertising, promotion, presentation, distribution, and solicitation of child pornography. The PROTECT Act also penalizes speech accompanying or seeking the transfer of child pornography, via reproduction, or physical delivery, from one person to another. 18 U.S.C. § 2252A(a)(3)(B).

The PROTECT Act classifies primary producers as including "all those who actually create a visual representation of actual sexually explicit conduct, through videotaping, photographing, or computer manipulation." 28 C.F.R. § 75.1(c)(1) (2006). Secondary producers upload such images to a website or otherwise manage the content of the website. 28 C.F.R. § 75.1(c)(2). The producer must inspect the depicted individual's government-issued picture identification and determine her or his name and date of birth. 18 U.S.C. § 2257(b)(1) (2006); 28 C.F.R. § 75.2(a)(1).

In *United States v. Williams,* 128 S.Ct. 1830 (U.S. 2008), the U.S. Supreme Court upheld the pandering provision of the PROTECT Act of 2003. The PROTECT Act makes it illegal to send material, or purported material, in a way that "reflects the belief, or is intended to cause another to believe," that the material contains illegal child pornography. 18 U.S.C. § 2252A(a)(3)(B). In *Williams*, the defendant used a sexually explicit screen name, signed in to a public Internet chat room and conversed with a Secret Service agent masquerading as a mother of a young child.

The defendant offered to trade the agent sexually explicit pictures of his four-year-old daughter in exchange for similar photos. His chat room message said "Dad of toddler has 'good' pics of her an [sic] me for swap of your toddler pics, or live cam." The defendant was charged with one count of promoting, or 'pandering,' material intended to cause another to believe the material contained illegal child pornography and carried a sixty-month mandatory minimum sentence. The defendant challenged the constitutionality of the PROTECT Act's pandering provision and the Eleventh Circuit found this part of the statute both substantially overbroad and vague, and therefore facially unconstitutional. In a 7–2 opinion, the U.S. Supreme Court reversed the Eleventh Circuit. Justice Scalia's majority opinion concluded the federal anti-child pornography statute did not, on its face, violate the First Amend-

ment right to free speech. The *Williams* Court
found offers to provide or obtain child pornography
to be "categorically excluded from the First Amendment." *Id.* at 1842.

In *Connection Distributing Co. v. Keisler*, 505
F.3d 545 (6th Cir. 2007), the Sixth Circuit struck
down the PROTECT Act's record-keeping provisions for producers of sexually explicit conduct reasoning the provision was overbroad. The record-keeping obligation for producers "to include anyone
who created such visual representation and those
laterly publishing such images, could not be narrowly construed." *Id.* at 552. The individual plaintiffs were a couple who sought to publish their
photograph in Connection, a swingers' magazine.
Id. at 550. The couple was not unwilling to create
and maintain the required records, nor did they
wish to provide Connection with identification. *Id.*

The *Connection Distributing* court noted, "couples who take photographs for their own personal
use, must create the required records upon creation
of the image because either one has or both have
"produced" regulated images." *Id.* The court further noted, "[w]hile the government is indeed aiming at conduct, child abuse, it is regulating protected speech, sexually explicit images of adults, to get
at that conduct." *Id.* at 556.

§ 9.3 First Amendment in Cyberspace

(A) Content–Specific Regulations

Content specific speech is either protected or unprotected. As a content-based restriction on expres-

sion, the statute may only be upheld if it survives
strict scrutiny. A court will strike down government
regulations unless the legislation has narrowly tailored it to serve that interest. Prior restraints prohibit specific content or communications in advance. "Permitting government officials unbridled
discretion in determining whether to allow protected speech presents an unacceptable risk of both
indefinitely suppressing and chilling protected
speech." *11126 Baltimore Boulevard, Inc. v. Prince
George's County*, 58 F.3d 988, 994 (4th Cir. 1995).
The government needs very compelling government
interests to overcome a prior restraint. An injunction enjoining Internet speech is a prior restraint
available only in the most exceptional circumstances.

(B) Content–Neutral Regulations

In the context of the First Amendment, "a content-neutral regulation with an incidental effect on
speech component, ... must serve a substantial
governmental interest, the interest must be unrelated to the suppression of free expression, and the
incidental restriction on speech must not burden
substantially more speech than is necessary to further that interest." *Universal City Studios, Inc. v.
Corley*, 273 F.3d 429, 454 (2d Cir. 2001). A content-
neutral regulation need not employ the least restrictive means but it must avoid burdening "substantially more speech than is necessary to further the
government's legitimate interests." *Id.* at 450.
Courts uphold content-neutral restrictions on time,
place, or manner of protected speech so long as the
government narrowly tailors the regulation to serve

a significant governmental interest. *City of Renton v. Playtime Theatres, Inc.,* 475 U.S. 41 (1986) (upholding municipal zoning of x-rated theatres. Content neutral rules are unrelated to specific topics or subjects).

In *DVD Copy Control Association, Inc. v. Bunner,* 75 P.3d 1 (Calif. 2003), the California Supreme Court ruled an injunction barring a defendant from disclosing on his website a decryption program known as DeCSS did not violate the First Amendment. DeCSS is software which decrypts or circumvents CSS encryption which is an abbreviation for Content Scrambling System for protecting copyrighted contents of motion pictures in DVD format.

The court ruled DeCSS code was protectable expression but an injunction prohibiting dissemination of the code as a trade secret is a valid content-neutral speech regulation. The *DVD Copy Control* court found the injunction burdened no more speech than necessary to serve the government's interests in encouraging innovation and development and protecting trade secrets. Moreover, the California Supreme Court ruled the preliminary injunction was not a prior restraint on speech because it is a content-neutral measure adopted in response to the defendant's prior unlawful content in publicly revealing the DeCSS code in violation of California trade secrets laws.

The Digital Millennium Copyright Act, 17 U.S.C. § 1201(b) banned the manufacture and trafficking in technology, designed to circumvent software usage, is an example of protected speech. *United States v. Elcom Ltd.*, 203 F. Supp. 2d 1111 (N.D. Calif. 2002). The *Elecom* court ruled a ban on the sale of an item which contains protected speech, even if it is in the form of object code used in circumvention devices, triggers First Amendment protection. In *A.B. v. State*, 863 N.E.2d 1212 (Ind. Ct. App. 2007), a lower court held a middle schooler's incendiary postings about her school principal's disciplinary policies, were protected political speech dismissing a state criminal harassment claim. The Indiana Court of Appeals, however, affirmed on different grounds; they reasoned the state failed to prove the requisite elements of criminal harassment.

(C) Facial Attacks on Internet Speech

A court considering a facial challenge on either overbreadth or vagueness must first determine "whether and to what extent the statute reaches protected conduct or speech. The second [step] is determining the "plainly legitimate sweep" of the statute, that is, the sweep justified by the government's interest. The third [step] is determining . . . the statute's burden on speech" *Connection Distributing Co. v. Keisler*, 505 F.3d 545, 555 (6th Cir. 2007).

(1) Vagueness

Plaintiffs may challenge content-based restrictions of speech on vagueness grounds. The vagueness doctrine is an outgrowth of the Due Process Clause of the Fifth Amendment. In *Reno v. American Civil Liberties Union*, 521 U.S. 844 (1997), the

Court struck down a part of the Communications Decency Act ("CDA") on grounds of vagueness and overbreadth. The Court reasoned the CDA's use of the undefined terms "indecent" and "patently offensive" would have a chilling effect on speakers and therefore, raised special First Amendment concerns. The CDA's vagueness undermined the likelihood it had been carefully tailored to the congressional goal of protecting minors from potentially harmful materials.

(2) Overbreadth

The First Amendment's "overbreadth doctrine" is a tool for striking down Internet related content regulations as facially invalid if they prohibit a substantial amount of protected speech. Courts will strike down content regulations on overbreadth "grounds if less restrictive alternatives would be at least as effective in achieving the legitimate purposes the statute was enacted to serve." *Ashcroft v. ACLU*, 542 U.S. 656, 666 (2004). The Court in *Reno v. American Civil Liberties Union*, 521 U.S. 844 (1997) found the CDA's expansive coverage of content was wholly unprecedented; and the Court acknowledged the breadth of the content-based restriction placed a heavy burden on the Government to explain why they could not enact a less restrictive provision. Void for vagueness in contrast, is when a regulation is so ambiguous a person can not know with certainty what acts are proscribed.

(D) Categories of Unprotected Speech

The Virginia Supreme Court struck down a notorious spammer's criminal conviction on First

Amendment overbreadth grounds. Overbreadth is the constitutional infirmity where a regulation prohibits more conduct or protected speech than is necessary. In *Jaynes v. Commonwealth of Virginia*, 666 S.E.2d 303 (Va. 2008), the defendant was convicted of violating Virginia's Computer Crime Act for sending over 10,000 emails within a 24–hour period to subscribers of America Online, Inc. (AOL) on each of three separate occasions. The spammer used routing and transmission information trespassing onto AOL's proprietary network. He sent tens of thousands of emails to AOL subscribers intentionally falsifying the header information and sender domain names before transmitting the emails to the recipients. The *Jaynes* court found Virginia's statute criminalizing the falsification of IP addresses as overly broad and burdening the right to engage in anonymous speech. The court explained the state statute therefore criminalized otherwise unprotected speech such as pornography or defamation. The court applied a strict scrutiny standard and therefore required the statute to be narrowly drawn. The court found the computer crime statute was overbroad in prohibiting communications "containing political, religious, or other speech protected by the First Amendment to the United States Constitution." *Id.* at *12.

In *United States v. Williams,* the U.S. Supreme Court relied on the Court's long held view "that obscene speech—sexually explicit material that violates fundamental notions of decency—is not protected by the First Amendment." *United States v.*

Williams, 128 S.Ct. 1830, 1835 (2008). Governments are free to regulate obscene materials. In *Miller v. California*, 413 U.S. 15 (1973), the Supreme Court set out a three-prong test for obscenity, whether: (1) " 'the average person applying contemporary community standards' would find the work, taken as a whole appeals to the prurient interest;" (2) it "depicts or describes, in a patently offensive way, sexual conduct specifically defined by applicable state law;" and (3) "the work, taken as a whole, lacks serious literary, artistic, political, or scientific value." *Id.* at 24. The *Miller* Court reasoned basic First Amendment protections should not vary from community to community, but fell short of articulating a fixed national standard as to what "appeals to the 'prurient interest' or is 'patently offensive.' " *Id.* at 31. The *Miller* Court's standard is for a jury to determine obscenity by applying the standard of "the average person, applying contemporary community standards." *Id.*

The emergence of the Internet raises difficult questions as to whose community standard should apply to Internet-related obscene material. One danger is websites subject to content regulations of all jurisdictions will adopt the "legal norms of the most restrictive community." Bellia, et. al. *Cyberlaw*, Id. at 97. Another possibility is foreign courts will be unable to reach websites based in other jurisdictions. If foreign courts cannot reach websites outside their territory, the "legal norms of the least restrictive community will be adopted." *Id.* Courts will have difficulty determining the impact of website content on the average Internet user as opposed to a particularly susceptible or sensitive person such as an Islamic fundamentalist.

In *United States v. Thomas*, 74 F.3d 701 (6th Cir. 1996), the Sixth Circuit was the first U.S. court to determine which state's community standard for obscenity should apply in an Internet related transmission of pornographic materials. Robert Thomas and his wife Carleen Thomas operated the Amateur Action Computer Bulletin Board System ("AABBS") from their California home. Members paid a fee for access to the Thomas' bulletin board and where they could download pornographic materials in a GIF file format. A postal inspector conducting an investigation of the couple, downloaded x-rated photographs in Tennessee.

The *Thomas* court found jurisdiction in Tennessee based upon a postal inspector's downloading of obscene materials from the defendant's website. *United States v. Thomas*, 74 F.3d 701 (6th Cir. 1996). The Sixth Circuit held "obscenity" is determined by the standards of the community where the trial takes place" rejecting the defendants' argument it was unconstitutional to impose local community standards on Internet transmissions. The court reasoned the computer-generated images were electronically transferred from the Thomas' home in California, to the Western District of Tennessee where that state's community standard applied. The court noted the defendants had a method in place to limit user access in jurisdictions where the risk of a finding of obscenity was greater than in

California. The defendants were convicted of the federal crime of transporting obscene materials in interstate commerce. The idea underlying protected speech is the government has no power to restrict expression. In addition to obscenity, libel is not protected speech because this categories has no social value.

§ 9.4 Cyberbullying

In 2008, the U.S. House of Representatives introduced the Cyberbullying Prevention Act in response to a middle-aged woman whose cyberbullying caused a thirteen-year-old girl to commit suicide. This federal statute states: "Whoever transmits in interstate or foreign commerce any communication, with intent to coerce, intimidate, harass, or cause substantial emotional distress to a person, using electronic means to support severe, repeated, and hostile behavior, shall be fined under this title or imprisoned." Cyberbullying Prevention Act, H.R. 6123, 110th Cong. (2d Sess. 2008).

The proposed statute would make cyberbullying a federal crime, but it is likely overbroad or too vague. Electronic Law & Commerce, *Federal Anti– Bullying Bill Raises First Amendment Questions* (June 11, 2008). It will be difficult to enact such a federal statute to withstand constitutional scrutiny. *Id.* South Korea, too, is considering criminalizing the cyberbullying after a popular actor committed suicide in the wake of vicious Internet rumors.

§ 9.5 Countering Hate on the Net

The Internet is a haven for hate groups and Germany alone has three hundred registered hate websites. The Anne Frank Foundation estimates the number of hate websites advocating racist violence to be at least 8,000. Thousands of websites are dedicated to advancing the cause of white supremacy. A typical website seeks to "destroy and banish all Jewish thought and influence" echoing Hitler's call for a "final solution." Cloud, *Is Hate on the Rise?* (1999). In *Planned Parenthood of the Columbia/Willamette, Inc. v. American Coalition of Life Activists,* 290 F.3d 1058 (9th Cir. 2002), pro-life activists posted "GUILTY" posters identifying the names, addresses, and photographs of physicians that provided abortions. *Id.* at 1062. The website, developed by the American Coalition of Life Activists ("ACLA"), personally identified the plaintiffs on "Deadly Dozen 'GUILTY' posters."

ACLA compiled the "Nuremberg Files" to collect evidence against abortion doctors in the hopes a court would convict them for crimes against humanity. The defendants acted knowing doctors who performed abortions were murdered after the initial circulation of the posters. The plaintiffs argued the distribution of the Old West-style Deadly Dozen "WANTED" posters identified the abortion providers constituted a threat of force against the doctors performing abortions, violating the the federal Freedom of Access to Clinics Entrances Act. Pro-life radicals later murdered three physicians featured in the "WANTED" posters.

The jury returned a verdict in the physicians' favor, and awarded $108.5 million in punitive damages. The district court also "enjoined ACLA from publishing the posters or providing other materials with the specific intent to threaten [the physicians]." *Id.* at 1063. On appeal, the Ninth Circuit held the website constituted a true threat as defined under the Freedom of Access to Clinics Entrances Act and affirmed the ACLA's liability, but vacated the $108.5 million punitive damages award for the district court to determine whether it comported with due process. *Id.* at 1063, 1086. The Ninth Circuit's decision sent a signal to ISPs, which unplugged the "Nuremberg Files" site.

§ 9.6 Local Internet–Related Regulations

The City of Tampa, Florida sought to restrain an Internet related adult entertainment website charged subscribers to view 25–30 young women undressing and performing sexual acts. Subscribers to "voyeurdorm.com" paid a subscription fee of $34.95 a month to watch the women employed at the premises 24 hours a day, seven days a week, and could pay special fees to "chat" with the women. The City of Tampa Zoning Board charged the operators of the Voyeur Dorm with a zoning violation for conducting adult entertainment in a residential area.

The *Voyeur Dorm* court found the Tampa residence was not offering adult entertainment given they were broadcasting the videotaped images over the Internet. The court ruled the city's zoning code does not apply to the Internet because the site did not offer adult entertainment to the public. The court reasoned zoning restrictions are anchored to a particular geographic location so they cannot apply to Internet transmissions. The court found the defendant's public offering occurred over the Internet in "virtual space" rather than in Tampa, Florida.

§ 9.7 Foreign Government Censorship

Governments throughout the world impose content regulations on Internet activities. During the 2008 Olympics, China blocked Internet content. The BBC cited a University of Washington reporting sixty-four bloggers were arrested in 2007 around the world for their Internet opinions. Bloggers were arrested for such acts exposing human rights abuses, government corruption, and the suppression of protest. Since 2003, half of the arrests relating to content regulations arose in three countries: China, Egypt, and Iran.

The number of Chinese Internet users is estimated to range between 165 million to 210 million, and that number is growing by the tens of millions each year. Pew Institute, *China's Online Population Explosion*, July 12, 2007. This skyrocketing number of Chinese Internet users is emblematic of increased struggles for human rights in many less developed countries. Information will be more accessible to the public, yet this may exacerbate struggles over human rights.

In Hong Kong, under the Control of Obscene and Indecent Articles Ordinance, it is illegal to distribute any material "not suitable to be published to any person" or "not suitable to be published to any juvenile." Hong Kong Ordinances, Ch. 390 § 2

(1998). A Malaysian deputy minister warned bloggers "that there were laws pertaining to sedition, defamation, and libel." BBC (May 8, 2008). Gopalan Nair, a former Singaporean living in the U.S., "became the first foreign blogger to be arrested and charged with "threatening, abusing, or insulting a public servant." Zhong, Cyberspace, ASIA MEDIA FORUM (2008). The French Government mounted a number of challenges to liquor advertisements on the Internet, which were non-compliant with French law. A court ruled Heineken shut down its French website because the Internet was not on a 1991 list of approved media for alcohol publicity. *French Legal Tangle*, AFP (June 6, 2008). These examples are emblematic of the radically different cultural and political systems of countries connected to the Internet.

CHAPTER TEN

COPYRIGHTS IN CYBERSPACE

§ 10.1 Overview of Copyright Law

Copyright law creates property interests in expression that is a product of the human intellect. Copyright law is purely a federal law branch of intellectual property law, as is patent law. Copyright is the brick and mortar of the knowledge economy. The U.S. "core" copyright industries accounted for an estimated $819.06 billion or 6.56% of the U.S. gross domestic product ("GDP") in 2005. The U.S. "total" copyright industries accounted for an estimated $1.38 trillion or 11.12% of GDP. Stephen Siwek, COPYRIGHT INDUSTRIES IN THE U.S. ECONOMY (2006 Report). Courts have had little difficulty in applying well-worn groves of intellectual property law to cyberspace. "This has led to a series of cases and statutes that enshrine the idea of property interests in cyberspace." Dan Hunter, *Cyberspace as Place and the Tragedy of the Digital Anticommons*, 91 Cal. L. Rev. 439, 443 (2003). Copyright issues are a significant part of Internet-related intellectual property. Copyright law potentially protects all facets of a website: materials, documents, computer programs, pictures, artwork, photographs, sounds, video text, designs, HTML code, as well as the content of many other works posted on the Internet.

An Internet-related business must protect its copyrighted materials and avoid infringing the copyrights owned by others. An online company is potentially liable for copyright infringement if its employees post unauthorized materials or use unlicensed software on its website. The Internet challenges copyright law on several fronts. E–Businesses will find it more difficult to protect copyrighted materials on the Internet. A 24/7 website operator must own, license, or have been assigned the right to use all images, artwork, photographs, and content subject to copyright law.

(A) The Path of Copyright Law

In the United States, copyright is rooted in the U.S. Constitution. U.S. copyright law was prefigured in England when Queen Mary chartered the stationers by letters patent on May 4, 1557. The first statute to grant rights to authors, as opposed to stationers, was the Statute of Anne enacted in April 10, 1710. The Statute of Anne set the term of copyrights for authors at twenty-one years. Benjamin Kaplin, AN UNHURRIED VIEW OF COPYRIGHT LAW (1967). The sole rights of copyright owners were to print and reprint works. *Id.* at 7.

The Patent and Copyright Clause of the U.S. Constitution grants Congress the power to "promote the Progress of Science and useful Arts, by securing for limited Times to Authors and Inventors the exclusive Right to their respective Writings and Discoveries." U.S. CONST. Art. I, § 8, cl. 8. The power to determine the duration of copyright terms rests with Congress. Congress enacted the first federal copyright statute in 1790. Congress has amended the Copyright Act many times over the last two centuries.

(B) Copyright Act of 1976

Copyright is a federal statutory privilege broadly applicable to works "fixed in a tangible medium" that meet a minimum level of creativity. The Copyright Act of 1976, codified at 17 U.S.C. §§ 101, et seq. governs U.S. copyrights. Section 102(a) of the Copyright Act describes copyright subject matter: "Copyright protection subsists in original works of authorship fixed in any tangible medium of expression, now known or later developed, from which they can be perceived, reproduced, or otherwise communicated, either directly or with the aid of a machine or a device." 17 U.S.C. § 102.

Works of authorship include the following categories: (1) literary works, (2) musical works, including any accompanying words, (3) dramatic works, including any accompanying music, (4) pantomimes and choreographic works, (5) pictorial, graphic, and sculptural works, (6) motion pictures and other audiovisual works, (7) sound recordings, and (8) architectural works." 17 U.S.C. § 102.

(C) Copyright Term Extension

In 1998, Congress enacted the Copyright Term Extension Act, which extended copyright protection for an additional twenty years. 17 U.S.C. § 304(b).

Corporate publishers have copyright term protection for ninety-five years from publication.

§ 10.2   Elements of Copyright Law

Copyright protects "original works of authorship" fixed in a tangible form of expression. 17 U.S.C. § 102. The 1976 Act explains copyright extends to "original works of authorship," 17 U.S.C. § 102(a).

(A) Originality

Article I, § 8, cl. 8, of the Constitution mandates originality as a prerequisite for copyright protection. The constitutional requirement necessitates independent creation plus a modicum of creativity. "Original, as the term is used in copyright, means only the work was independently created by the author, and that it possess at least some minimal degree of creativity." *Feist Publications, Inc. v. Rural Telephone Service Co.*, 499 U.S. 340 (1991). In *Feist*, the U.S. Supreme Court held the plaintiff's white pages in *Feist* were not entitled to copyright because they did not fulfill the minimum threshold of originality required under the U.S. Copyright Act. The *Feist* Court explained the requirement of originality is satisfied if it is shown the work have some slight degree of creativity. However, the Court found the compilations of telephone numbers lacked this slight amount of originality. The Court conceded a compilation of facts could possess the requisite originality if the author made choices as to what facts to include, their ordering, and arrangement. However, even under these circumstances copyright protection extends only to those components of the work original to the author, not to the telephone numbers themselves.

This fact/expression dichotomy severely limits the scope of protection in fact-based works such as databases. In *Feist*, the Court reasoned there was no creativity in Rural Telephone's directories comprised only an alphabetical list of facts. The *Feist* Court rejected a "sweat of the brow" theory adopted by some courts, which extended a compilation's copyright protection beyond selection and arrangement to the facts themselves.

(B) Fixation

An author must fix a work of authorship in a tangible medium of expression to satisfy the fixation requirement. The creator may communicate the fixation with the help of a machine or device and need not be directly perceptible. A work is "fixed" in a tangible medium of expression when it is "sufficiently permanent or stable to permit it to be perceived, reproduced, or otherwise communicated for a period of more than transitory duration." 17 U.S.C. § 101. Merely loading a computer operating system into a computer's random access memory ("RAM") creates a copy under the Copyright Act. *MAI Systems Corp. v. Peak Computer*, 991 F.2d 511, 517–19 (9th Cir. 1993). Similarly, the acts of transmitting an email or viewing a web page, both of which store copies in the user's computer RAM, qualify as copies for purposes of the Copyright Act.

Internet copying, such as caching temporary copies of websites, would qualify as a fixed copy under the reasoning of the *MAI* court.

Generally, a "cache" is "a computer memory with very short access time used for storage of frequently or recently used instructions or data." *United States v. Ziegler*, 474 F.3d 1184, 1186 n.3 (9th Cir. 2007)

(C) Works of Authorship

Copyright law protects "original works of authorship fixed in any tangible medium of expression." 17 U.S.C. § 101. Software is classified as works of authorship so long as they are original and tangibly fixed. Writing a poem on the sands of Rexhame Beach would not satisfy fixation. Software inscribed on a diskette or CD–ROM is sufficiently tangible to meet the fixation requirement. *Id.* Similarly, any content on a website is a work of authorship copyrightable so long as it satisfies the statutory requirements of originality and fixation.

(D) Derivative Works

A "derivative work" is a work based upon preexisting works including translations, musical arrangements, dramatizations, fictionalizations, motion picture versions, and any other work "recast, transformed, or adapted." The movie, *A Civil Action*, for example, is the motion picture version of a novel of the same name by Jonathan Haar. Derivative works include preexisting works such as "a translation, musical arrangement, dramatization, fictionalization, motion picture version, sound recording, art reproduction, abridgment, condensation, or any other form in which a work may be recast, transformed, or adapted." 17 U.S.C. § 101. Editorial revisions, annotations, elaborations, or other modifications such as an altered or updated website, may qualify as a derivative work.

(E) Automatic Creation & Notice

Copyright arises automatically during creation of a work of authorship, even if the author does not include a copyright notice or fails to register the work with the U.S. Copyright Office. It is advisable, however, to include a copyright notice (the letter c in a circle: ©, or the word Copyright and the first year of publication of a work (e.g. Copyright © 2009 Michael L. Rustad) because registration and notice confer benefits on the copyright owner. A copyright registration certificate is evidence of the validity of the copyright, such the holder of the registration certificate need not put on evidence of ownership or originality in the copyrighted work. 17 U.S.C. § 410(c).

A defendant in a copyright infringement suit cannot use an "innocent infringer" defense to mitigate actual or statutory damages if there is a proper copyright notice affixed to a work. 17 U.S.C. § 401(d). Consequently, when a copyright symbol is present, even an innocent infringer is liable. *Playboy Enterprises, Inc. v. Webbworld,* 968 F.Supp. 1171 (N.D. Tex. 1997).

(F) Work Made for Hire

In general, the creator of a copyrightable work is the rights holder. The "work for hire" doctrine is an exception to the general rule where a person creates, but is not the owner of a copyrightable work. The "work for hire" doctrine makes the employer the copyright owner for works prepared by an employee within the scope of employment even if they do nothing more than hire the employee who creates the work.

§ 10.3 Types of Copyright Infringement

American copyright law recognizes three types of copyright liability: direct copyright infringement, contributory copyright infringement, and vicarious copyright infringement.

(A) Direct Liability

To prove a claim of direct copyright infringement, a plaintiff must show she owns the copyright and the defendant herself violated one or more of the plaintiff's exclusive rights under the Copyright Act. Copyright owners must therefore satisfy two requirements to prove a *prima facie* case for direct copyright infringement: (1) ownership of the allegedly infringed material and (2) copying of original works violate at least one exclusive right granted to copyright holders under 17 U.S.C. § 106. Liability for direct copyright infringement arises from the violation of any one of the exclusive rights of a copyright owner, which include the exclusive right to, and to authorize others to, reproduce, distribute, perform, display, and prepare derivative works from the copyrighted work. Sharing music files or video files with other Internet users is infringement of the copyright owner's distribution right. Courts have recently held there is a difference between distribution and merely making illegal content on shared files available on a peer-to-peer network such as BitTorrent. See, e.g., *Atlantic Recording Corp. v. Howell*, 554 F.Supp. 2d 976 (D. Ariz. 2008) (holding making available content is not the equivalent of distribution).

One who reproduces or distributes a copyrighted work during the term of the copyright has infringed the copyright, unless licensed by the copyright owner. Assuming a plaintiff establishes a *prima facie* direct infringement case, the defendant may avoid liability if he can demonstrate fair use or another copyright defense. *Playboy Enterprises Inc. v. Frena*, 839 F.Supp. 1552 (M.D. Fla. 1993). A plaintiff in a direct infringement suit must prove the defendant copied the constituent elements of work that are original. If the plaintiff cannot show the defendant directly copied a work, it must submit "fact-based showings that the defendant had access to the plaintiff's work and that the two works are substantially similar." *Funky Films, Inc. v. Time Warner Entm't Co., L.P.*, 462 F.3d 1072, 1076 (9th Cir. 2006).

(B) Secondary Infringement

Free peer-to-peer sharing programs ("P2P") permit users to swap music, software, video, and other copyrighted materials. The users of these P2P services are direct infringers. However, during the first wave of P2P infringement cases, large copyright owners seldom targeted direct infringers such as college students doing the illegal downloading of music and videos. P2P computers programs include WinMX, BiTorrent, Shareaza, eDonkey/Overnet, and eMule. Nearly all P2P copyright infringement enforcement actions until the last few years targeted the secondary infringers rather than the primary users. The U.S. Supreme Court has been active in reforming the law of indirect infringement consists of contributory and vicarious infringement. One can be liable for vicarious copyright infringement even without knowledge of the infringement. In the second wave, copyright owners are targetting direct infringers.

(1) Contributory Infringement

A defendant contributorily infringes when she: (1) has knowledge of another's infringement; and (2) (a) materially contributes to, or (b) induces that infringement. To prevail in a contributory copyright infringement lawsuit, the plaintiff must prove: (1) direct copyright infringement by a third party, (2) knowledge by the defendant the third party was directly infringing, and (3) defendant's material contribution to the infringement. The idea underlying contributory infringement is proof the defendant actively encourages infringement. *Gershwin Publ'g Corp. v. Columbia Artists Mgmt., Inc.*, 443 F.2d 1159, 1162 (2d Cir. 1971). Thus, to state a claim of contributory infringement, a plaintiff must show knowledge as well as material contribution to the infringing conduct. *Perfect 10, Inc. v. Visa Int'l Serv. Ass'n,* 494 F.3d 788 (9th Cir. 2007). Contributory infringers must either know or have reason to know of the direct infringement.

(2) Vicarious Infringement

Vicarious infringement evolved out of the common law and is now well established in copyright law. To state a claim for vicarious copyright infringement, a plaintiff must allege the defendant has: (1) the right and ability to supervise the infringing conduct, and (2) a direct financial interest in the infringing activity. A defendant is subject to vicarious liability if the defendant is "profiting from direct infringement while declining to exercise a right to stop or limit it." *MGM Studios v. Grokster*, 545 U.S. 913, 930–31 (2005). Where credit card companies did not induce or materially contribute to the infringement of a publisher's copyrighted material, the court found they were not contributorily or vicariously liable for copyright or trademark infringement; rather, they merely processed credit card payments to allegedly infringing websites. *Perfect 10, Inc. v. Visa Int'l Serv. Ass'n.*, 494 F.3d 788 (9th Cir. 2007).

In *Perfect 10,* the publisher of an adult entertainment site operated a subscription website and published a magazine, both of which featured copyrighted images of models owned by a magazine publisher. The magazine publisher asserted defendants were contributorily and vicariously liable because they processed credit card payments to allegedly infringing websites.

The appellate court found defendants did not induce or materially contribute to the infringing activity. The infringement stemmed from the failure to get a license to distribute, not from processing payments. The court held the defendants were not vicariously liable because they had no right or ability to control the infringing activity.

§ 10.4 P2P File Sharing

(A) Napster

"About as many American consumers are trading music over peer-to-peer file sharing networks as voted for President Bush in 2004." Jessica Litman, *War and Peace*, 53 J. OF COPYRIGHT SOC. OF THE U.S.A. 101, 112 (2006). Napster was the pioneering P2P sharing permitting to exchange MP3 music files stored on individual computer hard drives with other Napster users. Many record companies and music publishers filed a copyright infringement lawsuit against Napster for facilitating peer-to-peer transmission of copyright content. Napster defended its actions asserting fair use. *A & M Records, Inc. v. Napster, Inc.*, 239 F.3d 1004 (9th Cir. 2001).

The court found Napster had diminished the copyright owners' commercial sales because users were downloading content without paying royalties or fees. The court rejected Napster's fair use argument finding Napster's users "repeated and exploitative unauthorized copies evidenced commercial use." *Id.* at 1015. The federal appeals court rejected Napster's argument it was not liable for direct or contributory copyright infringement. The Ninth Circuit in the *Napster* case ruled DMCA § 512(a) did not protect Napster's referencing and indexing activities. The federal appeals court upheld the lower court finding visitors to the Napster site engaged in direct infringement. In addition, the court held Napster liable for contributory infringement because Napster not only had knowledge of the infringing activity, it also contributed to the infringing conduct. The *Napster* court also found Napster vicariously liable because it had a direct financial interest in the visitor's infringing activities. *Id.* at 1020–22.

(B) Grokster's Inducement Theory

In computer terms, the personal computer used by the consumer is the "client" and the computer that hosts the web page is the "server." The client is obtaining information from a centralized source, namely the server. In a P2P distribution network, the information available for access does not reside on a central server. "In a peer-to-peer network, each computer is both a server and a client." *Metro–Goldwyn–Mayer Studios, Inc. v. Grokster Ltd.*, 380 F.3d 1154, 1158 (9th Cir. 2004). Peer-to-peer ("P2P") networks make widespread copyright infringement inevitable. The central server of most P2P networks will index the information made available by end-users on the network and allow individual users to connect to each other.

In *Metro–Goldwin–Mayer Studios, Inc. v. Grokster, Ltd.*, 545 U.S. 913 (U.S. 2005), the Supreme Court found "[o]ne infringes contributorily by intentionally inducing or encouraging direct infringement." *Id.* at 930. The Court based its inducement theory upon evidence the P2P networks intended and encouraged their products for file sharing. The *Grokster* Court unanimously held the P2P defendants distributed their software promoted copyright infringement. The "mere knowledge of infringing potential or actual infringing uses would not be enough here to subject [a defendant] to liability." *Id*. at 937. The Court described how Grokster induced direct infringement in its advertising and business model targeting millions of consumers. "The probable scope of copyright infringement," just with respect to the two networks at issue there, was "staggering." *Id*. at 923.

In *Grokster*, the Court imported the doctrine of inducement from Section 271(b) of the Patent Code which states "[w]however actively induces infringement of a patent shall be liable as an infringer." 35 U.S.C. § 271(b). A patent infringement action based upon inducement requires the plaintiff to prove the defendant encouraged another's infringement, and mere knowledge of the direct infringer's activities is not enough. Inducement in copyright law as well as patent law is the active aiding and abetting theory of infringement.

More recently, Viacom International, Inc. filed a $1 billon copyright infringement claim against YouTube for enabling users in uploading 150,000 unauthorized copyrighted videos on its service. A federal court ruled Viacom must produce it logging database and data fields for all YouTube videos. *Viacom Intern., Inc. v. YouTube, Inc.*, 2008 WL 2260018 (S.D. N.Y. 2008).

§ 10.5   Links to Third Party Sites

"The power of the Web stems from the ability of a link to point to any document, regardless of its status or physical location." *ACLU v. Reno*, 929 F.Supp. 824, 837 (E.D. Pa. 1996). "Links may also take the user from the original Website to another Website on another computer connected to the Internet. These links from one computer to another from one document to another across the Internet are what unify the Web into a single body of knowledge, and what makes the Web unique." *Id*. at 836–37.

Typically, there is no copyright infringement when linking to a third party's website contains infringing materials. A federal court dismissed a copyright infringement claim against J.C. Penney for linking to a Swedish website with infringing content. In that case, the site with the infringing material was several links removed from J.C. Penney's site. *Bernstein v. J.C. Penney, Inc.*, 1998 WL 906644 (C.D. Calif. 1998). Deep linking is when a link bypasses the principal web page containing the trademark owner's log and third party advertising. Ticketmaster claimed a deep link from Microsoft's web page exploited its trademark. Microsoft removed the deep link and settled the case before a court ruling.

Framing is displaying content from another website while still maintaining advertisements from the original site. Framing allows the user to visit one website "while remaining in a previous website." This method of online advertising causes a second website to appear on a part of another site. *Digital*

Equipment Corp. v. AltaVista Technology, Inc. 960 F.Supp. 456, 461 (D. Mass. 1997). "The framed page moves simultaneously with the outer window. If the outer window is closed or minimized, the framed page also closes or minimizes. The purpose of framing is to create a single seamless presentation that integrates the content of the two webpages into what appears to be single webpage." *Wells Fargo & Co. v. WhenU.com, Inc.* 293 F. Supp. 2d 734, 748–49 (E.D. Mich. 2003).

The practice of framing causes the plaintiffs' website to appear in a form not envisioned by the website developer. Framing allows a party to superimpose its advertising on all linked websites. To date, no appellate court has weighed in on framing. In *Washington Post v. Total News, Inc.*, No. 97–1190 (S.D. N.Y. Feb. 20, 1997), the newspaper contended Total News infringed its copyrights, trademarks, and misappropriated their news material. Total News displayed multiple publications including *Time Magazine*, *Entertainment Weekly,* and *The Los Angeles Times* in its Total News frame. *Id.* The district court did not decide the case because the parties reached a settlement. In-line linking is when a web page directs a user's browser to incorporate content from different computers into a single window. *Kelly v. Arriba Soft Corp.*, 336 F.3d 811, 816 (9th Cir. 2003) (remanding issue).

§ 10.6   Limitations on Exclusive Rights

(A)   First Sale Doctrine

Under the first sale doctrine, once the copyright holder has sold a copy of the copyrighted work, the owner of the copy could "sell or otherwise dispose of the possession of that copy" without the copyright holder's consent. *Bobbs–Merrill Co. v. Straus*, 210 U.S. 339, 350 (1908). The owner of software licenses sells software to side step the first sale doctrine. If a software vendor sold software rather than licensed it, the purchaser of the first sale of a copy of the software could copy the software and distribute it with impunity. Copyright owners therefore license software to circumvent the first sale doctrine. 17 U.S.C. § 109(a).

In *Microsoft Corp. v. Harmony Computers & Electronic, Inc.*, 846 F.Supp. 208 (E.D. N.Y. 1994), Microsoft sought declaratory relief, injunctive relief, and treble damages because Harmony sold Microsoft's MS–DOS Windows without a license. Microsoft contended Harmony exceeded the scope of its license agreement thus constituting copyright infringement. Harmony Computers bought Microsoft software bundled with personal computers. Harmony contended it had the power to resell Microsoft software under the first sale doctrine of the Copyright Act.

However, the court found Microsoft Products were not subject to the first sale doctrine of the Copyright Act because they were licensed, rather than sold. Microsoft's chain of distribution gives users or possessors of Microsoft Products a bare license to use rather than ownership of software. *Id.* The court found Harmony Computers infringed Microsoft's copyrighted software when it exceeded the scope of the license agreements.

(B) Public Domain Information

Copyright law does not encompass public domain information. The Fifth Circuit held a code-writing organization could not prevent a website operator from posting the text of a model code. The code was simply the building code of a city enacted as a model code as law. The court concluded the model building code was in the public domain and not protected by copyright, notwithstanding a software licensing agreement and a copyright notice that did not allow copying and distribution. The federal appeals court held when the operator copied only "the law" which he obtained from the organization's publication, and when he reprinted only "the law" of those municipalities, he did not infringe the organization's copyrights in its model building codes. The court reasoned the operator was merely posting laws on his website with precisely the form adopted by the municipalities. *Veeck v. Southern Bldg. Code Cong. Int'l Inc.*, 293 F.3d 791 (5th Cir. 2002).

(C) Fair Use

The fair use doctrine evolved as a common law doctrine but is now codified as Section 107 of the Copyright Act. Fair use is a statutory exception to copyright infringement allowing unauthorized use or reproduction of copyrighted work if it is "for purposes such as criticism, comment, news reporting, teaching ... scholarship or research." 17 U.S.C. § 107. The "fair use" doctrine limits the exclusive rights of a copyright holder by permitting others to make limited use of portions of the copyrighted work free of liability for copyright infringement. The four fair use factors are: (1) the purpose and character of the use, (2) the nature of the copyrighted work, (3) the amount, and substantiality of the part used in relation to the copyrighted work as a whole, and (4) the effect of the use upon the potential market for or value of the copyrighted work. 17 U.S.C. § 107.

Perfect 10, an adult entertainment site, sued Google to prevent access to copyrighted photographs of nude models. *Perfect 10, Inc. v. Amazon.com, Inc.*, 487 F.3d 701, 719 (9th Cir. 2007). The *Perfect 10* court held Google's use of thumbnails of copyrighted images owned by the adult entertainment company qualified as a transformative use. Google's software does not recognize and index the images, but provides search results with greatly reduced lower resolution images called thumbnails. The *Perfect 10* court noted fair issue "counterbalances copyright law's goal of protecting creators' work product." *Id.*

(D) Transformative Use

The first factor in a fair use inquiry is the "purpose and character of the use." Courts determine whether the new work "supersedes" the original work or is transformative in it "adds something new, with a *further purpose* or different character." *Harper & Row, Publishers, Inc. v. Nation Enterprises*, 471 U.S. 539, 562 (1985). Transformative use is a fundamental change in a plaintiff's copyrighted work or use of the copyrighted work in a radically different context. The plaintiff's copyrighted work is "transformed" into a new creation. *Campbell v. Acuff–Rose Music, Inc.*, 510 U.S. 569, 579 (1994). However, the *Acuff–Rose* Court reasoned: "If we allow any weak transformation to qualify as parody . . . we weaken the protection of copyright. *Id.* at 599.

"The more transformative the new work, the less important the other factors, including commercialism, become." *Kelly v. Arriba Soft Corp.*, 336 F.3d 811, 818 (9th Cir. 2003). The Ninth Circuit found Arriba Soft's use of thumbnails was transformative because the greatly reduced copies of copyrighted images were for a different purpose. In addition, the court found the use of copyrighted images in thumbnails did not harm the copyright owner's commercial market. In *Perfect 10, Inc. v. Google, Inc.*, 508 F.3d 1146 (9th Cir. 2007), the Ninth Circuit held Google's thumbnail-sized reproduction of entire copyrighted images in its search engine results page to be "highly transformative." Google's use of the copyrighted images was to find content, which was a radically different purpose than the original copyright owner's use. *Id.* at 1164–67.

§ 10.7 Digital Millennium Copyright Act

(A) Overview of the DMCA

The U.S. is a signatory to the Berne Convention for the protection of Literary and Artistic Works. The Stockholm Agreement of July 14, 1967, created a world organization for copyrights and for revision of related treaties. The U.S. agreed to the two Internet-related WIPO treaties in 1996, the WIPO

Copyright Treaty ("WCT") and the WIPO Performances and Phonograms Treaty ("WPPT"). The United States enacted The Digital Millennium Copyright Act ("DMCA") of 1998 to implement the WCT and the WPPT. The Digital Millennium Copyright Act strengthened the U.S. Copyright Act to address Internet transmissions, which fulfilled the United States' WIPO Treaty obligations.

Title I of the DMCA implements the WIPO Copyright and Performances and Phonographs Treaty Implementation Act by criminalizing the circumvention or removal of Digital Rights Management ("DRM") or digital locks on copyright materials. The DMCA defines circumvention to mean, "to descramble a scrambled work, to decrypt an encrypted work, or otherwise to avoid, bypass, remove, deactivate, or impair a technological measure, without the authority of the copyright owner." 17 U.S.C. § 1201(a)(3)(A). The encoding schemes used by DVD producers are technological measures because they control access to works protecting the rights of copyright owners. Apple's FairPlay and Microsoft Windows Digital Rights Managers, for example, provide controls on the viewing or playing of copyright materials. The latest DRM systems use forensics watermarking to augment traditional controls.

Section 103 also prohibits the selling of anti-circumvention devices. The WCT requires signatory powers to provide remedies against defendants circumventing digital rights management ("DRM") tools or tamper with copyright management information. DRM tools restrict the use and copying of digital information such as music or movies. Congress had the statutory purpose of facilitating "the robust development and world-wide expansion of electronic commerce, communications, research, development, and education in the digital age." S. Rep. No. 105–190, at 1–2 (1998).

Chapter 12 of the DMCA criminalizes the manufacture, distribution, or trafficking of technological devices for the circumvention of software encrypting copyrighted content. Congress provides for a penalty of up to five years imprisonment for a defendant's first offense in manufacturing, importing, offering to the public, or trafficking in circumventing a technological measure controlling access to a protected work.

Title II of the DMCA is entitled, The Online Copyright Infringement Liability Limitation Act ("OCILLA") which limits the liability of service providers for a wide range of ministerial activities. Congress followed the reasoning of *Religious Technology Center v. Netcom On–Line Communication Services, Inc.*, 907 F.Supp. 1361, 1368–83 (N.D. Cal. 1995) in protecting Internet Service Providers from liability for the infringing acts on others on its service. The *Netcom* court reasoned, "It does not make sense to adopt a rule leading to the liability of countless parties whose role in the infringement is nothing more than setting up and operating a system necessary for the functioning of the Internet." *Id.* at 1372.

(B) ISP's Four Safe Harbors

Title II of the DMCA is the OCILLA amended Section 512 of the U.S. Copyright Act to update the law for the age of the Internet. The OCILLA enacted section 512(a)–(d) of the DMCA to limit the liability of Online Service Providers ("OSPs" for copyright infringement: (1) Transitory digital network communications, (2) System caching, (3) Information residing on systems or networks at the direction of users, and (4) Information location tools. 17 U.S.C. § 512(a)–(d). The four OSP safe harbors limit the liability for all equitable relief as well as direct, vicarious, and contributory infringement so long as they meet qualifying conditions. The DMCA is a complex statute enacting a narrower definition for a qualifying OSP for the transitory digital network communications safe harbor than for the broad definition of OSPs enacted for the other three safe harbors.

OCILLA (Title II of the DMCA) protects OSPs who meet certain safe harbor requirements from liability for all monetary relief for direct, vicarious, *and* contributory infringement. *Hendrickson v. eBay, Inc.*, 165 F. Supp. 2d 1082 (C.D. Cal. 2001). OSPs are not eligible for any of the safe harbors unless they implement and adopt a policy to terminate the account of recidivist copyright infringers. OSPs interfering with "standard technical measures" are divested of the OSP or not entitled to the safe harbors of § 512(a)–(d). *Id.* at § 512(i)(1)(B). The service provider must also remove or block access to the material upon receiving notice of alleged infringement from the copyright owner or assignee. 17 U.S.C. § 512(c). The notice must give sufficient information to identify the various infringing or pirated items. *Hendrickson v. eBay, Inc.*, 165 F. Supp. 2d 1082 (C.D. Cal. 2001) (holding copyright owner did not give eBay sufficient information about pirated DVDs for sale on auction site). The next section is a guide to the four OSP safe harbors, which vary significantly in their preconditions.

(1) Transitory Digital Network Communications

The DMCA immunizes OSPs for all copyright infringement "by reason of the provider's transmitting, routing, or providing connections for, material through a system or network controlled or operated by or for the service provider, or by reason of the intermediate and transient storage of that material." *Id.* at § 512(a). The definition of an OSP is narrower for transitory digital network communications than the other safe harbors in Section (b)-(d). This safe harbor applies only to OSPs qualifying under OCILLA's narrow definition means those entities that transmit, route, or provide connections for digital online communications, between or among points specified by user." 17 U.S.C. § 512(k)(1)(A). To qualify for the transitory digital network communications safe harbor, OSPs may not modify content transmitted, routed, or connected. Someone other than the OSP must initiate the transmission of the material. *Id.* at 512(a)(1). To qualify for any of the four OSP safe harbors, they must adopt and implement policies for terminating the account of recidivist infringers. 17 U.S.C. § 512(i). Service providers must adopt, reasonably implement, and inform subscribers of a policy that it may terminate the accounts of repeat infringers. 17 U.S.C. § 512(i)(1)(A). A service provider must act "expeditiously to remove, or disable access to, the material" when it (1) has actual knowledge, (2) is aware of facts or circumstances from which infringing activity is apparent, or (3) has received notification of claimed infringement meeting the requirements of § 512(c)(3).

(2) System Caching

OSPs routine cache or replicate identifiable web pages to improve the speed of accessing information from a source server. OSPs make cached copies store web pages on a separate server called a proxy server. Before the DMCA's system caching safe harbor, there was uncertainty as to the liability of OSPs for the desirable practice of caching which is technically making a copy under the U.S. Copyright Act. OSPs also create mirror caches or identical web site on different servers. The DMCA immunizes service providers for caching and the other two safe harbors so long as they fall within the broad definition of "a provider of online services or network access" and those that operate such services. 17 U.S.C. § 512(k)(1)(B). Service providers qualifying for the transitory digital network communications may also benefit from the other three safe harbors.

Think of caching and the other safe harbors as the OSP serving as a pipeline for transmitting, routing, or storing information "without selection of the material by the service provider." *Id.* at § 512(a)(2)–(3). Service providers are divested of these "pipeline safe harbors" if they have neither a direct financial interest nor the right to control content. *Ellison v. Robertson, Inc.*, 189 F. Supp. 2d 1051 (C.D. Cal. 2002) (holding AOL qualified for a DMCA safe harbor). If the OSP is creating or modifying the content rather than serving as a pipeline, it will not have the benefit of the safe harbors.

A service provider may not select the recipients of the material except as an automatic response to the request of another person." *Id.* at § 512(a)(3). Service providers may not keep copies or modify materials transmitted except for temporary storage. *Id.* at § 512(a)(4)–(5). OSPs claiming the caching safe harbor must expeditiously respond to takedown notices and remove or disable objectionable content. Assuming these preconditions are satisfied, § 512(b) shields service provider from injunctive or monetary remedies for caching copyrighted materials. Caching is a desirable practice because it eliminates the delay of successive searches for the same material and thus decreases the demands on their Internet connection. *ACLU v. Reno*, 929 F.Supp. 824, 848–39 (E.D. Pa. 1996).

(3) Storage Exemption

OCILLA's third OSP safe harbor applies "for infringement of a copyright by reason of the storage at the direction of a user of material" residing on a service provider's system or network. 17 U.S.C.

§ 512(c)(1). The OSP's storage exemption can only be claimed if they satisfy certain qualifying preconditions. To qualify for an OSP safe harbor for information residing on systems or networks, a company will need to post its agent's name on its website and register with the Library of Congress' Copyright Office. *Id.* at § 512(c)(2). An ISP needs to provide the U.S. Copyright Office with the following information: name, address, phone number, electronic mail address of its agent and other contact information along with a filing fee. The Copyright Office maintains a directory of all service providers' agents and contact information.

The online service providers designated agent must communicate its policy of taking down infringing content and implement a reasonable takedown policy. A website must post information on how to report copyright infringement on its website. The Copyright Office's Form for the Interim Designation of Agent to Receive Notification of Claimed Infringement is remitted along with an $80 filing fee. The Copyright Office's Designation of Agent Interim Form currently requires service providers to designate the Agent's full name and all alternative names. The Register of Copyrights maintains a directory of agents and posts the list to the Internet.

The copyright owner must give the provider's designated agent a written takedown notice: (1) includes a physical or electronic signature of a person authorized to act on behalf of the copyright owner of the right allegedly infringed, (2) identification of the copyrighted works allegedly infringing,

(3) identification of the parts of the copyrighted work that is infringing and thus should be removed, (4) sufficient information to contact copyright owner or complaining party, (5) statement by the complainant in the good faith belief the material is infringing, and (6) a statement the information in the notice is accurate. The DMCA requires copyright owners to provide the website with a "statement that the complaining party has a good faith belief that use of the material in the manner complained of is not authorized by the copyright owner, its agent, or the law" as part of its takedown notice. 17 U.S.C. § 512(c)(3)(A)(v).

To qualify for this safe harbor, OSPs cannot have actual knowledge the material or activity is infringing or be aware infringing activities are apparent. In addition, they must: (1) perform a qualified storage or search function for Internet users; (2) lack actual or imputed knowledge of the infringing activity; (3) receive no financial benefit directly from such activity in a case where he has the right and ability to control it; (4) act promptly to remove or disable access to the material when his designated agent is notified that it is infringing; (5) adopt, reasonably implement and publicize a policy of terminating repeat infringers; and (6) accommodate and not interfere with standard technical measures used by copyright owners to identify or protect copyrighted works. *Verizon Intern. Inc., v. YouTube Inc.*, 253 F.R.D. 256 (S.D. N.Y. 2008).

The complex notice, takedown, and putback procedures are triggered when a copyright owner gives written notice to the designated agent of the service provider under § 512(c)(3)(A). The copyright owner is able to find the contact information for the service provider's agent because it is posted at the U.S. Copyright Office's website. The OSP provider is required to disable or take down infringing materials when it receives notice from the copyright owner and it is required to appoint an agent to receive notices. The OSP removes or disables the content immediately and the subscriber or user has no right to court hearing before this action.

Once the OSP's designated agent receives a notice that substantially complies with the DMCA's requirements, it must expeditiously remove the identified material. However, the service provider's duty to remove or block access to infringing materials is not triggered by constructive notice. Copyright owners need not identify all infringing works when multiple copyrights are infringed. The DMCA requires only substantial compliance with the notification the copyright owner provide a representative list if multiple infringements. *ALS Scan v. RemarQ*, 239 F.3d 619, 625 (4th Cir. 2001).

The next step is for the service provider to give notice to the user or subscriber that posted the allegedly infringing copyright content it has removed or disabled. *Id.* at § 512(g)(2)(A). After the user who posted the objectionable material receives notice, it has a statutory right to send a written counter notification to the OSP has designated agent. The counter notice must minimally contain the subscriber's signature (physical or digital), identify the material removed, and give a statement under penalty of perjury the material was removed or disabled because of mistake or misidentification. The agent then transmits this notice the counter-notification to the copyright owner, § 512(g)(2)(B). The OSP puts back the disputed material unless the copyright owner shows it has filed a copyright infringement lawsuit or other judicial action. *Id.* at § 512(g)(2)(C).

The copyright owner's complaint must declare, under penalty of perjury, that he is authorized to represent the copyright holder, and that he has a good-faith belief the use is infringing; thus, a notification must do more than identify. *Id.* "Congress imported the "red flag" test of § 512(c)(1)(A)(ii)" which divests service providers of their immunity if they "fail to take action with regard to infringing material when it is "aware of facts or circumstances from which infringing activity is apparent." *Perfect 10, Inc. v. CCBill LLC,* 481 F.3d 751, 763 (9th Cir. 2007). It is unclear what red flags would constitute an OSP's actual notice assuming they received no notice from the copyright owner.

The OSP immunity for information residing on systems or networks at the direction of users is the subject of most OCILLA generated litigation. In *ALS Scan v. RemarQ Communities, Inc.,* 239 F.3d 619 (4th Cir. 2001), the Fourth Circuit ruled the service provider could not be liable as a direct infringer by allowing its members to access to news-groups containing infringing "adult" photographs. ALS Scan displayed these images on the Internet to paying subscribers. RemarQ was a Delaware Internet Service Provider that hosted tens of thousands of news groups on diverse topics. The news groups included "alt.als" and "alt.binaries.pictures,erotica.als" containing infringing copies of ALS Scan's copyrighted images. ALS Scan's notice to RemarQ of the infringing materials was not compliant with the DMCA. The district court ruled ALS Scan's notice failed to comply with § 512(c)(3)(A) because it filed to identify a list of infringing materials in enough detail. The Fourth Circuit disagreed finding ALS Scan's notice substantially complied with DMCA's written notice of infringement requirements so the provider could disable or remove the infringing adult photographs.

Another drafting problem of OCILLA's notice, takedown, and putback procedures was Congress' failure to provide direction to copyright owners in taking fair use into account when they request takedowns. An empirical study of almost 900 takedown notices revealed many were questionable because they targeted materials protected by fair use. The authors concluded the DMCA notice, takedown, and putback procedures have a chilling effect on expression. Jennifer M. Urban & Laura Quilter, *Efficient Process or "Chilling Effects"? Takedown Notices Under Section 512 of the Digital Millennium Copyright Act*, 22 Santa Computer & High Tech. L.J. 621, 683 (2006)

In *Lenz v. Universal Music Corp.*, 2008 WL 3884333 (N.D. Cal. 2008), the court ruled the copyright owner had to consider fair use doctrine in formulating good faith belief in connection with takedown notice under Digital Millennium Copyright Act (DMCA). The court further concluded the "use of the material in the manner complained of is not authorized by the copyright owner, its agent, or the law." 17 U.S.C. § 512(c)(3)(A)(v).

A California court held Universal to be acting in bad faith by issuing a takedown notice for a home video of a child dancing uploaded to YouTube.com with a part of Prince's *Let Go Crazy* playing in the background. The videographer issued a counter-notification pursuant to 17 U.S.C. § 512(g) asserted her family video constituted fair use of "Let's Go Crazy" and thus did not infringe Universal's copyrights. Universal sent her a removal notice asserting Prince's wishes not to have his songs posted on YouTube. The court's found Universal's failure to consider fair use as sufficient to state a misrepresentation claim pursuant to the Digital Millennium Copyright Act ("DMCA"). 17 U.S.C. § 512(c)(3)(A)(v). The court also ruled the plaintiff alleged a cognizable injury in responding to a bad faith takedown notice.

(4) Information Location Tools

Section 512(d) is the OSP safe harbor used by search engines such as Google limiting liability for monetary relief as well as injunctive relief for copyright infringement for "referring or linking users to an online location containing infringing material or infringing activity, by using information location tools" such as "a directory, index, reference, pointer, or hypertext link." 17 U.S.C. § 512(d).

(C) Anti–Circumvention Provisions

Chapter 12 of the DMCA entitled "Copyright and Management System" prohibits any person from circumventing a technical measure effectively controlling access to a work protected under the Copyright Act. Data rights management ("DRM)" may take the form of software, encryption codes, digital walls, or other locks on digital data. The DMCA's anti-circumvention prohibitions essentially criminalize picking digital locks guarding copyrighted materials. The DMCA anti-circumvention provisions address the issue of access controls for digital content and target circumvention of those technological measures. Prohibited devices have three attributes: (1) it is primarily designed for circumvention, (2) it has limited uses for legitimate commercial purposes (other than circumvention), and (3) it is marketed for use in circumventing copyright protection. The DMCA Act makes it a crime:

(A). To "circumvent a technological measure" means to descramble a scrambled work, to decrypt an encrypted work, or otherwise to avoid, bypass, remove, deactivate, or impair a technological measure, without the authority of the copyright owner and

(B). A technological measure "effectively controls access to a work" if the measure, in the ordinary course of its operation, requires the application of information, or a process or a treatment, with the authority of the copyright owner, to gain access to the work.

17 U.S.C. § 1201(a)(3).

Specifically, Section 1201(a)(1)(A) provides "[n]o person shall circumvent a technological measure that effectively controls access to a work protected under this title." Section 1201(a)(2) states

[n]o person shall manufacture, import, offer to the public, provide, or otherwise traffic in any technology, product, service, device, component, or part thereof, that—

(A) is primarily designed or produced for the purpose of circumventing a technological measure that effectively controls access to a work protected under this title;

(B) has only limited commercially significant purpose or use other than to circumvent a technological measure that effectively controls access to a work protected under this title [17 U.S.C. §§ 1 et seq.]; or

(C) is marketed by that person or another acting in concert with that person with that person's knowledge for use in circumventing a technological measure that effectively controls access to a work protected under this title.

17 U.S.C. § 1201(a)(2).

Section 1201(b) criminalizes the manufacture of anti-circumvention devise to bypass technical measures to control access to copyrighted work. Section

1201(b) prohibits circumventing a technological measure imposing limitations on the use of a copyrighted work, or in the words of the statute, that "effectively protects the right of a copyright owner." Section 1201(b) prohibits trafficking in software or other tools that avoids, bypasses, removes, deactivates, or otherwise impairs any DRM technological measure protecting digital copyrighted works. *United States v. Elcom Ltd.*, 203 F. Supp. 2d 1111 (N.D. Cal. 2002).

(D) DMCA's Trafficking Provisions

Congress banned trafficking in devices primarily designed for circumventing any technological measure "effectively protects a right of a copyright owner," or have limited commercially significant purposes other than circumventing use restrictions, or are marketed for use in circumventing the use restrictions. The DMCA distinguishes between circumvention and trafficking. Section 1201(a)(1) is the DMCA section against those who engage in unauthorized circumvention of technological measures. Section 1201(a)(2) is DMCA's anti-trafficking provision prohibits offering or providing technology used to circumvent technological means of controlling access to copyrighted works.

(E) Exemptions & First Amendment Challenges

The DMCA exempts nonprofit libraries, archives, and educational institutions so long as these organizations make a good faith determination as to whether to acquire a copy of a protected work. Congress's ban on anti-circumvention devices was a response to Hollywood and the music industry's goal of using protective technologies to protect their products that could otherwise be easily copied and distributed widely on the Internet. Academic commentators view these anti-circumvention measures as an inappropriate extension of copyright impediments to fair use.

Congress faced an insurmountable policy decision in its anti-circumvention and trafficking provisions, which had the effect of constraining fair use as well as infringing uses. The DMCA prohibits "offering to the public, providing, or otherwise trafficking in" any technology designed to circumvent a technological measure controlling access to a copyrighted work is implicated when one presents, holds out, or makes available a circumvention technology or device, knowing its nature, for the purpose of allowing others to acquire it. 17 U.S.C. § 1201(a)(2). Copyright management information," is limited to components of technological measures used to protect copyrights in automated systems.

Congress's intent was to preserve the traditional defenses to copyright infringement, such as fair use, and the DMCA was not intended to enlarge or diminish vicarious or contributory liability for copyright infringement. However, the courts have determined the proper balance between the DMCA's copyright protection measures and fair use. In *Universal City Studios, Inc. v. Reimerdes*, 111 F. Supp. 2d 294 (S.D. N.Y. 2000), several motion picture studios brought action under the DMCA to enjoin Internet web-site owners from posting for downloading computer software decrypting digitally encrypted movies on digital versatile disks ("DVDs") and from including hyperlinks to other web-sites making decryption software available. The federal court ruled the Internet posting of decryption software violated DMCA provision prohibiting trafficking in technology circumventing measures controlling access to copyrighted works.

The *Reimerdes* court also ruled posting hyperlinks to other web sites offering decryption software violated DMCA. The court rejected the defendant's First Amendment challenge finding the DMCA anti-trafficking provision to be content-neutral as applied to a decryption computer program. The court ruled the DMCA's anti-trafficking provision was not overly broad and the plaintiffs were entitled to injunction enjoining defendants from posting decryption software or hyper linking to other web sites making software available.

The Second Circuit upheld *Reimerdes* in *Universal City Studios, Inc. v. Corley*, 273 F.3d 429 (2d Cir. 2001). The Second Circuit held the decryption software qualified as "speech" for First Amendment purposes because the computer code combined nonspeech and speech elements. The court found the DMCA anti-circumvention regulation to have an incidental effect on a speech component. The court found the "government's interest in preventing unauthorized access to encrypted copyrighted material is unquestionably substantial." *Id.* at 454. The court also found the governmental interest to be unrelated to the suppression of free expression.

The federal appeals court upheld the injunction finding it to be a content neutral restriction on owners' speech. The court also found the injunction did not burden substantially more speech than necessary to further the government's interest. Finally, the injunction did not eliminate owners' "fair use" of copyrighted materials and was therefore not unconstitutional. *Id.* at 454.

(F) Critique of DMCA

The DMCA's takedown policy presents the risk content will be removed when it is not infringing. A study of DMCA takedowns documented the removal of content protected by "fair use or other substantive defenses, very thin copyright or non-copyrightable subject matter." Jennifer M. Urban & Laura Quilter, *Efficient Process or "Chilling Effects"? Takedown Notices Under Section 512 of the Digital Millennium Copyright Act,* SANTA CLARA COMPUTER & HIGH TECH. L.J. 621, 666 (2006).

(G) VARA Moral Rights

The Berne Convention protects artists' moral rights for the Protection of Literary and Artistic Works. Moral rights include the right of attribution, integrity, right of attribution, spirit, and personality. The United States enacted the Visual Artists Rights Act of 1990 ("VARA") to implement the Berne Convention. Regardless of assignment or ownership of rights, VARA protects the expectation a visual work will not be revised, altered, or distorted. VARA has little application to the Internet since it only protects works of visual art that have attained the status of "recognized stature."

CHAPTER ELEVEN

TRADEMARKS IN CYBERSPACE

§ 11.1 Overview of Trademark Law

This chapter summarizes Internet-related trademark issues. The federal Lanham Act gives nationwide rights to owners of federally registered marks. Federal law gives nationwide rights to owners of federally registered U.S. trademarks. The Internet's disregard of geographic borders creates conflicts between concurrent users which would never have arisen in the purely brick and mortar world. A trademark is a limited property right in a particular word, phrase, or symbol. The federal Lanham Act, 15 U.S.C. §§ 1051 et seq. protects marks used to identify and distinguish goods or services in commerce, subject to common law rights of another that used the mark before the registrant's filing date.

(A) What Is a Trademark?

"Trademark law serves the important functions of protecting product identification, providing consumer information, and encouraging the production of quality goods and services." *Lamparello v. Falwell*, 420 F.3d 309, 313 Cir. 2005). A "trademark" is either a word, phrase, combination of words, phrases, symbols, or designs, which identifies and distinguishes the source of the goods or services of one party from those of another. The emblem of a good trademark is distinctiveness. Trademark protection "is the law's recognition of the psychological function of symbols." *Avery Denison Corp. v. Sumpton*, 189 F.3d 868, 873 (9th Cir. 1999) (quoting *Mishawaka Rubber & Woolen Mfg. Co. v. S.S. Kresge Co.* 316 U.S. 203, 205 (1942)). Thus, a consumer purchasing an Apple iPhone knows it can expect the degree of quality consistent with the Apple brand. Apple.com, *iPhone* (2008).

(B) Federal Trademark Registration

Trademark applicants register marks in the United States Patent and Trademark Office "(USPTO). Registration with the USPTO gives the owner exclusive rights only in the U.S.; although trademarks are registerable in different countries, especially those where goods and services are sold on the Internet. The registration of trademarks signals constructive notice of mark ownership and create a legal presumption in favor of ownership. Trademark registrants have the right to bring infringement or dilution actions in federal court. Federal trademark registration also confers a basis for registering the mark in other countries where protection is sought. Finally, U.S. registration is a predicate to the U.S. Customs preventing the importation of infringing goods.

The federal registration of trademarks is governed by the Trademark Act of 1946, as amended, 15 U.S.C. §§ 1051 et seq. The term of a federal trademark registration is 10 years, with 10–year renewal terms. Trademark owners must file an affidavit or declaration of continued use with the USPTO to keep the registration alive, between the fifth and sixth year after the date of initial registration. Failure of the registrant to provide the affidavit results in cancellation of the trademark registration. Trademark priority is determined by the first to use a mark in interstate commerce. Factors determining first use include which party first affixed the mark to a product or whose party's name appeared with the trademark. Another factor is which party maintained the quality and uniformity of the product or created the good will associated with a product.

(C) State Trademark Law

States vary widely in their trademark registration procedures. Online companies, for example, need not register their trademarks to receive protection under the Massachusetts' state trademark law. In 2006, Massachusetts adopted the International Trademark Association's Revised Model State Trademark Bill. An online company, or a person may register a trademark or service with the Corporation Division, so long as the mark is used in the Commonwealth. The use must be *bona fide* and not to merely reserve a right in the mark. A trademark is considered in use when it is affixed on the goods or containers, and on the tags, labels, displays or documents associated with the goods, and the goods are sold or transported in the Commonwealth. Similarly, service marks are used or displayed in the sale or advertising of services. The Internet marginal-

ized the value of state trademark registration because, by definition, cyberspace is rarely intrastate.

(D) Trademark Applications

Trademark applications must include five things:
(1) the name of the applicant, (2) a name and
address for correspondence, (3) a clear drawing of
the mark, (4) a listing of the goods or services, and
(5) the filing fee for at least one class of goods or
services. The federal Lanham Act's requires proof of
"use in commerce." The mark cannot only be used
to reserve a right to a particular mark. In the brick
and mortar world, the term "use in commerce"
originated when trademarks where affixed on goods
or containers. On the Internet, trademarks are used
in website sales.

The Lanham Act allows two types of use applications: (1) actual use, and (2) intent to use (ITU).
ITU applications require an intent to use the trademark in commerce in the future. The PTO may
accept evidence an applicant has used a mark "in
commerce" for five years as *prima facie* evidence of
distinctiveness. 15 U.S.C. § 1054(f). A trademark
owner will typically use trademarks on the product
and its packaging, while service marks advertise
services.

(E) Distinctiveness Continuum

The *sine qua non* of a trademark is it identifies
the source of particular goods. To qualify as a
trademark, the mark must be distinctive. Marks are
classified on a continuum of increasing distinctiveness: (1) generic, (2) descriptive, (3) suggestive, (4)

arbitrary, or (5) fanciful. Fanciful or coined marks are the strongest marks, followed by arbitrary, suggestive, and descriptive marks.

Suggestive, arbitrary, or fanciful trademarks, due to their intrinsic nature, serve to identify a particular source of product. Suggestive marks require imagination and creativity. Microsoft's mark is suggestive in it connotes software for microcomputers. Descriptive marks describe the goods or services being sold, and receive protection only upon a showing they have acquired secondary meaning. *Northern Light Technology, Inc. v. Northern Lights Club,* 97 F. Supp. 2d 96 (D. Mass. 2000). For example, the mark "Super-encrypted software" describes computer security. A descriptive mark which is quite weak, may gain secondary meaning through online advertising or publishing.

The general rule is a mark must be distinctive, either inherently or by acquiring a secondary meaning. A mark originally distinctive may lose its distinctiveness or become generic if it does not relate only to the trademark owner's product. See, e.g., *Kellogg Co. v. National Biscuit Co.,* 305 U.S. 111 (1938) (holding "shredded wheat" to be a generic term).

Although a trademark may be found distinctive, the Lanham Act may not protect it if it "comprises immoral, deceptive, or scandalous matter; or matter which may disparage or falsely suggest a connection with persons, living or dead, institutions, beliefs, or national symbols, or bring them into contempt, or disrepute." 15 U.S.C. § 1052(a). A trademark is protectable if it is inherently distinctive, or has acquired distinctiveness through secondary meaning, such as the décor of a Mexican restaurant chain. *Two Pesos, Inc. v. Taco Cabana, Inc.,* 505 U.S. 763, 769 (1992). A company may not register generic marks such as "email" or "web services." Generic marks may not be registered as a trademark. 15 U.S.C. §§ 1052, 1127.

(F) Trade Name

Apple is a trade name, which means it is a name used by a person to identify his or her business or vocation. 15 U.S.C. § 1127. ABC is also a trade name; ABC Marks includes ABC trademarks, service marks, and trade names, covering their Internet website, ABC.com™, as well as television, radio, cable, and other Internet websites.

(G) Service Marks

The USPTO uses the terms "trademark" and "mark" to refer to both trademarks and service marks whether they are word marks or other types of marks. A service mark, like a trademark is a source identifier. The single difference is the service mark identifies and distinguishes the source of a service rather than a product. Those claiming rights in a mark will label their products with the symbols "TM," "SM" or "®." The Trademark Office allows a company to use the "TM" (trademark) or "SM" (service mark) designation, which signals rights even if it had not registered their marks. However, a company may not use the federal registration symbol "®" until the Trademark Office of the USPTO actually *registers a mark,* not while an examination is pending.

§ 11.2   Website Trade Dress

In the *Two Pesos, Inc. v. Taco Cabana*, 505 U.S. 763, 770–76 (1992) case, the U.S. Supreme Court found trade dress to be protectable under Section 43(a) of the Lanham Act. Section 43(a) of the Lanham Act creates a cause of action for any false designation of origin or misrepresentation likely to cause confusion, mistake, or deception as to origin or sponsorship. Unfair competition law includes false designation of origin.

The Supreme Court held that trade dress which is inherently distinctive is protectable under § 43(a) even if the plaintiff can not demonstrate secondary meaning since the trade dress itself identified products or services as coming from a specific source. The Court noted the shape and general appearance of the restaurant as well as "the identifying sign, the interior kitchen floor plan, the decor, the menu, the equipment used to serve food, the servers' uniforms, and other features [all reflected] on the total image of the restaurant." *Id.* at 765, n.1. A website's "look and feel" may be classifiable as trade dress. Xuan–Thao Nguyen, Should It Be a Free for All? The Challenge of Extending Trade Dress Protection to the Look and Feel of Websites in the Evolving Internet, 49 Am. U.L. Rev. 122 (2000).

In *Peri Hall & Assoc. v. Elliot Institute*, 2006 WL 742912 at *6 (W.D. Mo. March 20, 2006), the plaintiff was a web design company hired to create a website to promote a company's views on certain public issues. However, the defendant later launched a website with inconsistent positions on related public issues. The defendant copied the plaintiff's website's look and feel, graphics, coding and photographs, and used the company's trademarks as metatags. The court ruled the plaintiff proved a *prima facie* case of copyright infringement as well as trade dress.

§ 11.3   Direct Trademark Infringement

The Lanham Act of 1946 provides a federal cause of action for trademark infringement or false designation of origin claims. The Lanham Act recognizes trademark infringement claims under § 32(1) of the Lanham Act, 15 U.S.C. § 1114(1). The Lanham Act prohibits unauthorized persons who "reproduce, counterfeit, copy, or colorably imitate a registered mark ... in connection with the sale, offering for sale, distribution, or advertising of goods or services on or in connection with which such use is likely to cause confusion." 15 U.S.C. § 1114(1)(b). Trademark owners can seek remedies for infringement including: (1) injunctive relief, (2) accounting for profits made while misusing the owner's trademarks, (3) damages including treble damages for willful infringement, (4) attorneys fees in the "exceptional case," and (5) costs.

(A) *Prima Facie* Direct Infringement Case

To prove trademark infringement under the Lanham Act, a plaintiff must show: (1) it owns a valid, protectable, and nonfunctional mark, (2) is inherently distinctive or acquired secondary meaning, (3) the defendant uses, produces, counterfeits, copies, or imitates that mark in commerce without the plaintiff's consent, and (4) the consuming public is likely to be confused with the defendant's goods or services. 15 U.S.C. § 1114(a) (2005). The core element of any trademark infringement cause of action or false designation of origin is the "likelihood of confusion." 15 U.S.C. § 1125(a). To state a claim pursuant to 15 U.S.C. § 1125(a) of the Lanham Act, a plaintiff must allege: (1) the defendant uses a false designation of origin; (2) such false designation of origin occurs in interstate commerce in connection with goods or services; (3) is likely to cause confusion, mistake or deception as to the origin, sponsorship or approval of the plaintiff's goods and services by another person; and (4) the plaintiff has been or is likely to be damaged.

(B) Likelihood of Confusion Test

To prevail in a trademark infringement case, the plaintiff needs proof to show the defendant's use of the mark would likely cause an appreciable number of the purchasing public to be misled or confused as to source, sponsorship, or affiliation of defendant's goods or services. *McGregor–Doniger, Inc. v. Drizzle Inc.,* 599 F.2d 1126 (2d Cir. 1979). It is unclear how channels of trade for purposes of the likelihood of confusion are to be determined because many virtual stores sell diverse products.

The usual test used to measure a likelihood of confusion is whether the similarity of the marks is "likely to confuse consumers about the source of the products." *North Am. Med. Corp. v. Axiom Worldwide, Inc.*, 522 F.3d 1211, 1218–20 (11th Cir. 2008). No single factor is determinative, as the likelihood of the confusion test considers the totality of facts under the circumstances. *Hotmail Corp v. Van$ Money Pie, Inc.*, 1998 WL 388389 *5 (N.D. Cal. 1998).

Courts consider the following factors in determining whether there is a likelihood of confusion or unfair competition: (1) strength or weakness of plaintiff's mark, (2) the degree of similarity with defendant's mark, (3) class of goods, (4) marketing channels used, (5) evidence of actual confusion, and (6) intent of the defendant. The Lanham Act prohibits a person from unauthorized "use in commerce [of] any reproduction, counterfeit, copy, or colorable imitation of a registered mark in connection with the sale, offering for sale, distribution, or advertising of any goods or services on or in connection with which such use is likely to cause confusion." 15 U.S.C. § 1114(1)(a).

Courts also often apply the *Sleekcraft* factors to determine the likelihood of confusion in trademark infringement lawsuits: (1) the similarity of the marks, (2) the relatedness or proximity of the two companies' products or services, (3) the strength of the registered mark, (4) the marketing channels used, (5) the degree of care likely to be exercised by the purchaser in selecting goods, (6) the accused infringer's' intent in selecting its mark, (7) evidence of actual confusion and (8) the likelihood of expansion in product lines. *AMF Inc. v. Sleekcraft Boats*, 599 F.2d 341, 348–49 (9th Cir. 1979).

§ 11.4   Contributory   Trademark   Infringement

To be liable for contributory trademark infringement, a defendant must have: (1) "intentionally induced" the primary infringer to infringe, or (2) continued to supply an infringing product to an infringer with knowledge that the infringer is mislabeling the particular product supplied. When the alleged direct infringer supplies a service rather than a product, under the second prong of this test, the court must consider the extent of control exercised by the defendant over the third party's means of infringement. For liability to attach, there must be direct control and monitoring of the instrumentality used by a third party to infringe the plaintiff's mark. *Sony Corp. v. Universal City Studios*, 464 U.S. 417 (1984). In *Sony*, the Court determined the manufacturers of Betamax video tape recorders were not secondarily liable because these machines had a substantial legitimate use. *Id.* at 442–56.

§ 11.5   Vicarious Trademark Infringement

Vicarious liability for trademark infringement requires "a finding that the defendant and the infringer have an apparent or actual partnership, authority to bind one another in transactions with third parties or exercise joint ownership or control over the infringing product." *Hard Rock Café Licensing Corp. v. Concession Servs Inc.* 955 F.2d 1143, 1150 (7th Cir. 1992). Courts apply a four-part test to determine partnership: (1) parties' sharing of profits and losses; (2) parties' joint control and management of business; (3) contribution by each party of property, financial resources, effort, skill, or knowledge to business; and (4) parties' intention to be partners.

In *Perfect 10 v. Visa International*, 494 F.3d 788 (9th Cir. 2007), the Ninth Circuit refused to find Visa vicariously liable for its role in enabling payment of website access to content violating the copyrights and trademarks of a third party magazine publisher. The appeals court uncovered no affirmative acts by the defendants suggesting third parties should infringe the publisher's trademarks. The Ninth Circuit said even if defendants allowed the infringing merchants to use their logos, trade name, or trademarks, they would not be liable for false advertising because they had no duty to investigate the truth of the statements made by others. Moreover, the court found Visa did not encourage the improper conduct at issue; they merely processed credit card payments.

§ 11.6   False Designation of Origin

Section 43(a) of the Lanham Act provides rights and remedies for unfair trade practices such as the "false designation of origin, false or misleading description of fact, or misleading representation of fact." 15 U.S.C. § 1125(a)(1). Section 43(a) covers a false or misleading misrepresentation of fact which "is likely to cause confusion, or to cause mistake, or to deceive as to the affiliation, connection, or association of such person with another person, or as to the origin, sponsorship, or approval of his or her goods, services, or commercial activities by another person." 15 U.S.C. § 1125(a)(1)(A). Section 43(a) also covers unfair trade practices in the form of false or misleading advertising. The essence of a false or deceptive advertising claim under the Lanham Act is an advertisement that "misrepresents the nature, characteristics, qualities, or geographic origin of his or her or another person's goods, services, or commercial activities." 15 U.S.C. § 1125(a)(1)(B).

A plaintiff in a federal Lanham Act unfair competition action must prove five elements: (1) it possesses a mark, (2) the [defendant] used the mark, (3) the [defendant's] use of the mark occurred "in commerce", (4) the [opposing party] used the mark "in connection with the sale, offering for sale, distribution, or advertising" of goods or services and (5) the [opposing party] used the mark in a confusing way misleading consumers. *Lamparello v. Falwell* 420 F.3d 309, 313 (4th Cir. 2005).

§ 11.7   Anticybersquatting Act of 1999

Cybersquatters typically register well-known brand names as Internet domain names in order to force the rightful owners of the marks to pay a ransom for the right to engage in electronic commerce under their own name. A company may have a federal trademark action if a competitor registers a domain name identical or confusingly similar to their trademark, under the ACPA if it can prove bad faith and the defendant has no fair use or other defense. 15 U.S.C. § 1125(d)(1) (2006).

The core element in a cybersquatting case is proof of a bad faith intent to profit from a distinctive or famous mark. In *Panavision Int'l, L.P. v. Toeppen*, 141 F.3d 1316 (9th Cir. 1998), Dennis Toeppen registered scores of domain names containing the trademarks of famous companies, and then sought to sell them to the owners of the marks for a profit. Toeppen posted an aerial vision of Pana, Illinois on the website Panavision.com as a pretextual gesture to try to prove legitimate use. The federal court rejected this ploy finding Toeppen liable for misappropriating the trademark of Panavision through his practice of registering trademarks as domain names and then selling them to the trademark owners. *Id.* at 1325.

In another case, Mike Rowe, a Canadian teenager, registered MikeRoweSoft.com for his web design business. When offered $10 by Microsoft to sell the domain name, he countered with a demand for $10,000. Microsoft claimed this was evidence of bad faith dealing and filed suit. Todd Bishop, *Mikerowesoft vs. Microsoft: The Saga Continues*, SEATTLE POST-INTELLIGENCER REPORTER (Jan. 21, 2004). Rowe sold his domain name to Microsoft and settled the case.

The ACPA was enacted in 1999 to protect consumers and American businesses and to nurture electronic commerce by prohibiting the bad-faith and abusive registration of distinctive marks as Internet domain names. Cybersquatters have the intent to profit from registering domain names containing the marks of others. A plaintiff must prove three elements in an ACPA case: (1) the defendant had bad faith intent to profit from a domain name, (2) the defendant registered, used, or trafficked in a domain name, and (3) the name is identical, confusingly similar, or dilutive of certain trademarks.

(A) ACPA Purposes

The ACPA addresses "a new form of piracy on the Internet caused by acts of 'cybersquatting,' which refers to the deliberate, bad-faith, and abusive registration of Internet domain names in violation of the rights of trademark owners." S. Rep. No. 106–140, at 4 (1999). Congress enacted the ACPA to deter the practice whereby persons register domain names that consist of famous or distinctive trademarks and then try to sell (or perhaps more accurately, to ransom) those domain names to the trademark owners, thereby profiting from the goodwill associated with the trademark. *Sporty's Farm L.L.C. v. Sportsman's Market, Inc.* 202 F.3d 489, 495 (2d Cir. 2000). The ACPA of November 29, 1999, applies retroactively to domain names registered before Congress enacted the federal statute.

(B) In *Rem* Proceeding

The concept of *in rem* jurisdiction is seeking jurisdiction over property rather than persons. The ACPA allows the "owner of a mark" to bring an *in rem* action where a domain name allegedly violates the owner's right in a trademark. Trademark owners may seek an *in rem* remedy if the abusive domain name registrant is not locatable despite a diligent effort to find him. 15 U.S.C. § 1125(d)(2)(A). ACPA plaintiffs include all entities or persons that own trademarks or their assignees, not just persons owning famous trademarks.

The trademark owner must file its claim for *in rem* jurisdiction in the federal district court in which the domain name registry, registrar, or other domain names authority was located. *Fleetboston Financial Corp. v. Fleetbostonfinancial.com*, 138 F. Supp. 2d 121 (D. Mass. 2001). The remedies for the *in rem* action include forfeiture or cancellation of the domain name or transfer of the domain name to the trademark owner.

The Fourth Circuit affirmed the lower court's dismissal of the automobile manufacturer's *in rem* action in *Porsche Cars N. Am., Inc. v. Porsche.net*, 302 F.3d 248 (4th Cir. 2002). On February 23, 2001, the district court found it had jurisdiction over the British domain names under the Anticybersquatting Act (ACPA). Just three days before the scheduled trial in Virginia, the owner of the British domain names notified the court that their registrant had decided to submit to personal jurisdiction in California. The district court ruled an *in rem* remedy was not properly invoked. The circuit court disagreed ruling Porsche.net waited too long to object to *in rem* jurisdiction. The Fourth Circuit vacated the district court's order dismissing the case and remanded without reaching the question of whether there was a basis for *in rem* jurisdiction premised on Porsche's trademark-dilution claims.

§ 11.8   Trademark Dilution Revision Act of 2006 (TDRA)

(A)   TDRA's Basic Provisions

The Trademark Dilution Revision Act of 2006 ("TDRA") amended Section 43(c) of the Lanham Act, 15 U.S.C. § 1125(c), to enable trademark owners of famous trademarks to file a federal anti-dilution action. The TDRA gives the owner of a *famous*, and *distinctive* mark the right to an injunction against a person who uses the mark in commerce, in a manner that is likely to cause dilution by *blurring* or *tarnishing* the famous mark. Under the TDRA, there is still a cause of action "regardless of the presence or absence of actual or likely confusion, of competition, or of actual economic injury." 15 U.S.C. § 1125(c)(1).

To get relief under the TDRA, a trademark owner must first show that their mark is both famous and distinct. The TDRA extends to those marks that are inherently distinctive, and to those deriving distinctiveness from secondary meaning. Second, the owner must show dilution, the FTDA recognizes two forms of dilution: blurring and tarnishment, first developed under the common law. "Dilution by tarnishing occurs when a junior mark's similarity to a famous mark causes consumers mistakenly to associate the famous mark with the defendant's inferior or offensive product." *Eli Lilly & Co. v. Natural Answers, Inc.*, 233 F.3d 456, 466 (7th Cir. 2000). In contrast, blurring is a whittling away of the distinctive features of a trademark.

(B) Emerging TDRA Case Law

The 2006 TDRA overrules the Supreme Court's ruling in *Moseley v. V Secret Catalogue, Inc.*, 537 U.S. 418, 433 (2003), which interpreted the prior federal anti-dilution act to require prevailing plaintiffs to prove actual dilution. Before *Moseley,* this issue sharply divided federal appellate courts. Some courts reasoned dilution, in contrast to infringement, does not require a showing of consumer confusion because it protects only the distinctiveness of the mark, and not against consumer harm. However, other courts required the TDRA plaintiff to prove actual dilution. Trademark owners first need to establish they are famous trademarks under a multi-factorial analysis:

(1) the degree of inherent or acquired distinctiveness of the mark;

(2) the duration and extent of use of the mark in connection with the goods or services with which the mark is used;

(3) the duration and extent of advertising and publicity of the mark;

(4) the geographical extent of the trading area in which the mark is used;

(5) the channels of trade for the goods or services with which the mark is used;

(6) the degree of recognition of the mark in the trading areas and channels of trade used by the marks' owner and the person against whom the injunction is sought;

(7) the nature and extent of use of the same or similar marks by third parties.

15 U.S.C. § 1125(c)(1).

To prevail under the TDRA of 2006, the plaintiff must show: (1) he or she owns a famous mark that is distinctive, (2) a defendant used a mark in commerce that allegedly is diluting the famous mark, (3) a similarity between the defendant's mark and the famous mark gives rise to an association between marks, and (4) the association is likely to impair the distinctiveness of the famous mark or likely to harm the reputation of the famous mark.

In *Visa International Service Association v. JSL Corp.*, 533 F. Supp. 2d 1089 (D. Nev. 2007), the court held a domain name registrant's use of the domain name evisa.com, to promote its language service business, diluted the Visa trademark. The district court stated that the defendant's use of the trademark—evisa.com—created actual dilution because it was substantially similar to plaintiff's famous Visa mark. Moreover, businesses commonly place an 'e' before their trademark to denote the online version of their business.

The *Visa International* court reasoned the impact of both preventing Visa from using that domain to market its products, and of placing its reputation at the mercy of defendant, resulted in dilution. The more significant aspect of the decision was that the court did not rely on direct evidence of actual dilution, or on evidence that consumers actually associated defendant's evisa.com mark with the plaintiff or its products. The court said the FTDA of 1996 only required the holder of a famous mark to show a likelihood of dilution arising out of defendant's use of its mark to prevail on a federal dilution claim, and not the evidence of actual dilution.

However the district court was obligated to interpret the FTDA as directed by the Supreme Court in *Moseley*, because the case was filed before the 2006 amendment of the FTDA. Before *Moseley*, to prevail on a dilution claim, the owner of a famous mark needed to prove that a defendant's use actually diluted their mark. The court held the plaintiff need not prove actual confusion given the near identity of the parties' respective marks—Visa and "evisa." The court found the federal anti-dilution act protected Visa in this case because the evisa mark weakened the ability of the Visa mark to identify its respective goods and services. The evisa mark diverted Internet searchers, as they are not brought to Visa's website when entering evisa.com.

In this decision, the court found plaintiff's Visa mark was famous and distinctive, and entitled to protection under the FTDA. In its prior decision, the court had found the defendant was making a commercial use of the mark—to promote a language service business—that began after plaintiff's mark became famous. As a result, the court granted plaintiff's motion for summary judgment, finding the defendant violated the FTDA.

§ 11.9 State Anti–Dilution Actions

Dilution evolved as a state law remedy to protect trademarks from blurring or tarnishment. *Mead*

Data Cent., Inc. v. Toyota Motor Sales, U.S.A., Inc., 875 F.2d 1026 (2d Cir. 1989) (New York state anti-dilution action). State anti-dilution actions survive the FTDA and vary widely, depending upon the jurisdiction.

(A) Blurring

Blurring occurs "where the defendant uses or modifies the plaintiff's trademark to identify the defendant's goods and services, raising the possibility that the mark will lose its ability to serve as a unique identifier of the plaintiff's product." *Merck & Co., Inc. v. Mediplan Health Consulting, Inc.*, 425 F. Supp. 2d 402, 417 (S.D. N.Y. 2006) Courts determine blurring on a multi-factorial study of six factors, including: (1) the similarity of the marks, (2) the similarity of the products covered, (3) the sophistication of the consumers, (4) the existence of predatory intent, (5) the renown of the senior mark, and (6) the renown of the junior mark.

(B) Tarnishment

Tarnishment occurs where a trademark is connected to shoddy, unwholesome, or other seamy context so the public will associate the trademark with shoddy or low prestige products or services. In *Mattel Inc. v. Internet Dimensions, Inc.*, 55 U.S.P.Q. 2d 1620 (S.D. N.Y. 2000), the federal court enjoined an online pornographer's use of the phrase "Barbie's play pen" on its adult entertainment website because it diluted Mattel's trademark "Barbie" for dolls. In *Hasbro,* the court found Internet Dimensions' use of a domain name combination for a sexually explicit website tarnished Hasbro's trademark, "Candyland," a well-known children's game. *Hasbro, Inc. v. Internet Entertainment Group, Ltd.*, 1996 WL 84858 (W.D. Wash. 1996). In *Toys "R" Us*, the famous toy company filed suit against an online pornographer doing business as Adults "R" Us as a domain name. Adults "R" Us.com sold adult sex toys and other X-rated materials. *Toys "R" Us, Inc. v. Akkaoui*, 40 U.S.P.Q.2d 1836 (N.D. Cal. 1996). The court found Toys "R" Us' trademark was tarnished by Adults "R" Us.

§ 11.10 Online Keyword Litigation

Google has been the defendant in many high profile trademark/keyword infringement lawsuits. Trademark owners have filed suits against Google arising out of its use of the "AdWords" context-advertising program. AdWords lets an advertiser bid on keywords or terms an Internet user might enter into a Google search. Google will link advertisements and sponsored hyperlinks to given keywords it sells. "When an Internet user enters the keyword, it triggers the sponsored link to appear on the search results page either to the right or immediately above the search results. Another program the defendant offers is the 'Keyword Suggestion Tool,' which it uses to recommend keywords to advertisers." *Rescuecom Corp. v. Google, Inc.*, 456 F. Supp. 2d 393, 397 (N.D. N.Y. 2006).

Rescuecom filed suit against Google for selling its trademark as a keyword to its competitors. Thus, whenever an Internet user typed "Rescuecom" as a search term, the competitor's hyperlink appeared linked to the competitors' websites among the search results. A New York court found Google's use of Rescuecom's trademark in a keyword did not satisfy the "trademark use" requirement, in 15 U.S.C. § 1051, necessary for infringement and false origin actions.

Rescuecom was unable to establish "trademark use" because they were unable to prove: (1) any of the search results, except the links belonging to plaintiff, displayed plaintiff's trademark, (2) defendant's activities affected the appearance or functionality of plaintiff's website, or (3) defendant placed plaintiff's trademark on any goods, containers, displays, or advertisements.

In *Google, Inc. v. American Blind & Wallpaper Factory, Inc.*, 2007 WL 1848665 (N.D. Cal. 2007), the court found Google's sale of trademarked terms in its advertising program did constitute "use in commerce" for purposes of the Lanham Act, and denied summary judgment to Google. Rosetta Stone filed a trademark infringement, dilution, and unfair competition lawsuit against Rocket Languages, a competitor, for "piggybacking," which is the practice of using "trademarked words of big brands in the text of search ads to divert traffic from the sites of bigger advertisers to their own sites." Dan Slater, *Unhappy With its Google Search Results, Rosetta Stone Sues Competitor*, THE WALL STREET JOURNAL, July 7, 2008. Rosetta Stone charged Rocket Languages, a competitor, with misusing its trademark and variations in sponsored link advertisements. Rocket Language bought keywords so when potential Rosetta customers clicked the links in advertisements, seeking ROSETTA STONE products, they were instead taken to websites operated by Rocket Languages. Rosetta also contends Rocket Language advertisements diluted and tarnished the ROSETTA STONE mark and the reputation of its products. One Rocket Language advertisement asked: "Is Rosetta Spanish a Scam?" in the header of the advertisement and "Don't Buy Rosetta Spanish Before You Read This" in the text of the advertisement. Rosetta contends these "comparison reviews" gave the consumer the false impression they were unbiased statements. Rosetta Stone will not prevail unless it can overcome the "use" requirement, which is a necessary predicate to its trademark infringement and dilution causes of action.

§ 11.11   Sponsored Banner Advertisements

Trademark infringement claims may be predicated upon the defendant's use of unidentified banner ads on the Internet user's search page. Playboy, for example, objected to a competitor's ad appearing as a popup in a banner ad along the margin of the search result when the searcher entered "Playboy" and/or "Playmate," trademark terms owned by Playboy. *Playboy Enterprises Inc. v. Netscape Communications Corp.*, 354 F.3d 1020, 1023 (9th Cir. 2004). The search engine incorporated calibration keywords in its software application. *Id.* at 1022–23. The *Playboy* court found the banner advertisements objectionable because they did not clearly identify the sponsor of the ad, thereby creating a likelihood of confusion. *Id*. at 1023–25.

§ 11.12   Metatags

A metatag is a invisible code in Hypertext Markup Language that describes the contents of a Web page. Search engines in the 1990s used metatags to determine page rank; although, currently Google and other search engines have other methods for determining page rank. Trademark owners filed suit against individuals or companies that incorporated the metatags of popular companies in their website to jump-start their page rank.

In an Eleventh Circuit case, the defendant incorporated the plaintiff's trademarked terms within its metatags to influence Internet search engines. *North Am. Med. Corp. v. Axiom Worldwide, Inc.*, 522 F.3d 1211 (11th Cir. 2008). Adagen was an authorized distributor of North American Medical's ("NAM") traction devices. Axiom, a competitor of NAM, manufactured a physiotherapeutic device; NAM and Adagen allege Axiom engaged in unfair competition by infringing NAM's trademarks when it included their trademarks in metatags on its website.

Axiom used two of NAM's registered trademarks in its metatags on its website: the terms "Accu–Spina" and "IDD Therapy." Even though no mention was made of the trademarks, the trademarks in the metatags influenced Internet search engines. That is, when a computer user entered NAM's trademarked terms in Google's search engine, the search engine returned Axiom's website as the second most relevant search result. *Id*.

The Eleventh Circuit affirmed the lower court's finding this misuse of metatags constituted trademark infringement and false advertising. The court found a likelihood of success on the merits of the infringement claims under 15 U.S.C. § 1114(1)(a). The appeals court held there was a likelihood of confusion when the defendant included trademarks of competitors in metatags. Such a misuse of the metatags suggested the competitor's products and those of the manufacturer had the same source, or that the competitor sold both lines. The *Axicon* court also found a likelihood of success on the merits of the false advertising claims under 15 U.S.C. § 1125(a).

The Ninth Circuit determined that the defendant, a video specialty store, who used the term "movie buff" in certain slogans since the late 1980s, could not also use that term in its domain name or in metatags on its website. *Brookfield Communications, Inc. v. West Coast Entertainment Corp*., 174 F.3d 1036 (9th Cir. 1999). Brookfield, the plaintiff, claimed priority use in commerce of the phrase, having used the mark first in 1993, although it did not get federal registration until September of 1998. The defendant had planned to launch a website with the name http://www.moviebuff.com,but the court determined that the use of Brookfield's trademark as a metatag would divert traffic from Brook-field to the defendant's website.

The defendant had registered the domain name in February of 1996, but it did not use the name until the website was actually launched. The defendant also obtained a federal registration of the term "The Movie Buff's Movie Store," and used the words "movie buff" in advertising.

The *Brookfield* court compared the misuse of metatags and the diversion of web traffic from the rightful trademark owner's site to placing a sign employing another's trademark in front of one's store. The seamy side of using metatags of competitors is it causes consumers to make rapid cognitive mistakes, which is what courts refer to as initial interest confusion. The initial interest confusion is a corruption of rapid cognition. Malcolm Gladwell, *BLINK*: THE POWER OF THINKING WITHOUT THINKING (2005). A decisive glance at a trademark gives consumers a split second profile of the quality of goods and services. Terri Welles graced the cover of Playboy in 1981 as the "Playboy Playmate of the Year for 1981." Playboy Enterprises International ("PEI") challenged her use of the title "Playboy Playmate of the Year 1981," and her use of other trademarked terms on her website. PEI contended Welles infringed the following trademarked terms on her website: (1) the terms "Playboy" and "Playmate" in the metatags of the website, (2) the phrase "Playmate of the Year 1981" on the masthead of the website, (3) the phrases "Playboy Playmate of the Year 1981" and "Playmate of the Year 1981"

on various banner ads, and (4) her repeated use of
the abbreviation "PMOY '81" as the watermark on
the pages of the website.

In *Playboy Enterprises, Inc. v. Welles,* 279 F.3d
796 (9th Cir. 2002) the Ninth Circuit reversed a
federal district court's grant of a preliminary injunction that restrained former Playmate Terri
Welles from using the registered trademarks "Playboy" and "Playmate" as metatags in her websites.
The Ninth Circuit decided in Welles' favor, holding
her use of the Playboy mark constituted fair use.
The court also rejected Playboy's dilution claim,
ruling the defendant was selling Terri Welles products only. The court found Welles was not trying to
divert traffic from Playboy.

§ 11.13   Trademark Law Defenses

(A) Nominative Use

The nominative fair use analysis allows a defendant to use the plaintiff's mark to describe the
plaintiff's product so long as the goal is for the
defendant to describe her own product. A computer repair shop, for example, can advertise it fixes
Apple II Computers even though "Apple" is a registered trademark. Nominative use also lets a defendant use the trademark of another when no descriptive substitute exists. First, the product or
service in question must be one not readily identifiable without use of the trademark. Second, the
defendant may only use as much of the mark as is
reasonably necessary to identify the product or service. Finally, the defendant must not do anything

in conjunction with the mark that would suggest sponsorship or endorsement by the trademark holder. *New Kids On The Block v. News America Publishing, Inc.*, 971 F.2d 302 (9th Cir. 1992).

Nominative use allows comparative advertising, employing another's trademark such as the Pepsi Challenge that featured taste tests between Coca Cola and Pepsi in malls around the country in the 1980s. The *New Kids* court described how Pepsi or another soft drink manufacturer "would be entitled to compare its product to Coca–Cola or Coke, but would not be entitled to use Coca–Cola's distinctive lettering." *Id*. at 308.

(B) First Amendment in Cyberspace

Companies will find it difficult to enjoin websites critical of their goods and services, which have become ubiquitous on the Internet. As an example of complaint or "sucks" sites, a critic of Bally's chain of health clubs set up an anti-Bally website entitled, "Bally's sucks." *Bally Total Fitness Holding Corp. v. Faber*, 29 F. Supp. 2d 1161 (C.D. Cal. 1998). Bally's filed suit for trademark dilution because the defendant was using its trademarks in an unauthorized manner. The federal court in California granted summary judgment in favor of the defendant, reasoning, "no reasonable person would think Bally's is affiliated with or endorses" the anti-Bally site. The court also found "fair use" in the website's use of Bally's intellectual property.

The Fourth Circuit found the FTDA applies only to a "commercial use in commerce of a mark" leaving no doubt "that it did not intend for trade-mark laws to impinge the First Amendment rights of critics and commentators." *Lamparello v. Falwell* 420 F.3d 309, 313 (4th Cir. 2005). In *Lamparello*, the Fourth Circuit determined Lamparello's domain name, www.fallwell.com, a website critical of Rev. Jerry Falwell and his views on homosexuality, did not constitute cybersquatting. The appellate court reasoned Reverend Jerry Falwell was unable to show Lamparello had a bad faith intent to profit from his use of the fallwell.com domain name.

The court also noted Lamparello had not engaged in the type of conduct described in the statutory factors as typifying the bad faith intent to profit essential to a successful cybersquatting claim. The court distinguished Lamparello's use of his website from *PETA v. Doughney*, 263 F.3d 359 (4th Cir. 2001). The defendant in *PETA* engaged in cybers-quatting because www.peta.org was one of fifty to sixty domain names registered by the defendant, and because the defendant had evidenced a clear intent to sell www.peta.org to PETA.

(C) Parodies in Cyberspace

The Fourth Circuit ruled "Chewy Vuiton" dog chew toy was a successful parody of the manufac-turer's luxury handbags, and the "LOUIS VUIT-TON" marks and trade dress used in marketing and selling those handbags. *Louis Vuitton Malletier S.A. v. Haute Diggity Dog*, 507 F.3d 252 (4th Cir. 2007). The *Louis Vuitton* court reasoned the Chewy Vuiton dog toy was obviously an irreverent and intentional representation of the famous designer's handbag. The *Louis Vuitton* court found no doubt the dog toy was not an "idealized image" of mark created by the manufacturer. Moreover, the toy's name immediately conveyed a joking and amusing parody by using something a dog would chew on to poke fun at the elegance and expense of the famous French designer's overpriced handbags. Parodies are entitled to a degree of First Amendment protection.

§ 11.14   False Advertising

Website false advertising claims are cognizable under both the Lanham Act and state law. To prevail in a Lanham Act false advertising case the plaintiff must prove: (1) the online advertisements of the defendant were false or misleading; (2) the online ads deceived, or had the capacity to deceive, website visitors; (3) the deception had a material effect on purchasing decisions; (4) the misrepresented product or service affects interstate commerce; and (5) the plaintiff has been—or is likely to be— injured as a result of the false advertising. *Johnson & Johnson Vision Care, Inc. v. 1–800 Contacts, Inc.*, 299 F.3d 1242 (11th Cir. 2002).

The Eleventh Circuit in *1–800 Contacts* found that the defendant's use of the manufacturer's trademarks within its website's metatags was a "use in commerce" within the meaning of the Lanham Act. The appeals court found that the district court's finding of a "likelihood of confusion" was not clearly erroneous for purposes of plaintiffs' Lanham Act trademark infringement claims. The court also upheld the Eleventh Circuit's finding that the defendant made false statements in its advertising and the statements were material to a consumers' purchasing decisions.

The defendant's use of the manufacturer's "IDD Therapy" and "Accu–Spina" trademarks within its website's metatags, as part of its effort to promote and advertise its own products on the Internet, was a "use in commerce" within the meaning of the Lanham Act. *North Am. Med. Corp. v. Axiom Worldwide, Inc.*, 522 F.3d 1211 (11th Cir. 2008). Each time a consumer entered the trademarks into a search engine, the metatags caused the trademarks to be displayed to the consumer in the search results as the second most relevant search result. *Id.*

§ 11.15 Typosquatting

Typosquatting is the practice of registering a domain name to benefit from users who mistype a domain name and land on the mistyped domain. A classic example is the "typosquatter" who registered domain names that employed misspellings of popular child-oriented websites, such as Teletubbies and Disneyland, to attract children to adult entertainment sites and enhance clickstream revenue. The typosquatter took advantage of children's foreseeable misspellings, redirecting the children to adult entertainment sites where it received a fee for each child's clickstream.

Typosquatters rely upon adult Internet users mistyping domain names as well. Dotster, a domain name registrar, registered the domain name "wwwVulcanGolf.com," which is a period away from the domain name www.VulcanGolf.com. *Vulcan Golf, LLC v. Google Inc.*, 552 F. Supp. 2d 752, 760 (N.D. Ill. 2008). Vulcan filed suit against Dotster claiming the defendant "intentionally registered this domain name without the period after the "www" expecting a certain number of Internet users will mistype the name and will land on the webpage." *Id.* Dotster was liable because it benefited from their blatantly deceptive domain. "When a user clicks on the advertising, Google and the parking companies and/or the domain owners receive revenue from that advertiser." *Id.*

§ 11.16   Domain Name Hijacking

Domain names violate the right of trademark owners when they interfere or infringe with trademarks. An adult entertainment company, for example, modified a domain name to redirect traffic of a rival to its website—a practice known as domain name hijacking. *Telemedia Network Inc. v. Sunshine Films, Inc.*, 2002 WL 31518870 (Cal. Ct. App. 2d Dist. 2002). The *Telemedia* court described how the defendant "surreptitiously re-direct[ed] traffic" for www.sexnet.com to Sunshine's address—in effect "hijacking" the sexnet.com domain name using the Sexnet mark. The diversion of traffic occurred when customers trying to access Sexnet found a website operated by Sunshine with no content. Sunshine's purpose was to raise revenue through deceptive means.

§ 11.17 ICANN's Governance

The Internet Corporation for Assigned Names and Numbers ("ICANN"), created in 1998, has responsibility for the technical functions of the Internet. ICANN is a non-profit organization that oversees domain name disputes and controls domain name issues. ICANN coordinates the assignment of IP address numbers, protocol parameter and port numbers, and the stable operation of the Internet's root server systems. ICANN is a quasi-governmental forum for developing policies governing the Internet's core technical elements, including the domain-name system ("DNS"). ICANN operates based on a civil society consensus, with affected stakeholders meeting to coordinate policies. The Internet Assigned Numbers Authority ("IANA") delegates or redelegates top-level domains and manages the domain-name system root. The registration of domain names within two-letter country code top-level domains ("CCTLDs") such as UK (United Kingdom), SE (Sweden) or AU (Australia) are administered by country-code managers. The DNS consists of a directory, organized hierarchically, of all the domain names and their corresponding computers registered to particular companies and persons using the Internet. On November 25, 1998, ICANN and the Commerce Department entered into a Memorandum of Understanding, in which they agreed jointly to develop and test the mechanisms and procedures that should be in place in the new, privatized DNS. Specifically, ICANN and the Commerce Department agreed to collaborate on "written technical procedures for operation of the primary root server including procedures that permit modifications, additions, or deletions to the root zone file." *Name.Space, Inc. v. Network Solutions, Inc.*, 202 F.3d 573, 579 (2d Cir. 2000). The DNS is a "directory, organized hierarchically, of all the domain names and their corresponding computers registered to particular companies and persons using the Internet." ICANN, *What is the Domain Name System?* (2008).

(A) Network Solutions' Registry

Network Solutions LLC was in a monopoly position from 1979 until the 1990s and had the exclusive right to allocate .com, .org, and .net addresses. Before 1999, Network Solutions was the only registrar. Today it is one of hundreds of domain name registrars accredited by ICANN. Network Solutions, like many registrars, offers web-related services in addition to the registration of domain names. Currently, Network Solutions registers 7.8 million domain names. To register its domain name an eBusiness may choose from literally hundreds of registrars, it is both an inexpensive and quick process.

(B) Accredited Domain Name Registrars

The first step in registering a domain name is to choose an accredited registry from the ICANN list of accredited registrars. ICANN has approved and accredited hundreds of domain name registrars. The U.S., the United Kingdom, and Canada have the largest number of registries. Australia, France,

Germany, India, and Korea also have many registries. Under the DNS, the registrant is the company
or individual to whom the domain name actually
belongs. A website operator must signify an administrative contact at the point of registration. The
administrative contact is a person authorized by the
registrant to make changes in the domain name.
For example, the administrative contact may transfer, cancel, or assign rights to the domain name.
Charges for domain name registration are competitive, although some charge as little as $10.

(C) Internet Assigned Numbers Authority (IANA)

"No single entity—academic, corporate, governmental, or non-profit—administers the Internet. It
exists and functions as a result of the fact that
hundreds of thousands of separate operators of
computers and computer networks independently
decided to use common data transfer protocols to
exchange communications and information with
other computers (which in turn exchange communications and information with still other computers)." *ACLU v. Reno*, 929 F.Supp. 824, 832 (E.D.
Pa. 1996).

ICANN is the closest thing to a single entity
responsible for key infrastructure of the Internet.
The Internet Assigned Numbers Authority (IANA)
is the ICANN-operated entity that controls numbers for protocols, the Country Code Top-level Domains, and maintains the IP Address allotments.
The Internet Protocol Addressing system uses
"IPv4 addresses, which are 32–bit numbers often

expressed as 4 octets in "dotted decimal" notation (for example, *192.0.2.53*)." IANA, *Number Resources* (2008). IPv6 is a new IP address standard designed to succeed IP version 4. Beginning in 1999, "IPv6 addresses are 128–bit numbers and are conventionally expressed using hexadecimal strings (for example, *2001:0db8:582:ae33: 29*)." *Id*. IANA manages the DNSRoot Zone (assignments of ccTLDs and gTLDs), as well as the .int registry, and the .arpa zone. *Id*.

IANA also works with the Internet Engineering Task Force ("IETF") as Internet architects in formulating new protocols necessary for the functioning of the Internet. The IETF is a large international body of "network designers, vendors and researchers concerned with the evolution of the Internet architecture and the smooth operation of the Internet." IETF, *Overview of the IETF* (2008).

§ 11.18 Uniform Domain Name Resolution Policy

The World Intellectual Property Organization (WIPO) developed the Uniform Domain Name Resolution Policy ("UDRP") for the arbitration of domain name disputes. UDRP panels have the power to cancel or transfer domain name registration. ICANN can also order such relief upon receipt of an order from a court or arbitral tribunal. UDRP Policy, § 3. UDRP panels have no authority to award monetary damages, statutory damages, or any other remedies typically awarded for Lanham Act infringement or dilution claims.

§ 11.19　Abusive Registration Remedies

Trademark owners will prevail under the UDRP if they can prove a domain name is either identical or confusingly similar to their trademark or service mark. Domain name registrants with no right or a legitimate interest in a domain name may have their registration cancelled. Bad faith registrations may have their registration cancelled or transferred to the true owner. The emblem of bad faith is when a registrant obtains a domain name for the sole purpose of selling, renting, or transferring the registration to the true owner for a profit, which is the classic test for cybersquatting. Another test for bad faith is whether the registrant registers the domain name to prevent the true owners from using it.

§ 11.20　Remedies for Abusive Registrations

Five paradigmatic categories of cases are typically decided by WIPO arbitral panels in deciding whether a given domain name is "confusingly similar" to a trademark: (1) cases where the domain name and trademark are wholly identical, or, in cases where the trademark owner has a registered domain name, the generic Top-level Domain ("gTLD") might be different; (2) cases where a registrant's domain name incorporates the surname of a celebrity; (3) cases where a generic or descriptive word has been added to the trademark (such as "my", "direct", "e-"); (4) cases where anti-corporate websites append the word "sucks" at the end of trade names; and (5) typosquatting cases where the domain name registrant relies on Internet users mistyping famous trademark names.

(A) Incorporating Another's Trademark

The classic illustration of incorporating another's trademark in a domain name was *Playboy Enterprises International, Inc. v. Good Samaritan Program*, WIPO Case No. D2001–0241 (2001). In this WIPO case, Hugh Hefner, Playboy's founder and complainant in the case, objected to Good Samaritan's registration of the domain name <hughhefner.com> with BulkRegister, a domain name registry. Playboy, which holds the trademark "Hugh M. Hefner," met the three elements of UDRP Policy 4(a) because: (1) Good Samaritan's domain name was identical to Playboy's trademarks, (2) Good Samaritan had no rights or legitimate interests in the domain name, and (3) Good Samaritan's domain name was registered and was used in bad faith.

The UDRP panel decided the case on the complaint given compelling evidence Good Samaritan was a cybersquatter. The panel noted that "although the consideration Good Samaritan solicits for transfer of domain names back to celebrities may (or may not) involve direct cash payment, it appears from Good Samaritan's own statements it sought substantial consideration in the form of celebrity endorsement or linkage to successful commercial websites in return for its services." *Id*. The UDRP panel concluded, "Good Samaritan registered <hughhefner.com> for the purpose of transferring it to Playboy in return for valuable consideration in excess of its costs directly related to the domain name." *Id*.

(B) Common Law TM Rights of Celebrities

The USPTO maintains a database of trademarks. The complainant must prove common law rights if the trademark or service mark is not registered. A celebrity's name alone is not protected under the UDRP, or the common law. The *sine qua non* of common law rights is the personal name means a source of goods or services. *Nicole Kidman v. John Zuccarini*, WIPO Case No. D2000–1415 (2001) (ruling nicholekidmannude.com was confusingly similar to Nicole Kidman's common law mark in her name).

The purpose of trademark law is to protect consumers by providing accurate product identification. *Qualitex Co. v. Jacobson Prods. Co.*, 514 U.S. 159 (1995). Kevin Spacey, for example, has common law rights in his name because he uses his name as a trademark as a way of identifying his performances. A single cybersquatter took advantage of the goodwill in the names of well-known personalities by registering domain names that contained the celebrities' names. UDRP panels ruled against the cybersquatter who registered Kevin Spacey's name, as well as domain names containing the name of certain well-known celebrities including Larry King, Pierce Brosnan, Celine Dion, Pamela Anderson, Carmen Electra, Michael Crichton, and Julie Brown. *Jeffrey Archer v. Alberta Hotrods tda CELEBRITY 1000,* WIPO Case No. D2006–0431 (2006); *Kevin Spacey v. Alberta Hot Rods*, NAF Case No. FA114437 (1992).

UDRP panels typically refuse to transfer or cancel domain name registrations of surnames unless the plaintiff proves he or she has common law rights or that their name has a secondary meaning in the marketplace. Many celebrities and public figures have filed UDRP complaints to transfer or cancel domain names based upon common law rights, including "Madonna, Julia Roberts, Eminem, Pamela Anderson, JK Rowling, Michael Crichton and Ronaldo." IPFrontline, *WIPO Continues Efforts to Curb Cybersquatting* (2005). In *Julia Roberts v. Russell Boyd*, WIPO Case No. D2000–0210 (May 29, 2000), the cybersquatter registered a domain name with famous actress Julia Robert's name and launched the website http://www.juliaroberts.com, which featured a photograph of a woman named "Sari Locker." The cybersquatter then placed the domain name up for auction on eBay. Asserting common law trademark rights, the famous actress contended the domain name <juliaroberts.com> is identical and confusingly similar to the name "Julia Roberts."

The WIPO panel agreed the name "Julia Roberts" has sufficient secondary association with the famous actress, and that she had common law trademark rights under U.S. trademark law. The panel transferred the domain name to Ms. Roberts, finding bad faith registration on the part of the registrant because he had registered more than fifty other domain names, including movie stars' names "within <madeleinestowe.com> and <alpaci-

no.com> and a famous Russian gymnast's name within <elenaprodunova>." *Id.*

Many UDRP panels have recognized common law rights in a trademark sufficient to enable a celebrity to succeed in a UDRP proceeding, The famous person must show their surname serves as a source for goods or other common law trademark usage. "It has now become well established jurisprudence that the Policy does not discriminate between those marks in the U.S. that are based on common law usage (unregistered marks) or grounded in federal registration." *Office of Personnel Management v. MS Technology, Inc.*, 2003 WL 23472306 (2003). In many of the famous surname cases, the respondent owns hundreds or even thousands of names. Typing a celebrity's name creates initial interest confusion when they are taken to the cybersquatter's website rather than to the celebrity's site.

In *Springsteen v. Burgar*, WIPO Case No. D2000–1532 (2001), the panel departed from established surname cases, finding very well known celebrities may acquire common law rights in their surname. The panel in *Springsteen* concluded no evidence has been given of the name "Bruce Springsteen" was entitled to common law trademark protection. The panel also concluded the respondent was not using the disputed domain name for goods or services. Consequently, Springsteen was unable to sustain a UDRP complaint. In *Jason Giambi and Jeremy Giambi v. Tom Meagher,* NAF Case No. FA114745 (2002), a UDRP panel rejected a request to transfer giambi.com to the baseball-playing brothers as the

Giambi surname had not yet attained a secondary meaning in the marketplace.

(C) Appending   Descriptive   or   Generic Words

Cybersquatting registrants with no rights to famous trademarks palm-off on their goodwill by simply adding one or more generic or descriptive words to the celebrity or company's name. A UDRP panel is likely to find a domain name confusingly similar when it is used in the same industry as a well-known   trademark,   as   with   "statefarm-claimshelp.com." *State Farm Mutual Automobile Insurance   Co.   v.   LaFaive*,   NAF   Case   No FA0008000095407 (2000). However, in *Safeguard Operations LLC v. Safeguard Storage*, NAF Case No. FA0604000672431 (2006), the NAF panel ruled the respondent had a legitimate interest in the domain name "safeguard-storage.com" because of the preparations it undertook to operate a self storage business under the name "Safeguard Storage" before receiving notice of the instant domain name dispute. As a result, the UDRP panel refused to direct the respondent to transfer the disputed domain to Complainant Safeguard Operations LLC, owner of several federally registered trademarks containing the word "Safeguard," which marks its uses in connection with its operation of self-storage facilities.

(D) Anti–Corporate Websites

The fourth category of UDRP cases deal with complaint sites, a.k.a. "sucks" domain names (i.e., names with the complainant's trademark and a negative term such as "sucks"). Most panels facing the issue have found such domain names are confusingly similar to the complainants' marks. In one case, the "sucks" site was found to be confusingly similar to the complainant's mark because a search engine would bring up the "sucks" site when the mark itself was entered as a search term. *Cabela's Inc. v. Cupcake Patrol*, NAF Case No. FA0006000095080 (2000).

UDRP panels distinguish between complaint websites expressing feelings about products and services, and websites constructed for the sole purpose of extorting money from the trademark owners. In general, rather than asking whether the domain name causes confusion as to source, the panel should compare the domain name and the mark for similarity. *Wal–Mart Stores, Inc. v. MacLeod,* WIPO Case No. D2000–0662 (2000). In *Wal–Mart*, the panel acknowledged the importance of protecting protest sites as trademarks to identify the object of their criticism. However, the panel found the Wall–Mart sucks site was not being used for protest but rather was offered for sale for far more than the costs of registration. The court found the defendant's site to be in bad faith constituting trademark piracy.

Other panels have noted many Internet users do not speak English or do not know the word "sucks"; ultimately, these panels have held domain names adding the word "sucks" to a trademark of another company was confusingly similar to the mark incorporated. *Koninklijke Philips Electronics N.V. v. In Seo Kim*, WIPO Case No. D2001–1195 (2001). A minority of panels have ruled "sucks" sites are not confusingly similar. In *Homer TLC, Inc. v. Green People*, NAF Case No. FA0508000550345 (2005), a panel refused to transfer "Home Depot Sucks.com" to Home Depot. The website "Home Depot Sucks.com" was operating as a "protest site" and the panel found no basis for transferring the protest site's domain name. The pejorative terms "sucks" added to the trademark did not create a likelihood of confusion. The Panel further found the protest site had a legitimate interest in this domain because respondent had used the domain as the home of a website critical of Home Depot for seven years; hence, it was not registered in bad faith.

(E) UDRP Typosquatting

The fifth paradigmatic UDRP case is the "typosquatting" case, i.e., where one letter in a well-known brand is replaced with another letter in order to direct traffic to the typosquatter's website. UDRP panels generally disfavor such strategies, especially when evidenced by bad faith. In *Toronto–Dominion Bank v. Karpachev*, WIPO Case No. D2000–1571 (2001), the WIPO panel concluded the domain name "tdwatergouse.com" was confusingly similar to the TD WATERHOUSE mark.

John Zuccarini, a recidivist typosquatter, was the respondent in *Six Continents Hotels, Inc. v. John Zuccarini*, WIPO Case No. D2003–0161 (2003). The

WIPO panel found Zuccaarini acted in bad faith, and transferred the domain name "hoildayinn.com" to the owner of the Holiday Inn hotel chain. In *TIPI Holdings v. Zuccarini*, WIPO Case No. D2001–0791 (2001), the Delaware corporation charged Zuccarini with registering the domain names "autotader.com" and "autotradr.com." Zuccarini omitted in one case the letter "r" in "trader," and in another case, the letter "e" in "trader" in order to divert website users who mistakenly mistyped or misspelled "autotrader" in trying to reach the "autotrader.com" website. The court observed Zuccarini had been on the respondent side in cases filed by *Encyclopedia Britannica, Dow Jones & Company, Inc. Yahoo!, Inc., Abercrombie & Fitch Stores, Inc., Saks & Company, America Online, Inc., United Feature Syndicate, Inc., Disney Enterprises, Inc.,* and scores of other famous trademark owners.

In *IMDb, Inc. v. Seventh Summit Ventures*, NAF Case No. 050300436735 (2005), the panel refused a request from the world's largest online movie database to transfer the domain name "indb.com" because in "the Internet context, consumers are aware that domain names for different Websites are quite often similar, because of the need for language economy, and that very small differences matter." *Id*. The panel even considered the scarcity of useful and recognizable domain names.

(F) UDRP Panels v. Domain Name Litigation

U.S. trademark owners have a choice as to whether to file federal trademark lawsuits under the

ACPA or pursue UDRP remedies. The advantage of
the UDRP is speed and low expense. Trademark
litigation may cost hundreds of thousands of dollars
and take years to complete the appellate process.
UDRP panels, in contrast, make decisions in a few
weeks and there is no appeals process. However,
UDRP panels have no power to award damages,
attorneys' fees, or costs. Another advantage of the
UDRP is that every domain name registrant is
subject to its jurisdiction, whereas a plaintiff will
need to demonstrate minimum contacts to haul a
defendant into federal court. In many instances, a
trademark owner is only seeking transfer or termination of the domain name, which can be accom-
plished more efficiently under the UDRP. The
UDRP proceeding has resulted in tens of thousands
of domain names transferred to their rightful trademark owner over the past decade.

§ 11.21   International Issues

A French court awarded famous French designers
$63 million against eBay for its gross negligence for
enabling the sale of counterfeits of famous French
luxury brands on its online auction service. EBay's
liability was based on its duty to prevent the sale of
counterfeits of Louis Vuitton, Christian Dior, and
Givency on its service. Foreign companies seek the
protection of U.S. courts to protect their trademarks from cybersquatters. The Casino de Monte
Carlo filed a trademark infringement suit against
offshore defendants who registered scores of dot.
com and dot.net domain names incorporating, in
various ways, the name "Casino de Monte Carlo."

International Bancorp., LLC v. Societe Des Bains De Mer Et Du Cercle Des Etrangers, 192 F. Supp. 2d 467 (E.D. Va. 2002). The famous casino claimed the companies' use in U.S. commerce of the term "Casino de Monte Carlo" in the disputed domain names and on various websites constituted trademark infringement in violation of the Lanham Act. The *Int'l Bancorp.* Court concluded the cybersquatter's use of forty-three domain names created a likelihood of confusion because the plaintiff's mark had secondary meaning. In the past decade, trademark owners around the world have sought protection in U.S. courts because of its strong anti-cybersquatting laws and American style damages.

CHAPTER TWELVE
TRADE SECRETS IN CYBERSPACE

Trade secrets deserve the same protection as in the bricks-and-mortar world but are especially vulnerable because the interconnected system of computers makes it easy for hackers, ex-employees, and corporate spies to steal information without leaving physical evidence. The death penalty for trade secrets occurs when a misappropriator posts it to a public website. The person who originally posted the trade secret on the Internet is liable for trade secret misappropriation. Anyone further downloading the post information has no liability as they did not improperly acquire the trade secret. Misappropriation is the improper acquisition or disclosure of a trade secret by one who "knew or had reason to know" that acquisition occurred, "under circumstances giving rise to a duty" to maintain confidentiality. *Avtec Systems, Inc. v. Peiffer*, 21 F.3d 568, 575 (4th Cir. 1994). "Thus, the hallmark of a trade secret is not its novelty but its secrecy." *Id*. An eBusiness must take reasonable measures to protect information classifiable as trade secrets, which includes reasonable Internet security. However, persons who later download the Internet will not be liable because the posting destroys its status as a trade secret.

§ 12.1   What Is a Trade Secret?

Unlike patents, copyrights, or trademarks, state tort law is the only protection for trade secrets. Trade secret misappropriation evolved as a business tort action at common law. Trade secrets are neither patentable nor subject to copyright because these forms of intellectual property mandate disclosure. Disclosure is the death knell of trade secrets destroying its emblematic feature of secrecy. A trade secret is proprietary information: (1) deriving economic value, actual or potential, from not being generally known; and (2) is the subject of efforts reasonable under the circumstances to maintain its secrecy. Cal. Civ. Code § 3246.1(d).

In order to qualify as a trade secret, the information must be secret, and must not be of public knowledge or of a general knowledge in the trade or business. Secrecy is the principal issue in most trade secret litigation. Coca Cola company officials have kept the recipe for Coca Cola® syrup locked in a vault for more than a century. Courts consider six factors in determining whether confidential information constitutes a trade secret: (1) the extent to which the information is known outside the business; (2) the extent to which it is known to those inside the business, i.e., by the employees; (3) the precautions taken by the holder of the trade secret to guard the secrecy of the information; (4) the savings effected and the value to the holder in having the information as against competitors; (5) the amount of effort or money expended in obtaining and developing the information; and (6) the amount of time and expense it would take for others to acquire and duplicate the information. *Heartland Home Finance Inc. v. Allied Home Mortg.*, 2008 WL 77785 (6th Cir. 2008).

Information does not have trade secret status if it is in the public domain or is general knowledge in an industry. However, information may be classified as a trade secret even if they were publicly available in government reports so long as no single document unveiled the entire secret. An online company must take reasonable precautions including undertaking physical, procedural, and technical measures in order to protect the information.

§ 12.2   Uniform Trade Secrets Act

The Uniform Trade Secrets Act ("UTSA") is a model law approved by the National Conference of Commissioners on Uniform State Law (NCCUSL) adopted in forty-six states. A trade secret "derives independent economic value, actual or potential, from not being generally known to" others and must be "the subject of efforts that are reasonable under the circumstances to maintain its secrecy." Uniform Trade Secrets Act, § 1. The Uniform Trade Secret Act ("UTSA") requires a prevailing plaintiff in a misappropriation case to prove two things. First, the plaintiff must prove its claims involve an actual trade secret. Second, a claimant must prove the information derives actual or potential value from not being disclosed or disclosed by improper means such as theft, bribery, misrepresentation, breach, or inducement of a breach of a duty to maintain secrecy, or economic espionage. *Id.* at § 1(1).

Information is not classifiable as a trade secret unless the owner takes reasonable measures under the circumstances to maintain its secrecy. UTSA, § 1.4. An e-commerce company will need to implement reasonable computer security to protect the confidentiality of online trade secrets. E-commerce companies will typically require employees to sign non-compete agreements. A broad definition of a trade secret includes information such as "a formula, pattern, compilation, program device, method, technique, or process." *Id.* UTSA § 1(4) defines secrets to mean

> information, including a formula, pattern, compilation, program device, method, technique, or process, that: (i) derives independent economic value, actual or potential, from no being generally known to, and not being readily ascertainable by proper means by, other persons who can obtain economic value from its disclosure or use, and (ii) is the subject of efforts that are reasonable under the circumstances to maintain its secrecy.

Courts may enjoin actual or threatened misappropriation of trade secrets under the UTSA. *Id.* at § 2. UTSA (1)(2) defines misappropriation as an:

> (i) acquisition of a trade secret of another by a person who knows or has reason to know that the

trade secret was acquired by improper means; or (ii) disclosure or use of a trade secret of another without express or implied consent by a person who (A) used improper means to acquire knowledge of the trade secret; or (B) at the time of disclosure or use knew or had reason to know that his knowledge of the trade secret was (I) derived from or through a person who has utilized improper means to acquire it; (II) acquired under circumstances giving rise to a duty to maintain its secrecy or limit its use; or (III) derived from or through a person who owed a duty to the person seeking relief to maintain its secrecy or limit its use; or (C) before a material change of his position, knew or had reason to know that it was a trade secret ad that knowledge of it had been acquired by accident or mistake.

UTSA provides a broad range of remedies, including preliminary injunctive relief, monetary damages, lost profits, consequential damages, lost royalties, attorney's fees, and punitive damages. *Id.* at § 3. Section 3 of UTSA also gives the court the power to award "exemplary damages in an amount not exceeding twice any award," upon a finding of "willful and malicious misappropriation." *Id.* The UTSA statute of limitations is three years after the owner discovers the misappropriation or should have discovered it. *Id.* at § 6.

§ 12.3 Restatement (Second) of Torts

The D.C., Massachusetts, New York, and Texas continue to follow the Restatement of Torts' approach to trade secrets and have yet to adopt UTSA. Trade secret misappropriation evolved as a tort and the Restatement (First) of Torts, §§ 757–58 (1939) was followed by most states until UTSA swept the country. The First Restatement of Torts defines a trade secret as "any formula, pattern, device, or compilation of information which is used in one's business, and which gives him an opportunity to get an advantage over competitors who do not know or use it." Restatement of Torts, § 757, cmt. b. The definition of a trade secret under Section 757 is based in part "upon the ease or difficult with which the information could be properly acquired or duplicated by others." *Id.* at § 757. The Restatement requires trade secrets to contain "a substantial element of secrecy so that, except by the use of improper means, there would be difficulty in acquiring the information." Restatement (First) of Torts § 757 cmt. b (1939). A key factor of secrecy is the ease or difficulty with which others can acquire information properly. *Id.* The Restatement lists the factors to be considered in evaluating a claim of trade secrecy:

(1) the extent to which the information is known outside of [the] business; (2) the extent to which it is known by employees and others involved in [the] business; (3) the extent of measures taken by [the business] to guard the secrecy of the information; (4) the value of the information to [the business] and [its] competitors; (5) the amount of effort or money expended by [the business] in developing the information; and (6) the

ease or difficulty with which the information could be properly acquired or duplicated by others.

Restatement (First) of Torts, § 757, cmt. b.

Courts have yet to carve out the contours of cyberspace trade secret protection. Companies failing to implement reasonable Internet security measures will likely endanger the status of their trade secrets under both UTSA or the Restatement.

§ 12.4 *Prima Facie* Case for Misappropriation

To prove misappropriation of a trade secret, the plaintiff must show: (1) it possessed a valid trade secret, (2) the defendant acquired its trade secret, and (3) the defendant knew or should have known the trade secret was acquired by improper means or by breaching an agreement, confidence, or fiduciary duty. A factfinder will calculate damages in a misappropriation case by several methods. First, damages may be computed by the plaintiff's losses including the cost of developing the trade secret. A second approach is to determine damages based upon a plaintiff's lost profits. Thirdly, if the first two methods do not adequately compensate the plaintiff, a court may award reasonable royalties. *In re Cross Media Mktg. Corp. v. Nixon*, 2006 WL 2337177 (S.D. N.Y. 2006).

Some of the initial cyberlaw cases involved litigation to vindicate the misappropriation of the Church of Scientology's secret religious doctrine. The first online trade secrets cases arose out

Church of Scientology's lawsuit to enjoin further electronic distribution of secret church doctrine A California federal court said, "posting works to the Internet makes them 'generally known,' " at least to the relevant people interested in the news group. *Religious Technology Center v. Netcom*, 907 F.Supp. 1361 (N.D. Cal. 1995).

In the Internet economy, employees are highly mobile. Courts often balance the employees' right to work against the employer's right to protect trade secrets. In *Doubleclick v. Henderson*, 1997 WL 731413 (N.Y. Sup. Ct. 1997), DoubleClick, the developer of proprietary online banner advertisements, sought an injunction to enjoin two ex-employees from working for a competitor for at least one year. DoubleClick required its employees to sign NDA agreements to maintain the confidentiality of information provided by its clients, and a covenant not to compete. Even in the absence of NDA, agreements not to compete, employees owed their employer a fiduciary duty not to divulge confidential information.

A covenant restraining an employee from competing with her former employer upon termination of employment is reasonable if the restraint is no greater than is required for the protection of the employer. Courts will also consider whether the non-compete agreement imposes an undue hardship on the employee and whether it is injurious to the public.

After hearing its employees were about to start their own company, DoubleClick confiscated one of the employee's laptops and found information stored on the hard drive, including emails, and future business plans, which provided evidence of misappropriation of trade secrets. DoubleClick discovered an email from his employee stating he "cut and pasted" DoubleClick's 1996 Business Plan to create Alliance's draft business plan. DoubleClick summarily fired the employees and sought an injunction to enjoin them from sharing trade secrets with competitors.

DoubleClick, alleged misappropriation of trade secrets and sued to enjoin the ex-employees from starting a competing business using their trade secrets. The ex-employees argued much of the information DoubleClick classified as trade secrets was already made public because it was displayed on the online company's website.

The court found there was evidence the ex-employees intended to use trade secrets to advise Alta Vista, DoubleClick's largest client. The court, however, refused to enjoin the ex-employees for a one-year period sought by DoubleClick, noting it was too long given the speed of the Internet advertising industry. The court limited the injunction to six months. The DoubleClick case illustrates many novel issues in Internet-related trade secret cases.

The Church of Scientology was the plaintiff in the first trade secrets cases arising out of Internet postings. Religious Technology Center filed suit against the Washington Post for misappropriating and publishing on the Internet portions of secret church doctrine, including the "Advanced Technology Works." The Washington Post defended reasoning church doctrine was not classifiable as a trade secret because it had been in public court files for more than two years, and had been published on the Internet. *Religious Technology Center v. Lerma*, 908 F.Supp. 1362 (E.D. Va. 1995). The Virginia federal district court denied an injunction against four ex-Scientologists, ruling the defendants were protected by fair use. One distinguishing factor in denying the injunction was despite the Church's best efforts, the Internet postings had destroyed the trade secret status.

Similarly, a Colorado court held in *Religious Technology Center v. F.A.C.T.Net, Inc.*, 901 F.Supp. 1519 (D. Colo. 1995), the online publication of a confidential document belonging to the Church of Scientology made the information "generally known," therefore destroying the trade secret. In *Religious Technology Center v. Netcom*, 907 F.Supp. 1361 (N.D. Cal. 1995), the court dealt further with the scope of intellectual property rights on the Internet. Two organizations sued a former minister who had been a vocal critic of the Church of Scientology for posting writings of the founder, L. Ron Hubbard, on the Internet.

The Scientologists had undertaken a variety of protection methods to keep the information secret, such as locked cabinets, electronic sensors attached to documents, locked briefcases for transporting works, alarms, photo identifications, security personnel, and confidentiality agreements. The court found the Church had made more than an adequate showing of reasonable efforts to maintain secrecy.

With respect to the Internet posting of information, the court found even though posting information on a site might not be akin to publishing it in a newspaper or on television, the information would nevertheless be stripped of its trade secret status. These cases stand for the proposition the posting of information onto the Internet results in a trade secret being generally known.

In *EarthWeb Inc. v. Schlack*, 71 F. Supp. 2d 299 (S.D. N.Y. 1999), an employee who had overall editorial responsibility for the content of the website decided to leave, prompting Earthweb to sue for preliminary injunctive relief enjoining him from commencing employment elsewhere, and disclosing or revealing trade secrets. Earthweb argued its trade secrets on the subject of strategic content planning, licensing agreements, advertising, and technical knowledge were all at risk of disclosure. The employee had entered into a non-disclosure agreement and a "Limited Agreement Not to Compete" with Earthweb. The court held a covenant not to compete for a period of one year was both unreasonable and too long, as the Internet industry exists in a constant state of fluctuation. The court elaborated by stating "a one year hiatus in the Internet field is like an eternity."

In *In re Cross Media Mktg. Corp. v. Nixon*, 2006 WL 2337177 (S.D. N.Y. 2006), an online company discovered an anonymous party was trying to auction its customer lists on the Internet. The plaintiff linked the IP number to a former consultant and his wife. The defendant had previously entered into a consulting agreement with Cross Media and had full access to customer lists. The court found the consultant's wife misappropriated Cross Media's trade secret when she either auctioned or conspired to auction the customer lists. In addition, the court found the defendant converted Cross Media's property; and had been unjustly enriched from access to the customer list.

The federal bankruptcy court awarded Cross Media $236,000 in compensatory damages and $50,000 in punitive damages. The court found even though the defendant was not successful in auctioning off Cross Media's customer lists, the defendant was responsible to pay the plaintiff for the cost of developing the customer lists she wrongfully obtained. The misappropriation of trade secrets is a popular cause of action to protect the intangible assets of companies connected to the Internet. The Internet economy is known for a rapid turnover in employees, and online companies face the constant danger an ex-employee will misappropriate trade secrets for use in a competitor's business. Monster.com, for example, settled a trade secret lawsuit against its former president and eighteen ex-employees who left the company to join a rival Internet company.

§ 12.5 First Amendment Issues

The First Amendment of the U.S. Constitution protects a website operator's posting of DeCSS enabled users to evade the "content scramble system" which both encrypts DVDs and is designed to prevent their unauthorized use and duplication. The California appellate court ruled since the DeCSS that the website operator posted was already public knowledge, the defendant could not be liable for misappropriation since there was no more trade secret. *DVD Copy Control Assn. Inc. v. Andrew Bunner*, 116 Cal.App.4th 241 (2004) (holding dissemination of DeCSS software on the Internet destroyed trade secret status).

§ 12.6 Economic Espionage Act

Congress enacted the Economic Espionage Act ("EEA") in 1996 to punish and deter foreign and domestic spies threatening America's economic well-being. The prosecution of trade secret theft as a criminal offense is a recent development. Before the EEA, prosecutors pursued the theft of trade secrets by using existing law such as the 1934 National Stolen Property Act, which was intended to punish thieves who also fled across state borders in automobiles. While the National Stolen Property Act applied to tangible goods, it was not clearly applicable to the unauthorized transfer of intangibles such as intellectual property. The EEA was enacted to bridge that gap in trade secret law by creating two new federal crimes for trade secret misappropriation.

The EEA criminalizes two types of offenses: (1) economic espionage that benefits foreign governments or entities (§ 1831); and (2) the theft of trade secrets benefits any person but the true owner (§ 1832). Section 1831 of the EEA addresses the problem of misappropriation by foreign governments or their agents and criminalizes data theft with fines of up to $500,000 and imprisonment of up to fifteen years. 17 U.S.C. § 1832. Offending organizations may be subject to fines of up to $10,000,000. Section 1832 covers misappropriation intended to benefit individuals and corporations.

In contrast, § 1832 applies to domestic trade secret theft. It is a broader provision, applying "to anyone who knowingly engages in the theft of trade secrets, or an attempt or conspiracy to do so." *Id*. at § 1832. Under § 1832, individuals are subject to fines and up to ten years of imprisonment, while organizations are subject to fines of up to $5,000,000. *Id*. Although the EEA provides criminal sanctions and civil damages for the misappropriation of trade secrets, it does not permit civil action filed by private attorneys general.

(A) EEA Definitions

Under the EEA, any tangible property and intangible information is potentially classifiable as a trade secret so long as the owner "has taken reasonable measures to keep such information secret," and the information "derives independent economic value from not being generally known to the public." 18 U.S.C. § 1839(1)(3)(a). The theft of trade secrets is criminalized if the defendant: (1) stole, or without authorization of the owner, obtained, destroyed or conveyed information; (2) knew or believed this information was a trade secret; and (3) the information was in fact a trade secret. 18 U.S.C. § 1839.

(B) Securing Trade Secrets

The government may not charge a defendant with violating the EEA unless "the owner thereof has taken reasonable measures to keep such information secret." *Id*. at § 1839(3)(a). If a company fails to implement reasonable computer security, the result is proprietary information is not classifiable as a trade secret. The U.S. Attorney General has the discretion to institute civil enforcement actions and to get injunctive relief for violations. The EEA provides for protective orders to protect trade secrets during litigation.

EEA prosecutions also require proof a trade secret has value. If the trade secret owner does not take reasonable measures, value can be destroyed. The EEA requires information must derive "independent economic value, actual or potential, from not being generally known to, and not being readily ascertainable through proper means by, the public." Id. at § 1839(3)(b). Trade secrets in the online world deserve the same protections as in the bricks-and-mortar world. Internet trade secrets are particularly vulnerable because the interconnected system of computers makes it possible for hackers, ex-employees, and experts in corporate espionage to steal information without leaving physical evidence.

CHAPTER THIRTEEN

INTERNET–RELATED PATENTS

§ 13.1 Overview of Patent Law

Congress enacted the first patent law in 1790 and the updated patent statute is codified in Title 35 of the United States Code. A patent for an invention is the grant of a property right to the inventor, issued by the United States Patent and Trademark Office ("USPTO") located in Crystal City, Virginia. Each country has its own patent office. European-wide patents are filed in Munich, Germany. A U.S. firm will likely seek protection in every country where it seeks to gain market share for its patented products. To get protection, the online company will need to file claims in each country's patent office, or alternately, an application can be filed under the Patent Cooperation Treaty ("PCT"), which will ease a company's later national applications in every country that is a signatory to the treaty.

The right conferred by the patent grant is exclusionary: in the language of the Patent Act and of the grant itself, it is "the right to exclude others from making, using, offering for sale, or selling" the invention in the U.S. or "importing" it for a limited period. Patent law is a negative monopoly or property right since the patentee has the right to exclude others from making, using, or selling his or her invention. Patent owners license their e-commerce related patents so others can use them.

The trend to propertization of software patents and eBusiness methods has led to a more complex online business environment. Many e-commerce related patent disputes center on the issue of whether a business method is patentable. Patent infringement lawsuits are typically over the issue of who was the first to get patent protection. This chapter will describe Internet-related patent issues.

§ 13.2 The Concepts & Methods of Patent Law

(A) Sources of Patent Law

A patent is a property right possessed or held by an inventor with constitutional roots in Article I, Section 8, Clause 8 of the U.S. Constitution. Congress has the power to legislate to "promote the Progress of Science and useful Arts, by securing for limited times to Authors and Inventors the exclusive Right to their respective Writings and Discoveries." U.S. CONST. art. I, § 8, cl. 8. Congress implemented this limited grant of patent protection by enacting a patent statute. Today, the federal statute governing patents is the Patent Act of 1952, 35 U.S.C. §§ 1–376. Title 37 of the Code of Federal Regulations sets forth patent regulations implementing the Patent Act. The Manual of Patent Examining Procedure ("MPEP") is the Office's own internal rules and interpretations of the statute and Title 37 for its examiners and other employees.

(B) Types of Patents

Patent law recognizes three types of patents: (1) Utility Patents, (2) Design Patents, and (3) Plant Patents. Utility patents are issued for four general types of inventions/discoveries: machines, human made products, compositions of matter, and processes. 35 U.S.C. § 101. Internet-related patents are typically utility patents subcategorized as process patents if they qualify as new and useful. The USPTO grants design patents to anyone who invents a new, original, and ornamental design for an article of manufacture, though the design must be purely aesthetic and have no functional benefit. The Patent Office grants plant patents to anyone who invents or discovers, and asexually reproduces any distinct and new variety of plant. USPTO, *What Are Patents*? (2008). Design patents are relevant to Internet inventions because the USPTO considers computer-generated icons, including full screen images and type fonts, to constitute surface ornamentation. Manual of Patent Examining Procedure, 1504.01(a) (2006).

(C) Patent Law Terms

Generally, the term of a new utility patent, which accounts for most Internet-related patents, is 20 years from the date on which the application for the patent was filed in the United States. In special cases, this can reach farther back to the date on which an earlier application for the same invention was filed. Plant patents also have a 20–year term, while design patents only have a term of 14 years from the issue date.

Utility or plant patents issued on applications filed before June 8, 1995 have a term of 17 years from the issuance of the patent or 20 years from the filing, whichever is greater. This rule was modified by the Uruguay Round Agreements Act, which gave the uniform 20–year rule in effect today. 108 Stat. 4809 (1994). In the United States, the patent term begins to run at the time of filing but patent rights in most cases are not available to the patent applicant until the patent issues. U.S. patent grants are effective only within the U.S., U.S. territories, and U.S. possessions.

(D) Statutory Elements

The Patent Act requires inventions to satisfy three conditions in order to be patentable: (1) novelty, (2) utility, and (3) nonobviousness. 35 U.S.C. § 103(a). The term "utility" means the subject matter satisfies a useful purpose and includes operativeness. A machine unable to perform its intended purpose would not be useful within the meaning of the Patent Act, and therefore would not be granted a patent. For example, the Patent Office has used this rationale in the past to deny patent applications for perpetual motion machines, which are impossible under the First Law of Thermodynamics. A patent can be properly construed and applied only "with a full understanding of what the inventors actually invented and intended to envelop with the claim." *Phillips v. AWH Corp.,* 415 F.3d 1303, 1323 (Fed. Cir. 2005) *(en banc).*

(E) Patent Applications

Inventors file applications in the USPTO, an agency of the U.S. Department of Commerce. The role of the USPTO is to grant patents for the protection of inventions and to register trademarks. Patent Office examiners determine whether the claims of an applicant are novel, useful, and non-obvious at the creation of the invention. Patent examiners also determine if the invention satisfies the statutory subject matter under 35 U.S.C. § 101. The examiners determine whether the applicant adequately describes how to make and use the invention which is a required disclosure under 35 U.S.C. § 112. This section has, in turn, been divided into three separate requirements by the courts: enablement, written description, and best mode. A patent application typically includes: (1) a specification, (2) a drawing; and (3) an oath by the applicant. Patent Act, *Id.* at § 111. The terms specification and claim are typically used in the practice world to mean separate things. Most patent attorneys would describe a patent application as containing a specification, drawings, and claims. Patent applications are filed and then either issued by the PTO or rejected.

(1) Patent Examiners

USPTO examiners are "persons of legal knowledge and scientific ability" who determine the patentability of inventions. 35 U.S.C. § 7. The patent examiners will make a decision to determine whether claims are obvious or anticipated in prior art. Patent applicants have the affirmative obligation of making adequate written descriptions of claims. A patent examiner may reject a claim because it is non-statutory subject matter. "Every case involving a § 101 issue must begin with this question: What, if anything, is it the applicant 'invented or discovered?' " *In re Alappat,* 33 F.3d 1526 (Fed. Cir. 1994). A patent claim consists of the elements comprising the invention. An examiner's job is to evaluate an application to determine whether the combination of claimed elements exist in prior art. Three categories of unpatentable subject matter are: (1) laws of nature (2) natural phenomena and (3) abstract ideas. *Diamond v. Diehr*, 450 U.S. 175 (1981).

(2) Patentability

The U.S. Supreme Court in *Diamond v. Chakrabarty*, 447 U.S. 303 (1980) interpreted Congress' intent "to include anything under the sun that is made by man" to be patentable subject matter. To be patentable, an invention must have some utility (§ 101). The subject matter must also be novel (§ 102) and non-obvious (§ 103). An invention must not be the functional equivalent of an invention covered by a previously issued patent. Nonobviousness is measured by prior art and what would not be obvious to a person skilled in the prior art. Any new or useful process, machine, articles of manufacture, composition of matter or improvements of these subjects are patentable. Patent Act, § 1. A patent application consists of an abstract, a description of the invention, disclosures of prior art, drawings, and one or more claims. The patent claim is the intellectual property protected when a patent is issued. The patent claim must meet the requirements for patentability set forth in Title 35 of the United States Code: novelty, utility, and non-obviousness. "A claim in a patent provides the metes and bounds of the right which the patent confers on the patentee to exclude others from making, using or selling the protected invention." *Burke, Inc. v. Bruno Indep. Living Aids, Inc.*, 183 F.3d 1334, 1340 (Fed. Cir. 1999). Claim construction is an issue of law for the court to decide. *Markman v. Westview Instruments, Inc.*, 52 F.3d 967, 970–71 (Fed. Cir. 1995). Courts conducting Markman hearings examine the claims, the specifications, and the prosecution history. *Id.* at 979.

U.S. patent law gives an inventor a one year grace period, which allows him or her to attempt to commercialize the invention prior to filing an application. 35 U.S.C. § 102(b). Most, if, not all other countries connected to the Internet, do not recognize a grace period. Thus, once the invention is disclosed to the public, patent rights are lost.

(3) Specifications

The specifications will generally summarize or describe the invention as a whole. "When a patentee thus describes the features of the 'present invention' as a whole, this description limits the scope of the invention." *Verizon Services Corp. v. Vonage Holdings Corp.*, 503 F.3d 1295, 1308 (Fed. Cir. 2007). "The specification is a written description of the invention and of the manner and process of making and using the same." Manual of Patent Examining Procedure, 608.01 (2006).

"The specification must be in such full, clear, concise, and exact terms as to enable any person skilled in the art or science to which the invention pertains to make and use the same." *Id.* Specifications are the part of the patent application showing the examiner how a claim is distinguished from other inventions. "It must describe completely a specific embodiment of the process; machine, manufacture, composition of matter or improvement invented, and must explain the mode of operation or principle whenever applicable." 37 C.F.R. § 1.71. "The best mode contemplated by the inventor of carrying out his invention must be set forth." *Id.*

(4) Enablement

Specifications must not only describe in full and exact terms the claim but also satisfy enablement. 35 U.S.C. § 112. Enablement means the claim must "enable" a person of ordinary skill in the relevant art or science to make and use the invention. The patent examiner's role is to determine whether the claim has sufficient descriptive support in its disclosures to meet the enablement requirement. Enablement is a separate requirement from the written description. An invention could be adequately described without being enabling, such as a chemical formula with no disclosed or apparent method of making; or be enabled without adequate description, such as a method of making a material without any specific formulation. *Manual of Patent Examination Procedure*, 2161 (2006).

§ 13.3   Internet–Related Patents

(A)   Software Patents

Software patents have been granted for hyperlinking, audio software, file formats, search engines, and thousands of other Internet-related applications. A software patent application must clearly describe what the computer does when it performs the steps dictated by software code. The electronic commerce infrastructure is built on bedrock of software patents owned by International Business Machines Corporation ("IBM"), Oracle Corporation, Novell, Inc., and Microsoft. IBM is the world's leader in revenues generated from its portfolio of software patents. Examples of software patents include compilers, application programs, and protection for "process or method performed by a computer game." *Atari Games Corp. v. Nintendo of America, Inc.*, 975 F.2d 832 (Fed. Cir. 1992).

The Internet enables online vendors to sell goods and render services. However, a company must avoid infringing software as well as business methods. CompuServe, Inc., the first major commercial online service in the United States, created a computer image format called the Graphics Interchange Format ("GIF"). GIF's compression algorithm, also known as Lempel–Ziv–Welch ("LZW") lossless data compression, was patented by U.S. Patent No. 4,558,302 (issued December 10, 1985) and owned by Unisys, Inc.

In 1995, Unisys entered into a licensing agreement with CompuServe. CompuServe's licensing of the LZW patent would require all commercial service providers to pay licensing fees for using GIF images. In response to the licensing fees, developers created the Portable Network Graphics ("PNG") format as an alternative to GIF, and allowed anyone to use it free of charge. The LZW patent expired in June 2003, its foreign counterparts expired in June, and July of 2004, so this technology is now in the public domain.

Similarly, JPEG, another popular image coding system, infringed on a patent owned by Forgent Networks. U.S. Patent No. 4,698,672 (issued October 6, 1987). When Forgent tried to enforce licensing fees for JPEG users, the Public Patent Foundation filed a motion to challenge the JPEG patent. In a reexamination proceeding, the USPTO ruled not only that Forgent's patent was invalid due to prior art, but also that Forgent knew about the prior art and failed to disclose it to the Office.

A hypothetical website developer's patented technologies allowing more rapid Internet downloads could be classified as utility patents. The value of this hypothetical software may be that Internet users may continue a download even if there was an interruption, such as the loss of a dialup connection during the download. Just as RealNetworks successfully challenged a functionally equivalent patented technology on grounds of obviousness and anticipation, an eBusiness may bring a patent infringement claim against another company using its patented technology without a license. For example, GaphOn Inc. claims YouTube's use of searchable media online violated its software patents.

Software patents are on the rise because of the increased competence of the USPTO and the formulation of Examination Guidelines for Computer–Related Inventions. United States Patent & Trademark Office, Examination Guidelines for Computer–Related Invention, 1184 U.S. PAT. & TRADEMARK OFF. OFFICIAL GAZETTE 87 (1996).

Algorithms and formulas are unpatentable, limiting patentable subject matter to "any process, machine, manufacture, or composition of matter." 35 U.S.C. § 101. Software was conceptualized as unpatentable subject matter until the 1980s because it incorporated algorithms. In *Gottschalk v. Benson,* 409 U.S. 63 (1972), the U.S. Supreme Court ruled a discovery of a novel and useful mathematical formula may not be patented. The inventor sought protection for a formula for converting a binary coded decimal signal to binary form. Justice William O. Douglas, writing for the majority, said a process must transform and reduce material to a different state and the formula was not patentable without Congressional authorization.

In *Parker v. Flook,* 437 U.S. 584 (1978), the Court considered whether a "Method For Updating Alarm Limits" was protectable where the only novel feature of the method was a mathematical formula claim for a method of calculation. In *Parker,* the Court did not automatically disqualify claim merely because it contained an algorithm, but without a tangible output, one cannot patent "a novel and useful mathematical formula". *Id.* at 585.

In *Diamond v. Diehr*, 450 U.S. 175 (1981), the U.S. Supreme Court for the first time recognized a process controlled by computer software as being patentable. In *Diamond*, the invention at issue was a computer program determined how rubber should be heated in order to be best "cured." The Supreme Court said in this case, the invention was not merely a mathematical algorithm, but the process for molding rubber, and was patentable. *Id.* at 188.

In *Akamai Technologies, Inc. v. Limelight Networks, Inc.*, 2008 WL 364401 (D. Mass. 2008), a jury found Limelight infringed an Internet content delivery patent asserted by Akamai Technologies, and handed down a $45.5 million verdict. In *Akami*, the patent claim covered software for delivering the embedded objects of a web page. Limelight argues a reasonable jury could conclude the company believed it did not infringe or cause others to infringe Akamai's patents because of Akamai's prior history of suing infringers.

(B) Business Methods

Business methods qualify as "patentable-eligible subject matter" if they are a new and useful process. The process must, at a bare minimum, produce a useful, concrete, and tangible result to qualify as a business method. *State Street Bank & Trust*

Co. v. Signature Fin. Group, Inc., 149 F.3d 1368 (Fed. Cir. 1998) (holding business methods are patentable). Technically, business method patents are utility patents for any process synthesizing software or code with business techniques or methodologies. The USPTO devised a classification system for patents and most e-commerce, Internet or data processing business methods are classified as Class 705. The number of Class 705 patents issuing skyrocketed from 120 to 1,191 from 1996 to 2006.

Most e-commerce methods, but not all, are related to financial and business data processing. The methods and apparatuses claimed in these applications are linked to financial and business data processing. Priceline, for example, holds a patent on an auction method for selling tickets. Netcraft filed suit against eBay and PayPal for infringing two related business method patents with variations on Internet Billing Methods. The USPTO has approved scores of business method patents for Internet purchasing, online advertising, and marketing.

The conventional wisdom was business methods were not patentable and were an exception to the general rule processes are patentable. In 1908, the Second Circuit held a bookkeeping system, whose purpose was to prevent embezzlement by wait staff, was an unpatentable algorithm, thereby carving out the business method exception. *Hotel Security Checking Co. v. Lorraine Co.*, 160 F. 467 (2d Cir. 1908).

Courts accepted this business method exception for ninety years until the Federal Circuit reversed course in *State Street Bank & Trust Co. v. Signature Fin. Group, Inc.*, 149 F.3d 1368 (Fed. Cir. 1998). In *State Street*, Judge Giles Rich, writing for the panel, accepted a patent held by Signature Financial Group for a "hub and spoke" method of computing interest in mutual funds. The business method made it possible for mutual fund managers to pool their assets into a partnership, allowing tax advantages and administrative savings. The mere presence of a mathematical algorithm does not preordain the USPTO will reject a patent claim. The Federal Circuit held a programmed computer using this mathematical algorithm was patentable so long as it produced a useful, concrete, and tangible result. The Federal Circuit overruled the "business method" exception to invalidate patent claims:

We take this opportunity to lay, this ill-conceived exception to rest. Since its inception, the "business method" exception has merely represented the application of some general, but no longer applicable legal principle, perhaps arising out of the "requirement for invention"—which was eliminated by § 103. Since the 1952 Patent Act, business methods have been, and should have been, subject to the same legal requirements for patentability as applied to any other process or method.

Id. at 1375.

In *State Street*, the court found an algorithm or formula produced a "concrete and tangible result," namely a final share price for each mutual fund within the partnership as determined by their contributions to the pool, was a practical application and thus patentable. *Id*. The validation of business methods patents was extended in *AT & T Corp. v. Excel Communications, Inc.*, 172 F.3d 1352 (Fed. Cir. 1999) when the Federal Circuit approved a patent incorporating Boolean algebra to determine the long-distance carriers involved in a telephone call creating a switching signal for billing purposes. The court reasoned because this was not an attempt to patent the Boolean principle, but rather a patent on the process to create the discrete switching signal, it was patentable subject matter. The patent created a concrete and tangible result, and was therefore patentable. *Id*. at 1358.

In the wake of *State Street* and *AT & T*, the USPTO required business method patents to press forward the technological arts. *Ex Parte Bowman*, 61 U.S.P.Q.2d 1669 (Bd. Pat. App. 2001). Only four years later in *Ex Parte Lundgren*, 76 U.S.P.Q.2d 1385 (Pat. App. 2005), the Board of Patent Appeals and Interferences found no statutory or legal requirement for a technological arts test.

The Federal Circuit recently shows evidence of reining in business methods perhaps in response to the gold rush in claims to 'processes,' many of which bear scant resemblance to classical processes of manipulating or transforming compositions of matter or forms of energy from one state to another." *Ex parte Bilski*, 2006 WL 4080055, at *7 (B.P.A.I. 2006). The *Bilski* application was to a method of managing risk in commodities trading by placing hedge bets on commodities with "counter-risk" positions to the primary trade. U.S. Patent Application No. 08/833,892. The Patent Office rejected the application for the commodity trading business method as an unpatentable abstract idea. The Patent Office reasoned the invention was a mathematical operation not coupled with a particular machine and did not physically transform matter or energy from one form to another and was therefore not patentable subject matter under 35 U.S.C. § 101. *Ex parte Bilski* at *19–20. The Patent Office's rejection of this business method is currently under appeal.

The Federal Circuit asked the parties to brief the issue whether it was appropriate to reconsider *State Street Bank & Trust Co. v. Signature Financial Group, Inc.*, 149 F.3d 1368 (Fed. Cir. 1998), and *AT & T Corp. v. Excel Communications, Inc.*, 172 F.3d 1352 (Fed. Cir. 1999), in their case and whether those cases should be overruled in any respect? Further, the *Bilski* decision coupled with another recent decision may imply the Patent Office is trending to restrict software patents. *Ex parte Bilski* said a process that was not "tied to a particular machine" might not be patentable. *Id.* at 15 (explaining a generic computer performing a mathematical algorithm does not qualify as a machine for patenting the algorithm).

In *Ex parte Langemyr*, the PTO Board said an algorithm for modeling a physical system "executed in a computer apparatus" was not tied to a particular machine, but could be performed on any general purpose computer, and was therefore a process, rather than a machine. *Ex parte Langemyr*, No. 2008–1495, at 22 (BPAI May 28, 2008). Because Langemyr's invention did not physically transform matter or energy from one form to another, it was not classifiable as a patentable process. *Id.* The majority of software programs can be executed on any general purpose machine, and manipulate data and numbers, rather than matter or energy.

(C) Emerging Case Law After State Street

Since 1998 hundreds of Internet-related business, methods have been issued as patents. Amazon.com's "one-click" technology for online shopping was issued a patent. Amazon.com's 1–Click, a "method, and system for placing a purchase order via a communications network" sparked one of the most famous Internet patent debates. U.S. Patent No. 5,960,411 (issued Sept. 28, 1999). The patent permitted customers to make online purchases with a single click, using a pre-defined address and credit card number.

A federal court granted Amazon an injunction enjoining Barnes & Noble for using a single-click Express Checkout on their online store. *Amazon.com, Inc. v. BarnesAndNoble.com, Inc.*, 73 F. Supp. 2d. 1228 (W.D. Wash. 1999). The parties settled before a trial to determine the validity of the one-click method. Richard Stallman, President of the Free Software Foundation, published a letter calling for a boycott of Amazon.com, saying the Barnes & Noble suit was "an attack against the World Wide Web and against E-commerce in general." Richard Stallman, *Please do not buy from Amazon*, LINUX TODAY, Dec. 22, 1999.

Jeff Bezos, Chairman and CEO of Amazon.com, published an open letter in response calling for patent law reforms. Bezo proposed to abbreviate the life of the patent term to three to five years for software and business method patents. Jeff Bezos, *An Open Letter from Jeff Bezos on the Subject of Patents*, March 9, 2000. The rationale for an abbreviated patent term is most software or business methods will have a short shelf life.

Amazon and Barnes & Noble settled their patent infringement dispute in 2000, with Barnes & Noble licensing the 1–Click patent. In 2006, in response to a request by blogger and patent enthusiast Peter Calveley, the USPTO opened the 1–Click patent for re-examination. *Amazon Surrenders on One–Click Shopping Monopoly*, OUT-LAW NEWS, Nov. 23, 2007. The USPTO Office rejected Amazon's patent, finding it obvious in light of prior art. *Id*. Amazon has amended its application to confine the patent only to items "purchasable through a shopping cart model". The Office has not yet ruled on the new amendment; its review is pending.

§ 13.4 Business Method Patent Litigation
(A) E–Business Patent Trolls

A patent troll is the owner of a patent that does not use its intellectual property to produce products, but rather to file suit against alleged infringers. *Taurus IP v. DaimlerChrysler*, 519 F. Supp. 2d 905 (W.D. Wisc. 2007). Trolls do not produce goods or services but rather use their inventions to threaten patent litigation. The danger of patent trolls is they will have a chilling effect blocking Internet-related innovations. Critics fear outsized Internet-related business methods will result in companies paying higher licensing fees in its online activities where they are not due. Patent law reformers call for Congress to act to thwart a litigation crisis created by abusive patent trolls. One of the problems with the concept of the patent troll is it is overinclusive including many universities and research institutes that do not practice any conventions, but nevertheless have patent portfolios. Patent reform has stalled in Congress because industries cannot agree on a legislative solution.

(B) Injunctive Relief

Injunctive relief is critically imperative in Internet-related patent litigation because of the rapidity with which online businesses can attain market share. In the Internet-based economy, the earliest mover has enormous advantages and patent law is a method for excluding others. In *eBay, Inc. v. MercExchange*, 547 U.S. 388 (2006), MercExchange owned a business method patent for the online marketplace designed to enable the sale of goods between private individuals by establishing a central authority to promote trust among participants. MercExchange sought to license its patent to eBay but could not reach an agreement. MercExchange filed a patent infringement suit against eBay and Half.com for infringing its patent while conducting on-line sales.

U.S. District Court ruled MercExchange's patent was valid and had been infringed and awarded damages, but denied injunctive relief. The Federal Circuit reversed the District Court, finding it had abused its discretion when it denied a permanent injunction. The Federal Circuit found eBay's online auction system infringed MercExchange's patent for method of conducting online sales. The appeals court ruled the lower court erred in not following the Federal Circuit rule once a patent was found to be valid injunctive relief should be granted unless absent "exceptional circumstances." This was the traditional Supreme Court rule before the eBay case.

The U.S. Supreme Court reversed the Federal Circuit, ruling federal courts should not automatically enter an injunction but rather apply the four-factor equitable test: (1) the plaintiff has suffered irreparable injury; (2) remedies available at law, such as monetary damages, are inadequate to compensate for that injury; (3) considering balance of hardships between plaintiff and defendant, remedy in equity is warranted; and (4) public interest would not be disserved by permanent injunction. The ruling in *eBay Inc. v. MercExchange* reverses the Federal Circuit practice of automatically granting injunctions in patent infringement lawsuits except under atypical circumstances.

§ 13.5   International Patent Developments
(A)   Patent Cooperation Treaty

The Patent Cooperation Treaty ("PCT") allows a U.S. business to file a single international application in the USPTO and have that application recognized as a regular national or regional filing in any PCT Contracting State. A U.S. firm will specify which PCT countries where it wants its application acknowledged, and later file national applications in each country while claiming the priority date of the international application, for overcoming prior art. Similarly, a foreign company may also file a PCT international application, designating the United States of America, in their home language and home patent office. Another feature of the PCT is it provides for international search report and written opinions for international applications. The International Searching Authority ("ISA") conducts a prior art search of inventions claimed in international applications, and the USPTO will use the ISA search report when considering a later national application.

After the PCT application is filed, an applicant must still fulfill the normal national procedures for obtaining patent protection in each of the designated countries within 30 months from the international application is filing date. The USPTO's MPEP expresses the underlying method for PCT applications. USPTO, MPEP, *Id*. at § 1842. The USPTO notes most patent applicants will file a national U.S. application first. The USPTO is the U.S. "receiving office" for international applications with the equivalent as WIPO's International Bureau.

(B) Business Patents

Business patents are not well established outside the U.S. In 2003, the Paris Appeals Court denied patent protection for an "electronic process for ordering products from sales points." *No Patents for Business Methods According to Paris Appeals Court,* PIKE & FISCHER INTERNET LAW & REGULATION (Feb. 10, 2003) (discussing *SA Sagem vs. M. Le Directeur de l'INPI,* Cour d'Appel de Paris, 2003). The business method enabled retailers "to conduct safe transactions with customers, via telephone or Internet, without recourse to the computer chip-equipped banking cards." *Id.* The court ruled the process was not protectable because it did not achieve a technical effect but merely enabled a commercial transaction. *Id.* Business method patents create many traps for the incautious online company and can negate influence online market entrants. The rise of the Internet creates new challenges for patent owners protecting intellectual property and avoiding infringing the rights of others. In less than two decades, the Internet has grown from an infant technology to becoming one of the world's greatest economic and cultural forces stimulated by eBusiness and software patents. Courts must be forward-looking in adapting patented technologies to the conditions of the information-based economy.

*

INDEX

References are to Pages

419

†